9780471101901

SOCIAL FOUNDATIONS
OF CANADIAN EDUCATION

SOCIAL FOUNDATIONS
of
CANADIAN EDUCATION

•

A BOOK OF READINGS

edited by

ANAND MALIK

•

PRENTICE-HALL ♦ OF CANADA LTD.
Scarborough h *Ontario*

©1969 by Prentice-Hall of Canada, Ltd.
Scarborough, Ontario

ALL RIGHTS RESERVED
*No part of this book may be reproduced in any form
without permission in writing from the publishers.*

PRENTICE-HALL, INC., ENGLEWOOD CLIFFS, NEW JERSEY
PRENTICE-HALL INTERNATIONAL, INC., LONDON
PRENTICE-HALL OF AUSTRALIA, PTY., LTD., SYDNEY
PRENTICE-HALL OF INDIA, PVT., LTD., NEW DELHI
PRENTICE-HALL OF JAPAN, INC., TOKYO

Library of Congress Catalog Card No. 68-26757
81561-*Pa*
81562-*Cl*
1 2 3 4 5 73 72 71 70 69
PRINTED IN CANADA

Preface

This book is a modest attempt to present the student of education with selected studies that discuss the basic social, economic, ethnic, and historical backgrounds of what goes on in our schools. The readings have been selected because of the sociological data they provide, and also because of the questions they raise regarding the purposes of Canadian education.

The book is divided into five Parts: Aims of Education, Education and Diversity in Canadian Society, Social and Economic Change, Levels of Education, and Society and the Teacher. Each Part contains significant readings that are Canadian in data and Canadian in aspirations. Each part has an introduction that traces the major idea in that section historically through major cultures of the world and relates it to the current Canadian situation. A basic bibliography is provided for each Part to help the student pursue some of the problems raised in the readings.

I must express my sincere appreciation to my colleagues in various university faculties and departments of education in Canada for their suggestions in relating this book to the needs of teachers. I am also indebted to the Humanities and Social Science Research Fund and the President's Publication Committee of the University of Saskatchewan for their generous grants in support of this project.

A.M.

TO

•

Anne, Arun, Ashwin, and Avinash

Table of Contents

Part One: AIMS OF EDUCATION   3

    I   Introduction   4
    I-1   The Aims of Education in a Free Society   7
            Neville V. Scarfe
    I-2   The Primary Ends of Education   27
            Very Rev. Henri Légaré
    I-3   A Mari Usque Ad Mare: Educational Problems   34
            H.T. Coutts

Part Two: EDUCATION AND DIVERSITY IN CANADIAN SOCIETY   39

    II   Introduction   40
    II-4   Democracies, Minorities and Education   43
            David Munroe
    II-5   Value Differences, Absolute or Relative: The English-Speaking Democracies   53
            Seymour Martin Lipset
    II-6   Social Class and Educational Opportunity   60
            John Porter
    II-7   Eskimo Education, Danish and Canadian: A Comparison   68
            C.W. Hobart and C.S. Brant

Part Three: SOCIAL AND ECONOMIC CHANGE   89

    III   Introduction   90
    III-8   Social Change and the Aims and Problems of Education in Canada   93
            John Porter
    III-9   Education and Economic Growth   98
            Economic Council of Canada
    III-10   A Schoolman's Guide to Marshall McLuhan   122
            John M. Culkin

Part Four: LEVELS OF EDUCATION   **133**

   IV   Introduction   *134*

   (a) Elementary Education
IVA-11   The Missing Component in Education   *138*
W.H. Worth

   (b) Secondary Education
IVB-12   The Loom Also   *144*
H.T. Coutts
IVB-13   Tomorrow's Secondary School   *149*
Lawrence W. Downey

   (c) University Education
IVC-14   The Modern University   *163*
Neville V. Scarfe
IVC-15   The University and Modern Man   *168*
Murray G. Ross

Part Five: SOCIETY AND THE TEACHER   **175**

   V   Introduction   *176*
V-16   Teachers as Civil Servants   *178*
Frank MacKinnon
V-17   Principles of Teacher Education   *186*
Neville V. Scarfe

Suggested Readings   **192**

SOCIAL FOUNDATIONS
OF CANADIAN EDUCATION

PART ONE

Aims of Education

1

Introduction

•

In Canada at the present time, intellectual training is considered to be the main objective of the school. However, an awareness that the school is also an agency for socializing the child—that is, conditioning him to the needs and values of society—has currently gained wide acceptance in educational theory, if not in practice.

Emphasis on the social function of education has persisted throughout history. Early tribal societies, concerned with survival of the group, emphasized total assimilation of the young in the life and customs of the community. Ancient Chinese education transmitted cultural heritage from one generation to the next by memorization of the great classics. Education in ancient India was based on curricula to meet the social needs of four sections of the community: the teachers, warriors, peasants, and labourers.

In Sparta, education was militaristic, emphasizing obedience to superiors and loyalty to the State. In Athens, the purpose of education was to train citizens. Plato (427–347 B.C.), in his *Republic*, advocated three kinds of education to prepare three types of citizens: the philosopher-king, the warrior, and the artisan. The labourer received no formal education. To Aristotle (384–322 B.C.) the highest aim of education was cultivation of the intellect. Roman education, on the other hand, was designed to develop the practical virtues of firmness, bravery, reverence for the gods, self-restraint, seriousness, prudence, and a sense of justice.

The aim of Christian education as exemplified in the monastic life of the Middle Ages was salvation of the soul. Later, St. Thomas Aquinas (1225–1274), basing his teachings on Aristotelian principles, broadened the aim of Christian education to include cultivation of moral and intellectual virtues. Humanistic concern for individual development was voiced by Desiderius Erasmus (1466–1536), Martin Luther (1483–1546), Michel de Montaigne (1533–1592), John Comenius (1592–1670), John Milton (1608–1674), and Jean Jacques Rousseau (1712–1778). European Latin grammar schools were based on a humanistic approach to education; this classical tradition still survives in some Canadian grammar schools.

Greek, Roman, and medieval education was confined to the upper and middle classes. The idea of universal education began to assume significance only in the nineteenth century. The principles expounded by such pioneers as Egerton Ryerson (1803–1882) helped open Canadian schools to all strata of society. Today, education is no longer viewed strictly as a selective academic discipline. The needs of democracy and an understanding of the social nature of man's development are creating a greater awareness of the social aspects of education. A consideration of "the whole man" is resulting in the broadening of curriculum offerings and the provision of technical and vocational schools and guidance opportunities. Since the end of the Second World War, the vast expansion of applied sciences and technology, the growth of urbanization, and the revolution in communications media have created new demands on education at all levels. The major challenge today is how to relate general and liberal education to technical and vocational education—that is, how to create a technician without losing sight of human values.

All Canadian provinces, at one time or another, have issued reports emphasizing the need for broadening the aims of the school. For example, the Royal Commission of Inquiry on Education in the Province of Quebec stated in its report of 1964:

> *The school, of course, has many functions. But its primary task is to instill a passion for the truth and a respect for the intelligence.... Even though the school's primary function concerns the intellect, the whole child is involved in education. Hence the school has a more encompassing responsibility, especially at the elementary and secondary levels. It plays a major part in training for citizenship. In and through the school, the child makes his first contact with an organized society outside the family circle; thus the school should afford him the richest possible experience of social and community life. The scholastic environment must not promote individualism; it must develop in the child respect and regard for others, team feeling, communal solidarity. This is particularly essential in modern society. For one thing, democracy requires of everyone an active participation in civic and professional associations, an interest in public affairs. For another, modern man is more and more called upon to work in teams and in groups. Thus in industry, smooth human relations have become almost as important as technical knowledge. Intellectual, cultural, moral and even religious training have too often been regarded from the individual point of view; they must be given social dimensions.*[1]

There are three readings in this section. In the first, Neville V. Scarfe points out some shortcomings in the present Canadian educational system which, he believes, is largely based on obsolete concepts and outmoded traditions. In the second reading, the Very Rev. Henri Légaré argues that, in a pluralistic society, the State should provide for those who wish to include religious aims in education. In the third, H.T. Coutts out-

---

[1] Royal Commission of Inquiry on Education in the Province of Quebec, *Report of 1964*, Part II (Quebec: Government of the Province of Quebec, 1965), p. 14.

lines the functions of education in a democracy and enumerates some of the problems facing Canadian education today.

I-1

The Aims of Education in a Free Society*

NEVILLE V. SCARFE

•

Whereas conservative caution, traditional virtues, and conformity to the law are properly taught in the home, in the church, and in the community, and by the society at large, it is the school that has the added special function of developing creativity, initiative, and originality by encouraging adventurous curiosity and enthusiasm for research types of activity. While the school promotes individuality and the development of the diverse gifts of each human being, all the agencies outside the school seem to combine to produce conformity. To the school alone is delegated the task of developing creative diversity and free-thinking individualism. It must foster curiosity and the inquiring mind. It must train future citizens to be questioning and critical of all that they see or hear or read. Destructive criticism is, however, quite insufficient. It is much more important to be constructively creative. We want our young people to be enthusiastic searchers for the truth, not energetic fault-finders.

The remarks which follow are directed almost wholly towards the high school, partly because high schools have met with the severest criticisms, and partly because the Conference booklet on Aims concentrated on that age level.

•

WHAT IS HAPPENING NOW?

Before the thesis, thus briefly outlined, can be developed, it is necessary to present some unquestioned facts and easily ascertainable truths about education so that subsequent argument may be soundly based.

1. There is ample evidence to prove that the public in general is at present dissatisfied with the schools of the nation. This Conference has been called because people feel that education in school could be improved substantially. They feel that the practices now commonly employed in schools are the results of aims that have long since outworn

---

* Reprinted with permission from *The Second Canadian Conference on Education, A Report* (Toronto: University of Toronto Press, 1962), pp. 65–84.

their usefulness. There are many people who think that we need aims different from those which satisfied our ancestors, and that these new aims should be higher and more challenging than in any previous decade.

2. The evidence of the Royal Commissions, which have been recently operative in Canada, and of investigations in the schools of America made in the last three years by Martin Mayer and James Conant, is that the practices in the high schools of North America do not derive to any important extent from the aims set forth by progressive educators. The progressive school of thought seems to have affected chiefly textbooks, some programs of study, a few administrators, and the odd professor of education. Here and there some of the best ideas of progressive educators filtered into our elementary schools, but, in general, progressive education has had relatively little effect in the classrooms of the nation and, in particular, almost no effect on the teachers in secondary schools. Martin Mayer writes:

> *The Progressive Education Association died in 1955. Progressivism, as its founders saw it, had been dead a long time by then. Dating the death is difficult. The general rule is that an idea is dead when an organization is formed to promote it. By this rule the headstone might read 1919. Certainly the intellectual calibre of the movement began to descend at about that time. The Progressive Education Association's job was to sell progressivism to teachers and in the course of the selling the problem changed. Progressivism as James, Dewey, Parker and Eliot had seen it has never been widely accepted by American teachers. Progressivism, however, did do two things: It made it respectable to be nice to children all day long: It showed that intellectualism can become a mere barren fooling with irrelevant symbols. The tragedy of American education in the twentieth century is not that Dewey's influence has been so great but [that] it has been so little. In speaking of Dewey's progressivism, one must copy Chesterton's remark on Christianity, that is, it has not so much been tried and found wanting as it has been found difficult and not tried.*

3. Unfortunately, what goes on in our secondary schools is much more obsolete than many of the critics have thought. In the main, the aims of education, as can be seen from the practices in the classrooms, are still those of the traditional, authoritarian, conformist educators who saw schools, in the last century and in the beginning of this, as a great means of unifying the nation and bringing some uniformity to very diverse groups of people. They did not realize fifty years ago that mass production, mass media of communication, and the tremendous speeding up of transport, would bring about a unity and a conformity in the nation far faster and far more effectively than any school could ever do. Thus, schools, so far from needing to bring about conformity, now need to be the great advocates of diversity, ingenuity, novelty, and research. It is because of this massive change in the function and purpose

of schools that Canada is looking most urgently for important changes in the aims of education. Jack Scott, columnist of the *Vancouver Sun*, wrote no more than a few months ago:

> *When in Heaven's name is the school board going to learn to make education a joyful adventure instead of a grim dare? When are they going to grasp the basic idea that a disciplined memory is not half as important in life as an aroused curiosity?*
>
> *My children hold their own and better with their classmates in the competition for total recall but it is mighty rare for them to be engrossed in an idea or to sort out a great truth and mystery from the vast file of inconsequential, unimportant, and immaterial data that is shovelled daily into their tender little craniums. The curriculum, in short, remains as ironbound and unimaginative as it was in my day and as diabolically contrived to discourage the meaning and understanding of knowledge as it ever was.*
>
> *No deliberate conspiracy could contrive a formula so brutal in clobbering the true spirit of enquiry as this tedious traditional mill of arbitrary fact and robot-like method. God only knows how many fine minds and bright intellects have been discouraged by it and prevented from going on to university by revolting from it.*
>
> *More than that, it negates the whole idea of teaching—the "art," as Anatole France put it, "of awakening the natural curiosity of young minds for the purpose of satisfying it afterwards."*

C.P. Snow says that our traditional culture responds by wishing that the future did not exist. "American education like the American theatre suffers today from a paucity of vital and controversial things. It is cluttred at the moment with trivia. A close correlation can be established between this and the swing toward conformity and conventionality in the American life as a whole. The American cultural climate is a mood of caution and complacency rather than one of moral audacity and social indignation."

4. More than ever before in the history of the human race our future citizens will need the skills, the courage, the confidence, the knowledge and the moral fortitude to face a dynamically dangerous future where flexibility, resilience, resourcefulness, and willingness to think for oneself, will be of paramount value. Dr. Brock Chisholm, the author of one of the outstanding papers available to this Conference in the Study booklets, has said that we have to start completely afresh in our thinking about future problems. They are so different from anything that we have faced in the past that we must free our minds of obsolete ideas, from prejudice and superstition, and develop new insights, new approaches, and novel skills.

5. At the same time as we plan to face change we must maintain a free society. Perhaps we should say we must still continue to work towards a free society, for it is obvious that even in the Western world the four freedoms are not universally enjoyed by all. The charter of human rights is still far from being ideally applied. The great challenge of the French Revolution has yet to be properly tried out. Rarely have the triple aims of equality, liberty, and fraternity been simultaneously used. Too often the third side of the triangle, fraternity, is omitted. Furthermore, people have long since realized that liberty and equality in their extreme forms are mutually exclusive.. There has to be a balance between liberty and equality. Even this balance is unworkable unless it is fully and properly seasoned by the golden rule of brotherly love. Put in other words, a free democracy cannot be a free society unless it is also an ethical society. Our high school students must be encouraged to discuss these important issues and act on them.

A free society has the obligation to create circumstances in which all individuals may have opportunity and encouragement to attain freedom of the mind. To be free, a man must be capable of basing his choices and actions on understandings which he himself achieves and on values which he examines for himself. He must understand the values by which he lives and the assumptions on which they rest. The free man, in short, has a rational grasp of himself, his surroundings, and the relations between them. He has the freedom to think and choose.

6. Everybody is saying that the future will see great changes and that knowledge which today seems true will be proven untrue within a decade, that skills learned now will be obsolete within four or five years. We do not know what problems will face humanity in the future, but we do know that there will be some very grave problems, some very difficult crises, which will demand the best thought and the most careful reasoning that men can summon. It will, therefore, be less important in the future to accumulate facts than to know how and where to find facts and how to verify them. Facts, no doubt, will be available in plenty—in books, in encyclopaedias, and in all other forms of record. Therefore, the important skills will be how to use facts, how to think through a problem, how to learn and how to relearn the skills of logical thinking and alert reasoning. Discrimination, judgment, and good taste must be carefully fostered, for not only will there be many new and unforeseen problems, but the mass means of communication will extend an ever increasing barrage of persuasion and propaganda over us. Education in the future, in fact, will be the only reasonable protective shelter against mass media fallout.

7. Schools must be a means of decreasing the incidence of public gullibility and susceptibility to emotional persuasion and subtle propaganda. Whereas schools have, in the past, tried to train their pupils to be critical of books and printed words, they must now take on the task of training future citizens to be critical of what they see and hear on radio,

television, and film, because more and more of the ideas which will reach the public will come through the media of expression other than printed words. We know enough of group psychology and social engineering to know the tremendous threats that mass means of communication present to human life. We know that human beings can be kept in chains economically, intellectually, and emotionally by clever suggestion and diabolical persuasion. If we are ever to maintain a free society, then schools must be the protectors and promoters of freedom of thought and freedom of expression by providing mental training in clear logical thinking freed from superstition, prejudice, and unnecessary taboos.

8. We know a number of things about how children learn. We know, for instance, that they learn most effectively when they devote energetic attention to important problems. We know that they become diligently thoughtful when they are actively investigating real and concrete problems that seem to them worthwhile solving. We know that they learn most effectively if they can persist with concentrated effort for a considerable length of time. We know that this can happen and does happen when the problem or topic of investigation retains their interest, awakens their curiosity, and develops their enthusiasm. We know, too, that children are different—that different things interest different children. We realize, therefore, that it is the business of the school to make sure that every child devotes concentrated attention and thought to important and challenging problems, bearing in mind that not all worthwhile problems or useful ideas are interesting to begin with. It is the teacher's job to make them interesting, attractive, and valuable educationally.

9. All schools of psychological thought agree that behaviour which is rewarded is more likely to recur. They also say that the kind of reward which is very effective in motivating learning is the opportunity for fresh, novel, and stimulating experiences. A.N. Whitehead said many years ago that: "For successful education, there must always be a certain freshness in the knowledge dealt with. It must either be new in itself or it must be invested with some novelty of application to the new world of new times. Knowledge does not keep any better than fish."

Psychologists are all agreed, too, that the most effective effort put forth by children is where success seems quite possible but not certain.

Children learn best in an atmosphere of trust and sympathy just as teachers teach best when they are trusted and given freedom and responsibility.

There is very little that need be boring or worthless in school. There are plenty of exciting and worthwhile things to learn. No teacher need be dull or lacking in enthusiasm. No lesson need be unstimulating or unprovocative. Learning can be and should be a very profitable experimental inquiry offering exciting rewards for diligent thinking and creative imagination.

10. Education can never be made easy. There is no labour-saving device which can save the child the effort of thinking for himself. Education cannot be mechanized even though instruction can. Wisdom and virtue are not achieved by effort expended in any form outside the child's brain. The art of education is to make use of a child's *natural* desire, needs, interests, curiosity, in order to tap the maximum energy and guide it towards the consideration of the important problems of our time and of the future. Since children spend maximum effort on those activities which interest them most, all such activities should be turned to intellectual profit and thought-provoking value by a clever teacher. The purpose of the teacher is to see that a maximum amount of high quality cerebration goes on in a given time—far more than normally goes on now. This is not done by regimentation, by prescription, by compulsion, or by direct frontal attack—but by subtlety, ingenuity, persuasion, stimulus and by working through the things that naturally attract the inquisitive curiosity of the child.

11. Education is something that the child must do for himself. Teachers cannot add to the power of the child's mind any more than they can add one cubit to his stature. The child must do all the thinking for himself if he is to be educated. Like digestion and exercise, thinking and wise action are self-operated, essential activities which no one can do for another individual. Teachers can only arrange conditions which stimulate, foster, and maintain a desire for mental activity. Without the desire no valuable intellectual effort is forthcoming. It needs consummate artistry and scientific skill to arrange conditions in school so that children *naturally* want to learn, because the emphasis must always be on learning rather than teaching. Yet neither of these are ever easy.

12. We know that no one subject in the curriculum is of itself any more effective than another in developing and encouraging the thoughtful and critical activities of the mind.

The idea that some subjects or some topics are intrinsically easy and some difficult is fallacious. Mathematicians have recently shown that many of the concepts which were once reserved for university students can now be understood by children in Grade 4.

Many have claimed that foreign languages are difficult, and yet we know that all but the very severely mentally retarded French children speak that language relatively easily before attending school. The facts are that our schools have often made French unnecessarily difficult by obsolete ways of teaching and by concentrating on grammatical rules that no Frenchman would consciously observe, instead of concentrating on French dialogue and French literature and France.

The Educational Policies Commission [of the United States] makes a claim for the equality of subjects:

The study of an abstract subject like mathematics or philosophy, in and of itself, does not necessarily enhance rational powers, and it is possible that experiences in areas which appear to have little connection may, in fact, make a substantial contribution to rational development. Music and vocational subjects may engage the rational powers of pupils equally well. There is a highly creative aspect in the processes of thought. All the higher mental processes involve more than simple awareness of facts; they depend also on the ability to conceive what might be as well as what is, to construct mental images in new and original ways. Experiences in literature and arts may well make a larger contribution to these abilities than studies usually assumed to develop abstract thinking.

Thinking is in no sense restricted to academic subject-matter of the traditional Arts and Science programs. Some of the best thinking is done by those who apply themselves to the practical business of the world. Engineering physics, chemical engineering, architecture, cancer research, plant breeding, etc., are often far more stimulating to thought, far more demanding intellectually than such subjects as history or mathematics as taught in university because the latter are so often a question of memorizing masses of inert facts or useless formulae.

13. There is no known or proven educational good derived from forcing children to undertake boring and apparently valueless tasks. This does not mean that any human being can avoid harshness, drudgery or boredom sometimes, but let us not justify these educationally. It does not do people good to be compelled to suffer hardship, deprivation, or indignity. To have come up the hard way is not necessarily beneficial to the character or the soul. These old puritanical and sadistical fallacies die hard.

We must renounce the fallacious notion that it is good for children to be made to do things they dislike. There is no educational advantage in pain, failure, threats of punishment, or appeals to fear. It does not do people good to have to suffer disappointment or disgrace. Spartan austerity and toughening-up tactics are simply illogical relics of a barbaric age. The Christian ethic of forgiving one another, of turning the other cheek, of love, of kindliness to little children is totally opposed to such brutality.

●

WHY ARE SCHOOLS LAGGING?

Having examined some of the factual information related to education, it is necessary to explain why obsolete emphasis on the accumulation of facts and insufficient attention to thinking effort is still characteristic of our schools despite the massive weight of evidence and public unrest which demands a change. The fact that our schools are still carrying on in dusty, obsolete, textbook-dominated, standardized classrooms is not primarily the fault of the teacher. It is primarily the fault of those who control education, and of the impersonal, highly conservative, and authoritarian system which deprives teachers of sufficient freedom to do better. There are many forces which combine to curtail freedom and teachers caught in this web find it difficult to exhibit initiative, to use new ideas and fresh practices proven by research, or to develop independently. The whole atmosphere discourages enthusiasm, eagerness, confidence, or imagination, all of which are essential ingredients in any good classroom. Many, many teachers are capable of teaching far better than they do, but they resort to orthodox and stereotyped practices because they lack freedom. What curtails or seems to curtail their freedom?

1. One of the reasons why the freedom of many is curtailed is that they have been inadequately educated for their profession. They are, therefore, hemmed in by ignorance and lack of understanding. All teachers should have as long and as rigorous a preparation for their profession as a doctor, an architect, an engineer, or a lawyer. This is just as true of those who teach in Kindergarten as those who teach Grade 13. Teachers must be educated men and women before they become teachers. Cultured maturity and worldly widsom are even more important than a complete knowledge of the subject, important though that is. Furthermore, every teacher needs to have a great deal of training in psychology and sociology, so that he knows why he is teaching the way he is. Those who send out adolescents with just one year of teacher training can expect adolescent behaviour to be imitated in the schools. A great deal of what is best learned in the school is acquired incidentally, as if by infection, rather than by direct instruction. Children are very imitative and they need, therefore, to have examples of high quality persons in the classroom. They need to see the way of life of a person who loves books, who loves learning, who is an enthusiastic searcher for knowledge and skill, who believes in high ethical standards and has excellent work habits. Children need to be in the company of mature, wise, and humane adults who have mastered the artistry and science of clever educational procedures. These highly educated, highly qualified persons are the only ones who are inwardly free to experiment, to adventure, to lead with confidence and competence.

2. The freedom of the teacher is restricted because the curricula and the textbooks are usually prescribed by a superior authority.

3. In many instances, but certainly not in all, the effect of inspectors and supervisors is to restrict the freedom of teachers.

4. Teachers have no legal powers vested in them.

5. Parental criticisms voiced publicly or to school boards or to principals and superintendents are taken so seriously that teachers often feel totally intimidated, if not persecuted, by these activities.

6. There have been occasions, especially in the past, when School Boards and School Trustees have exercised a curbing influence on teacher freedom.

7. Since there are very few direct rewards for excellent teaching and since excellent teaching is very demanding, fatiguing, and time-consuming, few teachers find it worthwhile to pursue excellent teaching to a point where it might be questioned by an old-fashioned inspector or criticized by a conservatively minded parent.

8. Perhaps one of the most obvious reasons why the freedom of teachers is restricted is the size of the classes they have to teach and the number of different classes they have to meet in a given week. A teacher who must teach five hours a day to five different classes of 35 children will find that he is exhausted at the end of the day and will find it impossible both to prepare good lessons for the following day and to mark the exercises or essays completed during the current session.

9. Large classes in small classrooms make it impossible to use the most up-to-date facilities and equipment necessary for excellent education. Most classrooms are built and equipped solely for the study of textbooks; they are not designed for any other form of inquiry.

10. The excessive emphasis that we in Canada put on examinations and the frequent incidence of these examinations exert a tremendously restrictive influence. Formal examinations occupy a very large portion of the secondary school year so that the amount of time during which children are learning new things is seriously reduced and far less than many people suppose. The passing of examinations is for many teachers and children the only purpose of school attendance. Education becomes a subsidiary, incidental, almost accidental, concomitant to the grind for examination success.

Since the easiest type of material to examine, measure, and mark is factual information, examinations very often degenerate into a factual recall process. Children are not required to understand what they put down; they are simply required to regurgitate or repeat uncomprehended syllables and verbalisms, or still more frequently, to make check marks or crosses on an objective test indicating that they have recognized by clever random sampling or inspired guesswork the right response to an anticipated stimulus.

Here is an example of the plaintive cry of one teacher. "The succession of tests and examinations which clutter the schools are a curse, for they interfere with the real business of teaching which is to stimulate curiosity and expose children to a few important truths."

Wilbur J. Bender of Harvard in a brilliant exposition points out the futility of relying too naively on examinations:

The student who ranks first in his class may be genuinely brilliant, or he may be a compulsive worker, or the instrument of domineering parents' ambition, or a conformist, or self-centred careerist who has shrewdly calculated his teachers' prejudices and expectations and discovered how to regurgitate efficiently what they want.

The adolescent with wide ranging curiosity and stubborn independence, with vivid imagination and desire to explore fascinating by-paths, to follow his own interest, to contemplate, to read the unrequired books, the boy filled with this sheer love of life and exuberance may well seem to his teachers troublesome, undisciplined, a rebel, may not conform to their stereotype, and may not get the top grades and the highest rank in the class.

Our present school system seems, in fact, to produce simply a high level of dull, competent, safe, academic mediocrities, an army of future Ph.D.'s. Competitive scholarship at the secondary school level is often the enemy of originality and creativity.

There are many kinds or aspects of intelligence which are important and grade-getting and test-scoring intelligence is not necessarily the most important even for purely intellectual pursuits. Judgment is important, and curiosity and independence and honesty and courage and sensitivity and generosity and vitality. Energy may well be the most important x-factor in determining the future contribution of an individual. Ten per cent of extra energy is probably worth at least 150 points on the scholastic aptitude test score. And judgment may be worth 200.

11. In general, therefore, teachers feel that they are inadequately trusted and are not given sufficient scope to carry on teaching in ways which they know to be better than the orthodox.

New York State and its school districts taken together employ more administrators than all of Western Europe. In Western Europe supervision is in the hands of men who understand that influence is at once more agreeable and more effective than authority. When the London County Council appoints the headmaster, they appoint the captain of a ship. And the headmaster, who may be teaching half a day, will usually extend similar courtesies to individual teachers. In France their system is held together not by orders from Paris, but by the general agreement of French teachers on what is important.

It is true, of course, that none of these restrictive influences need, in fact, curtail the freedom of the excellent teacher. If a first class person with a highly intelligent outlook feels that his freedom is curtailed by these influences he will likely move out of the profession. Unfortunately, because of the known restrictions, many of the great minds of the nation do not even attempt to enter the teaching profession; if they do, they leave it. Sometimes, therefore, the profession must make do with less than the most brilliant minds. Yet many such persons could do a first class job in the classroom if they were adequately trained, if the classes could be small, and if they could be given scope to develop original ideas, without undue inspection, criticism, and excessive domination by examinations.

People become trustworthy only by being trusted. They learn to be responsible only by being given freedom. They learn self-discipline only by *not* being disciplined from outside. They learn to think for themselves only by *not* having their thinking done for them.

●

TEACHING AND INSTRUCTION

Before spelling out more clearly how our future education should look, it seems necessary to distinguish between *instruction* and *teaching*.

An *instructor* is a performer and an informer. He tells a listening, attentive audience what they should know, how they should behave, what they should think. He presents problems and questions and then tells the answer with careful explanation and demonstration. He gives plenty of practice and drill. He relies mainly on memory and habit.

An instructor is often convinced, quite erroneously, that there is educational value in self-denial, in regimenting one's self, in doing one's duty. He feels, unjustifiably, some puritanism is a good training for future life and that a certain amount of asceticism builds character.

Instruction is authoritarian, or even patriarchal. It leads to conformity and preserves the status quo. It is a method of handing on, in easy doses, the distilled and accumulated wisdom and skill of the past. Instruction is a means of reproducing the type. It is designed to inculcate respect for tradition, for what society in the past has judged to be good, true, right and beautiful. Instruction produces well-informed conformists. It satisfies the conservative side of human nature only.

Instruction can, of course, be done by mechanical means, through mass media, through books, and simply requires that the learner be able to read. Instruction as described above does not, however, produce an educated person. It produces a well-informed person, but not a thinker, not a doubter, not an originator. By itself it is of little use for the future.

Teaching, on the other hand, is something entirely different. Teaching is human artistry in getting pupils to think for themselves, not by telling them answers but by asking questions. Pupils are no longer passively listening or patiently learning by heart what the textbook says. They are actively investigating original sources of information and data by experimental methods in order to draw their own inferences and their own conclusions.

The teacher is a resourceful person, a guide, a stimulus, one who opens cultural windows, suggests other approaches and other points of view. A teacher is a subtle adviser whose primary purpose is not to condition or to indoctrinate or to constrain, but to free future citizens of the trappings of prejudice, tradition, and custom, in order that they may arrive anew by thinking for themselves at the great truths of the ages and at great new truths.

A teacher has at least four main functions, none of which could be called direct instruction:

1. To see clearly the immediate and ultimate purposes of education for himself and for his class. He should also be able to state quite clearly the worthwhile, practical, immediate purpose for the children. That purpose is never passing an examination. The purpose is always intrinsic to the subject to be studied and its value for the children at the age and level at which they are.

2. The teacher should select and arrange the environment or the materials or the information or the experiences with which the children are to come into direct contact.

3. The teacher should guide, by suggestion, encouragement and stimulus, the children's investigation of and thought about the environment, materials, information, and experiences provided. Wherever possible the experiences should be direct experiences and not verbal substitutes for them. Obviously a laboratory type of research enquiry is intended for all subjects.

4. By some careful guidance the children should be led to draw conclusions and inferences and then apply acquired ideas to themselves and to the problems of the world around. They should also be given opportunities to express their ideas in various art forms. Obviously a studio type activity is implied again for all subjects.

The teacher, then, is one who sees to it that children are actively inquiring into and experimenting with new materials in order to gain new insights, new enlightenment, and new understandings useful to them and satisfying to their needs. A great teacher is one who can help them carry over their newly acquired insights to the improvement of the power of their mind, the quality of their character and wisdom. This final carry-over from acquired ideas to mind quality and power is the most fundamental part of education and the activity for which a personal teacher is most necessary.

●

EDUCATION AND LEARNING

Education is not just learning, that is, acquiring or mastering or understanding or achieving or accumulating. Education is a power, a quality, a richness, an ability to think and act wisely and virtuously. Education gives freedom, independence, assurance, confidence, a sense of perspective, powers of discrimination, and judgment. In fact, education gives personal quality.

Education, of course, cannot happen without learning, without information, and without skill. Learning is essential to education, just as food is necessary for bodily growth. Learning and education must go on together just as bodily growth and food consumption must go on together. Bodies must expend energy in order to eat, and in order to have energy a person must eat. One does not necessarily come before the other. They should happen simultaneously. Thus the learning of certain skills and the acquisition of certain information are not the necessary prerequisites to education, but they are necessary concomitants. Education may result from learning but learning always results from education. Therefore, it is best in school to concentrate on the educational side and to have learning as the incidental accomplishment that must come through concentration on education.

In our schools the instruction and the learning acts are still essentially those of fact-giving and fact-getting. This conception of fact as the basis of education process is both unnecessary and undesirable. The mental processes involved in the acquisition of facts about things as they are, are of a low order in the range of human intellectual potential.

Another very serious criticism of the fact type of education is that, in the life of the citizen, in his work, his play, his family life, his participation in civic, social, and religious institutions, the critical mental processes in use are not the simple recall and application of learned fact, but thought processes such as judgment, inference, and reasoning. It is, therefore, the development of the person in terms of increasing precision and appropriateness of thought processes which should form the continuing basis for educational experience rather than the mere addition of layer upon layer of descriptive fact through successive years of schooling. Rarely are problems solved by facts all of which are carried in the head. What a person understands of the functional relationship between classes of things, his understanding of the limits of such present knowledge as he has, and his insight into the need for particular kinds of additional facts, are the only truly effective understandings which lead to the successful adjustment of a situation to human needs. Fact collecting is, therefore, inadequate to the educative process.

There is a massive weight of opinion as well as undoubted evidence which favours emphasis on thinking rather than accumulation of facts. A few opinions only are provided. From Principal M. Woodside of University College, University of Toronto:

> *We should not teach facts at all. We shall have to make use of current facts for our purpose, but our purpose should be to teach the young to think in certain ways.*
>
> *The minimum of literacy required by the modern world is the ability to*

detect prejudice, special pleading and fraud and to reach conclusions by some valid form of reasoning. This cannot be deferred until the young reach the university or the technical institute. The process must begin in grade one. Most, if not all, of the evil in the world today is due to muddled thinking.

From Dean W. R. Niblett, University of London, Institute of Education:

Sheer knowledge is not necessarily educative. There is no proof and little evidence that if you do succeed in making a much greater proportion of men and women knowledgeable about all sorts of interesting things you will produce any great increase in the proportion of really educated people. Knowledge has to enter the heart as well as the head. School books tend to be looked upon as repositories of the dull truth in some absolute desiccated way. We all have to learn how to cope with feeling as well as how to cope with fact. To pretend that feeling hardly matters, or that the school need have no regard for such things, is to mistake part of the nature of our business.

John Dewey said: "The sole direct path to enduring improvement in the methods of instruction and learning consists in centering upon the conditions which exact, promote and test thinking." And A. N. Whitehead: "A merely well informed mind is the most useless bore on God's Earth."

Professor E. A. Peel, in his book *The Pupil's Thinking*, distinguishes four types of thinking. First he names "imaginative thinking." This is the type called up in creative writing, painting, music, and so on. Secondly, he identifies one called "explanatory thinking" which is connected with describing and explaining events or things in history, geography, science, or mathematics. The third kind is called "productive thinking," where the pupil is called upon to apply his knowledge or make use of his explanations in new situations. The fourth kind of thinking does not often appear in school but is called "integrative thinking" and is the type of thinking involved where great men such as Einstein develop new theories and systems of thought. Some people would call this speculative thought.

The conclusion to this study of teaching and education is that instruction will no longer suffice to help our future citizens face the problems of the future. Simple acquisition of the 3-R skills or the accumulation of information will no longer be of much avail by themselves. Instead, future citizens must be educated to speak for themselves, to learn the skills of argument and analysis, of logical deduction, of critical appraisal, and of experimental inquiry. They must learn how to sift, select, and assess evidence. They must learn how to counteract the effects of propaganda and persuasive appeals to the emotions. All this they must learn through their own efforts, not by instruction, by being in situations which cause them to think through what is presented to them, naturally and willingly.

•
CREATIVE EDUCATION FOR THE FUTURE

Since change is obvious in the future, we must concentrate more on the *creative* rather than on the conservative thinker in school; on freedom rather than conformity. The ingenious, the thoughtful, and the courageous must be encouraged.

If young people are to face new problems in a fresh situation they must learn to take nothing for granted, to make no false assumptions. They must learn the arts of thinking things out afresh for themselves by asking the most searching, appropriate, and fundamental questions. If this is so, we cannot expect them to accept education in school on trust. They must be convinced in their minds that what is provided in school is of value for them. They must not rely on authority, on custom, on precedent, or on time-honoured theory to solve future problems. They must learn that they cannot lean on or depend on adults or any other authorities to do their thinking for them. They must, in fact, resist all attempts to have thinking done for them. Unless they become independent thinkers, they will not be able to face future difficulties. Moreover, they will tend to conform to all the persuasive devices that vested interests can construct.

In the matter of traditional values schools start where other agencies leave off. Certain moral standards and codes of behaviour must be assumed. Schools can reinforce these but preservation of the past or of the status quo is not their major function. Schools should not primarily be devoted to passing on the accumulated wisdom of the past. This is already in books for all to read. They must perform the intellectual function which other agencies cannot easily undertake, which is to use the wisdom of the past to stimulate thinking and adventure with new ideas and with recent research findings. Schools must set children free to explore, to investigate, to experiment, and to construct. They must be essentially creative. Home and society will naturally be conservative. Without large-scale opportunity to create, schooling can never become education and knowledge will never become wisdom. That is why children must actively pursue education in laboratories and studios working with many more sources of information than books, and many more media of expression than words.

Real education, then, is not turning out well-rounded individuals in grey flannel suits, but young people with sharp-edged and uncowed consciences, persons with the character to be critics of society rather than conformists to it. They will be men of high understanding and broad principles who do not worship the god conformity, and do not mind sticking out their necks in favour of a moral principle.

The value of education lies in its power to enable students to invent and create new learning. Researchers have discovered that conformists are not the most useful citizens. The divergent thinker and those of complex temperaments are more useful to society than the convergent thinker and those who are only well-adjusted.

The divergent thinker is one who has an acute sensitivity to problems, a fluency of ideas, mental flexibility, and an ability to redefine familiar concepts. A creative soul has a quick humour and an ability to accept conflicts and tension. He is willing to let go all certainties and illusions.

It is the convergent thinker who rates high in I.Q. tests and on academic achievement tests, for he is able to give back the answers that the teacher wants. The divergent thinker, however, is the inventor, the originator of new ideas. He is the critic not only of the natural world but of the social world.

Creativity in adulthood is the natural sequence to play in childhood and both are the natural research activities of the human mind which flourish only in freedom. Creativity, however, does not develop in license and it isn't novelty just for the sake of being different. Creativity results from knowledge, understanding, and careful reflective thought, and depends for its success on thorough understanding of thought processes.

Unless children are allowed to be creative, unless they have opportunity to express their ideas, they can never become educated. Similarly, unless teachers in training are allowed to be experimental and creative, ingenious and imaginative in trying out new ways of teaching, we can never call the process teacher education.

Creativity implies that artistic pursuits are important in schools. Whitehead made this claim many years ago: "What is most precious and distinctive about any human being is his inner life, his appreciation, his sense of values. Art objectifies this subjective call of life. Civilization that neglects art for the sake of specialized education, competitive business, or scientific and technological advancement, is cutting the roots of its spiritual powers." Sir Julian Huxley also claims that "The essential distinctiveness of Art is that it provides a qualitative enrichment of life by creating a diversity of new experience. It is a process of discovery about ourselves and about life. Art opens the doors of that other world in which matter and quantity are transcended by mind and quality."

Jerome S. Bruner in his book *The Process of Education* very rightly advocates *intuitive learning* rather than formal understanding. When he uses the word "'intuitive" he means what others in education mean by "creative." He uses a rather telling phrase when he says that "children should have an intuitive feel for geometry."

Again, in attacking formalization in school, which he claims is dull and boring, he says that children when studying geometry should become skilful in discovering proofs, not in checking the validity of or remembering proofs already provided. Formalism in school has devalued intuition and creativity and debased imagination. Grading and examinations, rewards and punishments also inhibit intuitive thinking. He clinches his argument by quoting another writer as saying: "How do I know what I think until I feel what I do?"

●

THE POSITIVE DYNAMIC OUTLOOK

As in school, so out of school, adolescents should be encouraged to be critical of what they hear or see or read. They should be taught to verify statements, to investigate original sources of information and to avoid judgment without adequate data or evidence. To do this children must be freed from many of their prejudices and allowed to be accurately questioning and creatively original. C.P. Snow says:

> *Modern education should be completely antithetical to indoctrination. It should constantly require searching examination of the relevant evidence borne against every economic, political, moral or other proposal. It requires frank uninhibited communication about every aspect of all proposals. The major task of the school is not to transmit culture, rather its task is to lift the sights of the educational operation towards its innovative role. Educators must accept the thrilling opportunities of sharing in the creation of a new epoch both by and for mankind. The teacher is no longer a person whose main function is to impart information or even to demonstrate skills since so many resources are available and conveniently organized in a variety of published forms. In the age of mass media the teacher's function shifts to emphasis on selection, evaluation, interpretation, application, and individual guidance.*

John A. Irving in an article entitled "The Changing World Community," says most aptly that: "Those who tremble before the shape of things to come have failed to realize that our educational systems are already heavily weighted with propaganda—propaganda for the status quo. If we prevent educators from educating for social change, they will become pallid retailers of social reaction. Any education that is not education of the social change is missing fire."

●

A CREATIVE PHILOSOPHY

It seems appropriate to end by stating succinctly my own convictions about the aims of education in our schools.

1. The function of the teacher in school is to select and arrange materials and conditions which encourage and stimulate future citizens to reflect, contemplate, reason, cogitate, and think diligently, critically, constructively, and creatively for themselves and by themselves about the world of men and nature.

2. In order to think effectively future citizens need (a) to be alertly aware of and curiously inquisitive about the world of nature and man around them; (b) to acquire the mental skills necessary to face *new* problems courageously, constructively, and creatively.

3. In order to become effective future citizens, schools should encourage the maximum development of initiative, independence, and responsible use of freedom in their pupils.

4. In order to promote maximum mental growth and health, schools should concern themselves with the all-round development of the child—in particular, much care must be taken of emotional, aesthetic, and artistic development. Intellectual, physical, and spiritual growth depend on the care devoted to emotional harmony, balance, and well-being.

5. Education is an active, exploratory, discovery process of self-development and fulfilment. It is stimulated by using the child's native curiosity, love of adventure and experiment, and his desire to create and construct for himself. Education is stimulating chiefly when it deals with modern problems which have real and immediate significance for the child. The emphasis must always be on treading new ground, on possible future problems rather than on going over well-trodden ground or recounting past difficulties.

6. Education implies the development of future citizens who welcome change and are willing and able to modify society progressively and intelligently for the benefit of all mankind.

7. Education is not *primarily*: (a) handing on the heritage of the past; (b) moulding citizens to a type; (c) acquisition of factual information; (d) testing, by recall, of acquired facts; (e) training of regimented minds who accept traditional behaviour and thinking uncritically; (f) a passive absorptive process.

8. An educated person is one for whom facts, knowledge, and particularly experience have stimulated thinking so that independent ideas, conclusions, attitudes, and wisdom have developed to produce a harmoniously balanced personality devoted to freedom, honesty, impartiality, tolerance, and human virtue. An educated person not only knows facts, but has thought about them, has associated them into ideas, patterns of thought, connected argument and generalizations. Further the educated person has assimilated the ideas and principles derived from thinking about facts and experiences and is able to use and apply these ideas to understanding the world and himself. He has further developed attitudes, character, culture, maturity and wisdom. His mind has developed power, efficiency and humanity.

CONCLUSION

This dissertation has shown that there is a massive array of evidence to prove that the aims which animate the present practices in school are inadequate for the free Canadian society of the future. The evidence is also overwhelming that our children are not being educated as effectively as they should. The chief faults are caused by the obsolete aims of the traditional, authoritarian, and excessively academic school of thought with its emphasis on passive absorption of verbal information.

The future must put far greater emphasis on the thinking processes, on creativity, on self-directed inquiry, on problem-solving techniques. Far more effort and energy must be devoted to learning rather than teaching. Curiosity, initiative and interest must be kept alive. Fact-finding and fact regurgitation must no longer be the primary purpose of schooling or examinations.

To achieve these aims, teachers must be given a far better education not merely in professional work, but more particularly as persons. High quality individuals with wisdom and artistry in human relations are needed. Four years of immersion in the cultural excitement and intellectual turmoil of a university are an essential minimum.

Teachers must also be given a far greater measure of freedom and trust than they now enjoy, so that they can set an example of enthusiastic inquiry, independent initiative, and courageous creativity. Teachers must have much smaller classes and more ready access to a great variety of teaching materials, aids and apparatus.

Nothing, however, is more important than the quality of the person who becomes a teacher in the classroom. Dr. A. W. Trueman at the last Canadian Conference [1958] tried to crystallize the general feeling by saying: "Nothing is wrong with Canadian Education that a great deal more money will not put straight." He was wrong because he thought we simply needed more of the same. May I try to sum up our present thinking by using a slightly altered phrasing? "Nothing is wrong with Canadian Education that better quality teachers will not put straight." This implies that we need an education that is better and *different*. Dare I say exacting, positive, creative, thought-provoking, and experimental? Let us avoid tedious dullness, unchallenging drill, stereotyped repetition, useless content, and puritanical mistrust. Let us have faith in the goodness of our fellow men, our teachers, and our children.

REFERENCES

Barzun, Jacques, *The House of Intellect*, New York: Harper and Row, 1959.
Bender, Wilbur, *The Top-One-Per-Cent Policy*, Cambridge: Harvard University Press, 1961.
Bruner, J. S., *The Process of Education*, Cambridge: Harvard University Press, 1960.
Burton, Kimball and King, *Education for Effective Thinking*, New York: Appleton-Century-Crofts, 1960.
Conant, James B., *The American High School Today*, New York: McGraw-Hill Company, 1959.
Educational Policies Commission, *The Central Purpose of American Education*, 1961.
Fleming, C. M., *Teaching*, Toronto: Methuen, 1959.
Hullfish and Smith, *Reflective Thinking*, New York: Dodd Mead & Co., 1961.
Huxley, Julian, *The Humanist Frame*, London: Allen & Unwin, 1961.
Mayer, Martin, *The Schools*, New York: Harper and Row, 1961.
Niblett, W. R., *Objectives in Secondary Education Today*, London: College of Preceptors, 1961.
Peel, E. A., *The Psychological Basis of Education*, Toronto: Clarke Irwin and Company, Limited, 1956.
―――, *The Pupils Thinking*, London: Oldbourne Book Co., 1960.
Scarfe, Neville V., *Conflicting Ideas in Teacher Education*, Boyd Bode Lectures, Columbus: Ohio State University Press, 1959.
―――, *A Philosophy of Education*, Winnipeg: University of Manitoba Press, 1952.
Whitehead, A. N., *The Aims of Education*, London: Williams & Norgate, 1947.

I-2

The Primary Ends of Education*

VERY REV. HENRI LÉGARÉ

•

... If an educator can ... easily be brought to identify education with training, there are certainly grounds for believing that at the very outset he was victim of a confusion still more fundamental. It all goes back, I maintain, to an aboriginal ignorance of the importance of the first end of education. And having lost sight of that, we are led in no time at all in theory or in practice either to mistake means for ends or to promote the attainment of partial objectives at the expense of the integral formation of the person. And here—if I may make so bold—we touch upon the congenital weakness of many educational theories. You will forgive me, I am sure, the temerity of what I have to say when you remember that the task expressly assigned to me is to submit to you thoughts, of their nature, provocative.

Jacques Maritain, in those inspiring pages on the philosophy of education on which my own thought is so largely dependent, constantly harks back to this fundamental point. Our educators have devoted themselves successfully and excessively to a sort of animal training, having to do with psychological habits, conditioned reflexes and sensorial memorization. It is from there that they have become infatuated by learning methods and techniques of social adjustment. Let us not say, I beg you, that "these means are bad." Indeed, "they are so good" that we have lost or forgotten the essential *why* of them. Today, "the child is so well tested and observed, his needs so well detailed, his psychology so clearly cut out, the methods for making it easy for him everywhere so perfected, that the end of all these commendable improvements runs the risk of being forgotten or disregarded."[1]

What is at the root of this mistake? It is neither more nor less than a radical ignorance of the true nature of man. We hem and haw over the ends of education because we cannot decide on the specific characteristics of the person to be educated. Inevitably, ... the question "What is man?" comes back at every stage of the discussion on the

---

* Reprinted with permission from *The Second Canadian Conference on Education, A Report* (Toronto: University of Toronto Press, 1962), pp. 58–64.
[1] Jacques Maritain, *Education at the Crossroads* (New Haven: Yale University Press, 1943), p. 3.

subject of education. And this is our security, for in our constant awareness of its presence, we can be certain of keeping on the right track. We must keep on going on this same path in spite of the temptation to leave it because of its multiplying ramifications. Baffled by the very complexity of man, there is the constant temptation to take the short cut by monstrous over-simplifications, such as pragmatism, intellectualism, sociologism, etc. For it is readily admitted to be easier by far to concentrate on one aspect at the expense of others than to take the trouble to discover means of holding on to all. Too often our educators are allured by the idea that education is primarily adjustment to life in society and try to make of their students citizens, before making men of them and then citizens. No less frequent and equally dangerous is that educational theory which would have the educator hide beyond his blind confidence in either the *scientific idea* of man to the exclusion of the *philosophic idea*, or vice versa....

We see ... that man is without a peer in all the kingdom of creation. He is the only one to exercise the double rôle of knowing and loving, his power and his glory. Therefore all true education must revolve upon the axis of these two poles, and must seek as its first essential goal the edification of man in this double dimension. To build a man is to build a being of love and knowledge, that is, on the one hand, to free his intellect from that innate darkness which prevents his seeing clearly the path he is to follow, and, on the other, to free his will from that servitude to the instincts which deny the will in the lower orders of creating. Or to use the classical formula, to open the entire being to the values of goodness, truth and beauty. As for those other more particular ends, such as teaching techniques, learning for earning, learning for living, education for democracy, while they are not to be scorned, they must at all times be subordinate to the formation of a man as a being of knowledge and love....

"Training does not stretch the mind," nor does that education which would make knowledge and love exercise themselves in a vacuum. More is necessary than an intellect which merely functions well. Insight does not exist in an aptitude for juggling terms, not even for thinking, but in the capacity of *knowing*, of understanding *that which is*. And the reason is clear: our intellectual and affective faculties enter into a vital relation with specific objects, with values of goodness and truth, real objects which do not have to be invented, but rather to be revealed. And to cut off these faculties from what gives them their meaning is to condemn them to sterility. To explain what is in fact a very simple truth, but which is only now being re-discovered after two centuries of mentally paralysing idealism, our modern thinkers are devoting their attention to what is called the "intentional" character of the consciousness. Consciousness, they say, repeating Husserl, is always consciousness of something. The acts of consciousness, in other words, are essentially revelatory strokes that disclose the meaning and value of the world. In layman's language what this means is, as Jean Daniélou puts it, "what makes the intellect is to know the truth."...

... So, the primary duty of the educator, in conformity with the primary law of the intellect, is to help the student find himself, to help him find his place in the whole reality, in this world here below in which he exists, lives, loves, suffers, prays, follows his destiny and dies....

Today perhaps more than ever before one of our great needs is the formation of large numbers of technicians and men of science, and for them to accomplish, in keeping with the biblical vocation of man, the irreplaceable mission of penetrating the secrets of the cosmos, of liberating man from slavery to matter. Mankind can only be the better for their researches.

But it is no less imperative in our day to protect humanity, not indeed from science but from technocracy, that is to say from the despotic domination of man's life by techniques.... And here nothing on the human level will help as much as an education, during the school years, in the meaning and value of others, as much as a moral and social formation firmly grounded upon the respect due the dignity of another self. The Rt. Hon. Sir David Eccles, K.C.V.O., M.P., leader of the United Kingdom delegation to the Commonwealth Conference on Education held in New Delhi, quoted, in reference to this, the words of the English Professor, Dr. M. V. C. Jeffreys: "The most important thing about any household or school or system of education is the quality of human relationships which it sanctions and fosters." He went on to develop his own views by saying: "In practical terms what do these ideals mean for us? That we should curb the advance in scientific and technological education? Certainly not. But they do mean that the benefits and results of such education should be used in the service of a good society the principles of which are explicitly and consistently upheld as part of the education itself."

There is another question which we must ask in this regard. Will it be enough for the realization of such an ideal to limit ourselves to a program inspired on purely philanthropic grounds? Sir David does not seem to be of this opinion. Regarding the principles which are to be upheld, of which he had just finished speaking, he did not hesitate to speak his mind quite clearly by saying: "We should teach our religion to our children." For man infinitely transcends man, says Pascal. He must seek in a higher realm the animating principle of his social and interpersonal life in the world. I cannot see where such a higher principle can be found if it be not in God, the only Truth capable of giving internal unity and soundness to moral and social education. If the educator does not tap this source for the inspiration of his moral and social teaching, his only alternative will be to base it upon such precarious, unstable foundations as convention, caprice, social convenience or on no more than a vague humanitarian instinct. During the past two hundred years of progressive secularization, the Western world has suffered the illusion of defending the spiritual values inherent in its democratic way of life with such ineffectual weapons as these. But in fact, we have been able to resist up till now thanks to that residue of the Christian heritage on which, in spite of ourselves, we continue to live but which we continue to squander. But for how long can we resist attack, armed only with this poor humanitarian instinct? Atheistic communism shows no less a humanitarian face to the world, differing only from ours in that they push to the limit the logic of their atheism. They would prove to the world their ability to establish a universal brotherhood of men on the rejection of God. Apart from their colossal technological and economic advances which blind us to the true significance of their philosophy, the extent of their achievement to date lies in their success in launching great sections of humanity upon the most inhuman adventure yet known to the world. Nor should we be surprised by this! Brotherhood necessarily presupposes Fatherhood. It is sublimely contradictory to keep on treating men as brothers while forbidding them to recognize God as their Father.

And still we shut our eyes wilfully against these hard lessons of history, even when the most serious observers of the condition of man are unanimous in affirming that the cleavage between religion and life is at the very root of our spiritual malaise.

... To separate the child from religion during his school career, to divorce religious teaching from his humanist and moral formation, is to give him to understand at the very threshold of his intellectual life that religion is no more than a superfluous insignificant element. How can he avoid feeling bewildered, incapable of making a meaningful synthesis! Soon follows the conclusion that he has been fed fables at home and that school is a process of gentle rupture with the family's religious sentimentality.

Moreover, has not the child a valid right to receive from his education the knowledge of those things which are to play important parts in his life? And is not religion just such a knowledge which will help him to find his bearings as a *being-in-the-world*? Frequently, we hear that the goal of education is learning for living. What then about learning for dying? Unless it is that in our technological civilization even death has lost its meaning, or rather that it is regarded as no more than another function, when a mass of flesh is sloughed off as superfluous, eternally superfluous....

Those of our generation who, for opinions which they have every right to hold, oppose any form of religious education in our schools must come to understand this. All we would ask of them is, that if they be pleased to deny themselves the advantages of such instruction, they should at least show that tolerance towards their fellow citizens who have nevertheless the right to receive all the intellectual equipment necessary to the understanding of their culture and civilization.

From all that has been said so far, it follows inevitably that there can be no education independent of a philosophy of man. To refuse to recognize this is to admit it nonetheless, for a philosophy is denied only by a counter philosophy. And what is even more specific, any theory concerning the ends of education is bound not just to our idea of man but more profoundly to our philosophy of knowledge, to our epistemology, that is to say to our stand in the face of truth. I do not think we can overestimate the importance of such a philosophy or exaggerate the repercussions of such a philosophy upon the over-all behaviour of the educator. If the truth concerning the meaning of reality, of existence is no more than an outmoded relic which must be replaced by modern pragmatic or positivist substitutes, if that only is true which can be checked and measured in the laboratory or which has proved itself in experience to have succeeded, then is the situation of our education desperate indeed. We may as well give up any image of man worthy of inspiring our education programs. For what is sucking the life blood of all the wonderful theories of education which are proposed, and I include here what is called "progressive education" whose merits must be admitted, is not the contribution of science to the improvement of our methods but rather those philosophies which define man as *nothing but biological, psychological drives or reflexes, nothing but blood and matter.* We try to ward off the disastrous results of this impoverished concept of man by clinging madly, emotionally to a mass of values, a *consensus* of which the components—spirituality, liberty, justice, equality, the dignity and the rights of man—have been reduced to worn-out clichés. In this I wonder if we are not just going one better than the logomachy of certain defenders of democracy. For if while invoking their aid we are always to remain powerless to base these values on reason, I very much fear that we will be doing no more than playing with words of high emotional charge. . . .

. . . I am well aware that the views I have so far expressed will not find universal support. I would be deceived if it were the contrary. Else, where would be the need of our congress? But it does not follow that we are at odds all along the line. There is a definable area of agreement. Our differences need not, nay must not, prevent our having a common attitude regarding the plurality of our doctrinal tendencies. Indeed, it is upon just such plurality that we base our hope of building a common philosophy of education in Canada. . . .

My questioner may . . . admit the necessity of thus laying bare the doctrinal foundation of our faith in democracy, but will maintain the hypothesis that it is dangerous, unhealthy to do so, that it can but accentuate the walls that separate us, that it will make havoc of our precarious national unity. To which there can only be one answer— "What do you mean by 'national unity'?" If you continually confuse unity with uniformity, diversity with division, then indeed you may well seek to prevent young minds from reflecting upon the depths of their democratic convictions, for in so doing they will become aware of their differences. But have you considered who and what will be most hurt by such a prohibition? It will be no other than the young minds you vainly seek to protect and that national unity you spend yourself to safeguard; the first will be frustrated by your refusal to give them a reasonable answer; the second, that is our national life or rather the democratic ideal, will be irremediably weakened in the minds of our people for it will not be supported on firmly established convictions.

The educator's task, as you can well see, is no easy one. For he is set well and truly in the face of a dilemma which seems to escape any solution. He has two alternatives: either he must submit to the policy directives and accept the function of serving up watered-down truths, so vague and gratuitous that the intellect cannot get its teeth into them, in which case he denies his vocation as educator; or, he must hold out to the very end and educate, in which case he will be disobeying the policy directives. To the best of my knowledge, there is no possible solution to this impasse other than the official establishment by the State of a pluralism in education which will correspond to the desires of all citizens.

The State has a fundamental rôle to play in the realm of education. Its charge is, writes Louis de Naurois, "... to so arrange that teaching be given in the best manner possible...." Does that not mean precisely that the State must have as its primary object the development of man in all his social and personal dimensions? But it does not thereby follow that the school system *serving the true interests of all* will necessarily be the most egalitarian and the most conformist. For such a system, *suiting everybody's needs,* while promoting the sense of civic responsibility and national unity on the one hand, will on the other take full cognizance of the need to help the individual achieve his full stature as a man according to and in keeping with his intellectual aspirations. Needless to say this consideration must also govern the constant preoccupation of the State that education be given in the best manner possible. But it demands no less than that human education be ever closely associated with those ideological bases on which the student will construct his life philosophy, the reasons for his personal and democratic commitments.

I am covinced that only a pluralism in education can answer these legitimate claims, made as they are with the aim of guaranteeing the maximum educative value to our teaching. That is why, above and beyond any other plans to improve this or that point at issue, it is of pressing urgency to look first to the sound establishment of an over-all organization of such a nature as will permit it to realize the principal objective of any educational system: the integral human formation corresponding to the intellectual exigencies of a true education. This done, all other ends will be the more easily achieved, be it the formation of a citizen convinced of his responsibilities or the strengthening of the national and democratic consciousness of our people.

Such an ideal, however, in the context of pluralism in education, will ever remain in the realm of wishful thinking as long as the private school in Canada is forced to play the part of a poor relation, a tinker's makeshift, a rival instead of a partner....

We shall not have a viable Philosophy of Education in Canada until the day when in a spirit of healthy toleration we begin to work together for unity *in* and *by* diversity within the framework of a context typically Canadian, that of a duality of races and cultures.

I-3

A Mari Usque ad Mare: Educational Problems[*]

H. T. COUTTS

•

If as Canadians we are to receive optimum value from education, we must recognize and solve a number of inter-related problems. I want to pose some of the problems that impress me as being of common concern.

First, how can we develop, adapt and revise educational theory and practice to meet the needs of all sectors of a society that is moving more and more toward urban living? While the patterns of rural-urban migration show some regional variations, it is not difficult to verify the major trend toward urbanization. In its *Second Annual Review*, the Economic Council of Canada points out "... the drastic shift out of the farm areas of the Prairie Region...."[1]

Let us look briefly at the educational problems being faced in urban and semi-urban communities. They include provision of educational opportunities for a steadily growing enrolment with all that this means: expensive building programs, teacher recruitment and placement, administrative adjustments, expanded supporting services. But the number game is only part of the story. In urban centres especially, the trend is for the holding power of the schools at all levels to increase. This necessitates the planning of more diversified curricula to meet a wider range of student abilities and interests and of social needs. The urban situation lends itself more readily to pressures—both human and humane —to provide specialized programs for mentally, emotionally, and physically handicapped children and youth. The growth of large cities accentuates socio-economic and ethnic differences wtih unplanned but none-the-less real types of segregation. The problem of the so-called culturally disadvantaged is intensified as cities become larger. Because urban living offers little by way of natural and productive chores, educational agencies—formal or informal—must provide wholesome outlets for the energies of boys and girls. The school as one of the formal agencies of education must align itself with other persons, institutions, and agencies that exist to serve boys and girls. Urban school systems are called on to

---

[*] Reprinted with permission from *Canadian Education and Research Digest*, VI, 4 (December, 1966), pp. 247–264. Abridged with special permission from the author.

provide more equipment, more complementary services, and more programs than were formerly available in smaller communities. Instructional opportunities must be extended downward to provide nursery schools and kindergartens, and upward to include continuing, retraining, and cultural education programs for adults. To meet the challenge of change, urban school systems must provide leadership training for their administrators and in-service programs for their teaching staffs.

Second, how can we prepare Canadians adequately at one and the same time for living and making a living? The Economic Council of Canada in 1964 set as basic goals for the Canadian economy in the medium-term future full employment, a high rate of economic growth, reasonable stability of prices, and an equitable distribution of rising income.[2]

Because of the close relationship between economic growth and education, the demands for technical and skilled rather than unskilled workers in an increasing number of fields, and the uncertain effects of automation and cybernetics on types and nature of employment, Canadians are forced to re-examine, revise, and extend school and post-school programs.

If we are to meet the needs of Canada and Canadians, we are faced with providing every child, youth, and adult with as broad, deep, and rich a general education as possible while at the same time providing the specialized training necessary to prepare him to enter the world of work at some acceptable level—acceptable to himself and to society. While preparation for initial entry into employment is necessary, it may not be adequate for a world in which there is frequent transfer from one job to another. That is one reason why the Vocational and Technical Assistance Act (1960) limits its support to programs that include basic as well as specialized education and that emphasize general principles and cluster-type activities with transfer possibilities. Extension and continuous up-dating of vocational education programs is essential as occupations change. One of the great challenges facing the vocational high school and the technical institute is that of readiness to drop obsolescent training programs and to introduce new ones geared to changed conditions.

Third, how can we identify, nurture, and reward creative talent? The great revolution taking place in education today is the "Emphasis on the discovery of knowledge, as contrasted with the memorization of facts discovered by others. . . ." Our schools must more and more provide the motivation and offer the opportunity that arouses curiosity and that rewards creativeness. We need more intellectual exploration not only in the sciences and mathematics but in the social sciences, the languages,

---

[1] Economic Council of Canada, *Towards Sustained and Balanced Economic Growth, Second Annual Review* (Ottawa: Queen's Printer, 1965), p. 110.

[2] Economic Council of Canada, *Economic Goals for Canada to 1970, First Annual Review* (Ottawa: Queen's Printer, 1964), *passim*.

and the arts. We need more mental activity and less passivity and apathy. We need to stimulate students to pursue their interests beyond any formal level of education they may have reached. In the schools, we must provide optimum conditions for motivated learning to take place. This will mean well-selected and well-prepared teachers who themselves are stimulating, flexible and creative. It will mean well-equipped laboratories and classrooms and well-stocked libraries. It will mean a much more effective use of the resources of the community. Above all it will require guidance and counselling services far in advance of most that we now have.

We live by bread, but fortunately not by bread alone. Surely Canadians must be discoverers and innovators if they are to maintain self respect and to provide leadership. Hopefully we will take advantage of the contributions of our citizens with their diversity of ethnic and cultural backgrounds and their wide spectrum of talents.

Fourth, how can we through education help reduce the psychological tensions resulting from the pressures of change? In order to play its part education must attempt to give children and youth a sense of security and a means of facing and dealing with economic and social change. The environment of the school should itself contribute by providing clean, healthful, functional, and artistic surroundings. It is apparent that the program of the school must be planned to provide that type of education that is conducive to reducing tension, not in some negative fashion, but by giving pupils confidence in themselves and control over the tools of harmonious social living.

There must be a close relationship between the home, the school, and the other educational institutions and agencies of the community. We must work closely with parents, health authorities, social workers, and trained leaders of youth organizations. There must be a consistency of goals among us if we are to foster security and reduce the causes of tension.

Above all, we must provide strong guidance, counselling and psychological services in our school systems. We cannot afford to place the functions of such services in the hands of any but those who besides being well-adjusted themselves are competent and thoroughly prepared. We must not let tensions stand in the way of effective learning and personal development. Our responsibility, however, extends to assisting young people to make the transfer from the school to the adult world. Hence it involves provision of vocational as well as educational counselling, and provision of placement services in which there is cooperation between education, labor, and management.

Fifth, how can we best prepare students to accept a commitment to democratic government? Our best means of preparing for democratic participation and living is through education. To this end every boy and girl must have reasonable skill in the use of the tools of literacy and numeracy—must be proficient in the three R's. Beyond this, through the environment and the curriculum of the school, each should become familiar with democratic practices and learn to recognize the privileges and the responsibilities of Canadian citizenship. Through practice and precept all should come to the realization that difficult cultural, economic and social problems can be settled only on the basis of fact, reason, and carefully considered judgments. There must be an acceptance of the importance of give and take in relation to controversial matters. The schools must try to help maturing students to analyze the motivations behind different interest groups and the reasons for changes in support of political parties. If the dignity of man and the right of the individual are central to our concept of democracy, as I take them to be, the school must exclude all forms of discrimination and prejudice related to race, creed, or social class. Indeed the school must become a vital force against all forms of segregation on such bases.

Sixth, how can we best prepare our students for the wholesome use of leisure time? There are many ways in which the schools of Canada can develop programs that will lay the bases for the creative and profitable use of leisure. Physical education offerings should develop skills and promote activities that will have long lasting application. Those activities which hold promise through adulthood include golf, skiing, curling, bowling, boating, swimming, walking, fishing, and camping. These are all legitimate parts of a currently conceived curriculum in physical education for schools as well as for adult programs for those who somehow missed them.

The schools must also lay the foundation of the reading habit and use of the library. Schools must develop libraries of their own, but must also cooperate with public libraries in providing a wider variety and number of books and magazines. To accomplish this and other of its goals, the school of the future must remain open in the evenings and throughout the summer with programs both academic and cultural to meet the needs of those seeking retraining or preparation for leisure.

The programs of schools, colleges, and universities and all forms of continuing education must provide for developing skills and appreciations that lead to creative expression through writing, art, music, drama, and the dance. We need more art galleries and museums. Our schools, public buildings, and business establishments need to exhibit works of art. There must be more outlets in intimate theatres for the product of experimental drama, and more small concert halls for those who wish to show the results of their interest in music and dancing.

Seventh, how can we, through education, help to develop values that form the moral framework of our society? Faced with a rapidly expanding body of scientific knowledge, accelerating technological change, and unprecedented population growth, there is little wonder that the values that have served us in the past are being vigorously examined and in some cases questioned. Many of the institutions which have always been regarded as the bulwarks of traditional values based on emotion and faith are losing their appeal and support to vital new organizations which stress the primacy of fact and reason in decision making. Here again education must play an increasingly important role in Canada.

It is apparent to me that some of the values formerly held by our society need modification in light of changed conditions. On the other hand there are many basic values to which we continue to subscribe for the good of society. We believe, for example, in the dignity of the individual and demand that the school, through its practices, recognize this fact. We believe, too, that the school must help to develop and maintain the moral, spiritual, and ethical values which our democratic society continues to accept. These must be broad and inclusive and not narrowly conceived.

Through its practices the school must help its pupils to distinguish between right and wrong on values logically and reasonably determined. There must, of course, be an identification with commitments far beyond those of the self. These will involve concern for the welfare of the underprivileged and the less fortunate. It is this kind of concern that will motivate the increasing interest which Canadians must take in the people of the emerging nations.

•

BIBLIOGRAPHY

Baron, G., *Society, Schools and Progress in England*, London: Pergamon Press, 1965.
Economic Council of Canada, *Economic Goals for Canada to 1970, First Annual Review*, Ottawa: Queen's Printer, 1964.
———, *Towards Sustained and Balanced Economic Growth, Second Annual Review*, Ottawa: Queen's Printer, 1965.
"Educating the Culturally Deprived in the Great Cities," *Phi Delta Kappan*, XLV, 2, November, 1963.
Ellena, W. J. and Finis Engleman, "Man's Tomorrows," *Phi Delta Kappan*, XLVI, 10, June, 1965.
"Fifteen to Eighteen," Report to the Central Advisory Council for Education, England (Crowther), I, London: Her Majesty's Stationery Office, 1959.
Gardner, J. W., "The Anti-leadership Vaccine," *Annual Report of the Carnegie Corporation of New York*, New York: 1965.
"Half Our Future," A Report of the Central Advisory Council for Education, England (Newsom), London: Her Majesty's Stationery Office, 1963.
Imperatives in Education, Washington, D.C.: American Association of School Administrators, 1966.
"The Swing to Vocational Education," *Phi Delta Kappan*, XLVI, 8, April, 1965.

PART TWO

Education and Diversity in Canadian Society

II

Introduction

•

Canadian society is made up of a variety of subcultures. According to the 1961 census, 43.8 per cent of the population was of British origin, 30.4 per cent French, 10.3 per cent of German, Dutch, and Scandinavian origins, 12.3 per cent of other European origins, and 3.2 per cent of other origins, including Indian and Eskimo.

As pointed out by Ralph Linton in *The Study of Man* (1936), no cultural group has produced more than 10 per cent of the elements of its total culture, and all cultures are a product of "the principle of cultural diffusion." However, social prejudices still exist in our society. Sociological studies have shown that all groups have persistent elements of ethnocentrism—the belief that one's own cultural group is superior to all others. It is one of the products of unenlightened socialization that affects all children to some degree. Canada, with its history of several immigrant waves, has not been free of crude or insensitive expressions of prejudice. As quoted by William Peterson in his *Planned Migration* (1955), the early French nationalists were said to have resented the "drunkards, paupers, loafers, and jailbirds" from England that swamped French Canada. Stephen Leacock, in his *Economic Prosperity in the British Empire* (1930), said, "I am not saying that we should absolutely shut out and debar the European foreigner, as we should and do shut out the Oriental. But we should in no way facilitate his coming." Madison Grant, in *The Passing of the Great Race* (1921), attacked the open European immigration policies in the North American continent which allowed "poor" stock from eastern and southern Europe to dilute the "superior" breeds from England and northwest Europe. When Clifford Sifton tried to encourage populating the Canadian Prairies with immigrants from eastern Europe, he was accused of bringing in "the scum of Europe" to justify building a railway across Canada.

There is considerable evidence today to indicate that many of the prejudices of earlier years have been diminished, if not eliminated. Over a hundred national organizations pursue regular programmes to study and improve human relations in Canada. Educational sociologists analyse the structure of inter-group relations within the classroom. Government agencies—in particular, the Canadian Broadcasting Corporation and the National Film Board—university extension divisions, and community groups have tried in various ways to change attitudes by eliminating stereotyped perceptions.

In 1967 there were about 230,000 Indians living for the most part in 2,267 reservations and about 13,000 Eskimos, most of whom were living north of the 60th parallel. Education of Indians on the reserves has been a responsibility of the federal government since Confederation. The urgent need for an overhaul of educational and social policy concerning the Indians has been recognized, as the present policy has not had laudable results. Only one-half of one per cent of the entire Indian school population finishes high school and one-third of the Indian population earns less than a thousand dollars a year.

Eskimo education is also in need of improvement. Owing to difficulties in communication and lack of resources, only about 20 per cent of the Eskimo population receives formal schooling.

Even in democratic societies, communities reveal a hierarchy of social classes based on an index of status characteristics, such as occupation, income, and residential area. If the teacher aims to develop the child's whole personality rather than merely give formal instruction, he must understand the child's social class patterns. As Harold Laski said, people who live differently also think differently, and persons with different perceptions, to use Karl Manheim's phrase, "talk past one another."

There is a significant correlation between social class and school attendance. According to the Dominion Bureau of Statistics' report of 1956–57, Canadian families with an income of more than $10,000 comprised 3.3 per cent of the population, but the college student families in this group comprised 15.2 per cent. On the other hand, Canadian families with an income under $2,000 comprised 14 per cent of the population, but college student families in this group were only 7.4 per cent. The 1961 Dominion Bureau of Statistics' sample survey of 11,858 Canadian university students revealed that only 1.6 per cent of the students enrolled in the College of Arts and Sciences had fathers who were labourers. Regard for continuous education is not very high among the lower-income classes; the desire to stay in school has a strong correlation with a family's economic status.

This section contains four readings. In the first, David Munroe points out that one of the fundamental tests of a democracy is whether minority groups are treated on a par with the majority. He gives several examples to show that they have not always been in all Canadian provinces and that there is a compelling need for establishing a recognized channel of communication among our provincial governments to develop a better understanding of the place of minorities in a democracy. In the second reading, Seymour Martin Lipset compares some democratic values such as equalitarianism and universalism in Canada, the United States, Great Britain, and Australia. In the third, John Porter points out that the social factors of income, size of family, regional differences, and religion play an important part in determining the kind of education an individual may expect in Canada. In the fourth reading C. W. Hobart and C. S. Brant compare the Canadian philosophy of Eskimo education with the Danish philosophy. The Canadian philosophy is that of cultural replacement, where an attempt is made to replace the traditional culture with a modern one in a short period of time. On the other hand, the Danish philosophy is that of cultural continuity and cultural synthesis, where an attempt is made to preserve all basic features of the traditional culture.

II-4

Democracies, Minorities and Education*

DAVID MUNROE

•

The democratic state is a complex institution. It has a long history; it has developed a variety of forms, none of which is perfect or permanent; it has been merged with monarchy and blended with theocracy; it has been violated by dictators and abused by indifferent citizens; yet it is the form of government which a large proportion of mankind seeks to embrace.

Like all living organisms, it is subject to continuous change. Geographical discovery, economic expansion, technological invention, immigration, mass media of communication, rapid transport have inevitably created new patterns of social and political relationships that are reflected in the adjustments which have led to federalism, the enfranchisement of women, the growth of bureaucracy, the restraints of economic independence, the control of public health, the provision of educational services. It has never been possible to define democracy in exactly the same terms in any two countries even when they have inherited the same traditions. Republicanism is practised very differently in France and the United States; the principles of parliamentary government are applied very differently in London, Canberra, Pretoria and Ottawa. Nor is it possible to devise a democratic structure that will serve permanently in any one country. Radical changes have been introduced in the Victorian democracy in England, in the monarchies of Scandinavia, in the long succession of republican forms in France. In choosing democracy we have undertaken an endless task that can only be accomplished in the measure of tolerance, understanding and responsibility implanted in our citizens.

Increasingly in recent years, it has become apparent that one of the most fundamental tests of democracy is the treatment accorded to minority groups. This is something new. For many centuries it was considered perfectly reasonable to limit the privileges of democracy and power to a minority group such as the citizens of Athens or Rome, the theocracy of

---

* Reprinted with permission from the *Journal of Education*, the Faculty and College of Education, University of British Columbia, No. 9 (Vancouver and Victoria: January, 1964), pp. 57–67.

Geneva, or the English aristocracy of the 18th century, leaving a large number of subjects without the franchise and with very restricted rights. Under these systems minority problems could be solved in many ways. The British parliament, which professed certain principles of democracy in the 18th century, permitted religious minorities to remain within the Kingdom but denied them the rights to hold office or to practise their religion too openly. This was in rather sharp contrast with the policy of the autocratic Louis XIV, who simply drove the Huguenots out of his kingdom. The Congress of the United States, which has repeatedly affirmed its belief in democratic practice, wrote protective clauses in the Constitution assuring equal privileges and justice to all of its minorities but for almost a century did not take the action necessary to enforce these measures. It is only in the present century that we have come face to face with the full implications of democracy, by the inclusion in the rolls of citizenship women as well as men, immigrant as well as native, and persons of all religious, language, economic and social groups.

This presents obvious difficulties. Our loyalties may change, our economic status may improve or deteriorate, our attitudes may alter as the result of geographical, historical, occupational, political attachments. We may belong to a minority religious group but speak the language of the majority; we may be identified most closely with one political group in our youth and another as adults. Our attitudes alter when we change from one professional or occupational group to another. New causes [such as] nuclear disarmament may compel us to abandon old allegiances. Moreover, all these affiliations may change from one generation to another, and it is impossible to maintain a perfect equilibrium between the forces of culture, economics, politics, religion. Clearly we all belong to some minority group at some time or another and many of us belong to several at any one time. Indeed there is a danger of public opinion becoming so unstable under the pressure of referendums and public opinion polls that orderly government might be impaired. Obviously, it is not possible to devise a single formula by which all minority problems can be resolved, even problems such as those involving race, language or religion. We must depend on tolerance and understanding, and the closest we can come to a solution may be the spirit expressed in Voltaire's letter to Helvetius: "I disapprove of what you say, but I will defend to the death your right to say it."

●

The Education Act adopted by the Legislature of the United Provinces of Canada in 1841 provided for the establishment of common schools by local authorities with the direction and assistance of the provincial governments. This conformed to the pattern of public education elsewhere in North America and, indeed, in several European countries where national systems of education were organized in the early years of the 19th century. The significant difference in Canada was the provision for religious dissent, which, in a sense, was a reaffirmation of the principle recognized rather vaguely in the Quebec Act that assured the French Canadians of their right to their language and religion. This guarantee was now extended, insofar as it applied to religion, to the principal minority groups in both provinces.

However, it was one thing to recognize a principle, and quite another to confirm it in actual practice, as was perfectly apparent in the years that followed. The interpretations of "common school" and the "right of dissent" were very different among the citizens of Upper and Lower Canada, and even more radical differences of opinion were soon expressed by Egerton Ryerson and Bishop de Charbonnel and by Bishop Bourget of Montreal and Alexander Galt, the member of the Legislature from Sherbrooke.

During the quarter-century between 1841 and Confederation, two provincial systems became firmly established. Upper Canada was given a separate administration by an Act of 1843, Lower Canada in 1845 and 1846. In the one, a solid municipal structure was created with which the administration of "common schools" was closely linked. In the other, the parish divisions were retained and the confessional character of both common and dissentient schools was encouraged by the differences in curriculum, in textbooks, in the qualifications and, after 1857, in the training of teachers. These differences may be attributed, of course, as much to language as to religion, although at this time Roman Catholics and Protestants were in strong disagreement over the use of the Bible as a textbook in schools.

In 1855 a crisis developed over the demand of Roman Catholics in Upper Canada for concessions to their "separate" or dissentient schools. At this time the population of that province was still predominantly English-speaking and the policy of the Department of Public Instruction was favorable to the "common school." The Taché Bill, which was introduced unexpectedly at the end of the legislative session held in Quebec City and supported by a large number of members from Lower Canada whose constituents were not affected by the measure, was adopted over strong protests from George Brown and the Bill itself, and even more the tactics employed by John A. Macdonald in securing its adoption, aroused resentment among the Protestants of both provinces. Further concessions were granted by the Scott Act in 1862 and, as a result, the English-speaking minority of Lower Canada under Galt's leadership demanded that their rights be suitably recognized in the British North America Act. Thus, in Upper Canada, the "common school" was widely adopted through the advocacy of Egerton Ryerson, a clergyman; whereas in Lower Canada the confessional spirit of both common and dissentient schools was encouraged by two laymen, Dr. J. B. Meilleur and the Honorable P. J. O. Chauveau.

This helps to explain the provisions of Article 93, establishing the exclusive authority of each provincial legislature over education, and giving special protection to Protestant and Roman Catholic dissentient minorities in Upper and Lower Canada. Dissentient groups in any province were given the right to appeal for redress to the Governor General in Council against any law which contravened their privileges at the time of entry into Confederation. It may be said, therefore, that the Act recognized the right of the religious minority, either Roman Catholic or Protestant, to maintain dissentient schools in Upper and Lower Canada.

In the century following Confederation, the differences in the two systems became more pronounced. Ontario maintained a single unified department of education limiting the growth of separate schools. Serious complications arose after 1880, when French-speaking Roman Catholics began to settle in the Ottawa valley and Northern Ontario. They, not unnaturally, demanded the right to instruction in their mother tongue, and a number of regrettable incidents occurred which revealed a division of opinion and interest between English- and French-speaking Roman Catholics. Efforts have since been made to repair these injustices but the recent petition of the Roman Catholic Bishops of Ontario to the Provincial Government indicates clearly that some of the religious issues remain unsettled and the problems of language and culture are equally complex.

Quebec chose a different type of administration. After a brief experience under a Minister of Education, in 1875 the control of educational policy was vested in a Council of Education, which was divided on a confessional basis with the Roman Catholic bishops being given a dominant voice. The Council soon ceased to function as a united body, its authority being delegated to the two committees and a department of public instruction, which was also divided into confessional sections. Not unnaturally, the pressure of European movements in the last quarter of the 19th century was reflected in the Roman Catholic system. The influence of the ultramontane party became dominant from time to time and even the common schools became confessional. In contrast, the dissentient schools of the Protestants became steadily more secular, being attended by Jews and other non-Catholics. As in Upper Canada, social changes have also created new problems. A system which was originally designed to serve a population that could be divided between French-speaking Roman Catholics and English-speaking Protestants was not very well adapted to serve a pluralist society and, in spite of the provisions for English-speaking Roman Catholics, and recently for French-speaking Protestants, injustices still exist. The system which was eulogized by Dr. Weir thirty years ago as maintaining the spirit of the Fathers of Confederation "with reference to a satisfactory solution of the thorny problems arising from the educational rights and privileges of religious minorities," was faced with vexing difficulties even as he wrote. These and a wide variety of other problems—financial, pedagogical, administrative—are now under review by a Royal Commission of Enquiry on Education. Thus, it seems perfectly clear, that neither the provision of common schools in one province nor confessional schools in the other has provided a satisfactory solution to the minority problem.

•

Three incidents in the other provinces of Canada are pertinent in the study of minority problems in our educational history. The first occurred in New Brunswick. In 1871 the Common Schools Act was adopted, providing that "all schools conducted under the provisions of this Act shall be non-sectarian." This was followed by regulations which outlawed the catechism, prohibited the display of symbols and emblems and banned religious costume. Separate schools had not been recognized by law before Confederation but certain religious privileges had been accorded to Roman Catholics and these were seriously affected. Language differences were not a serious problem at this time. The spirit of the new order may be judged from the words of the Premier, who declared "New Brunswick is only following the general law of this continent; and because it does not follow the peddling, compromising policy of Ontario and Quebec, it is said the Government is tyrannizing over the consciences of Catholics." The legislation was challenged both by protest to the government of Sir John A. Macdonald in Ottawa and by appeal to the Privy Council in the case of Maher versus the Town Council of the Town of Portland. Macdonald decided that Section 93 could only be considered to apply if a law were held to be unconstitutional or if it might inflict injury in other provinces and he therefore refused to act. Maher petitioned against the payment of taxes for the support of a common school and his claim was rejected first by the Supreme Court of New Brunswick and then by the Privy Council. Thus, in the first application of the protective provisions of Section 93, no redress was granted the minority. Subsequently, however, another type of compromise was reached and in New Brunswick and two sister provinces it is customary in many municipalities to grant confessional privileges in certain schools to Roman Catholics and provision is also made in New Brunswick for the French-language minority.

The second incident occurred in Manitoba. When that province was established in 1870 the population was estimated at about 10,000, half being white and the others métis. While the territory had been administered by the Hudson's Bay Company, there was no organized civil government and the meagre educational services were provided by missionaries. When the Manitoba Act was drafted some questions were raised regarding the application of Article 93 and an amendment was accepted extending the phrase "such law" to "such law and practice." This change was significant.

In 1870 it was estimated that the population of English-speaking Protestants and French-speaking Roman Catholics was about equal but the lines of attachment with Quebec were strengthened by the structure of the new government. There were two houses in the Legislature and either English or French was recognized in debate, as well as in the courts of law. Separate schools were established for Roman Catholics and Protestants, each group having control over twelve districts. Radical changes occurred during the next twenty years. The population rose to over 100,000, only one-fifth of whom were Roman Catholic, and almost half of the new settlers came from Ontario, where they were accustomed to a system of common schools. External pressures were strong. On the one hand there was the example of Ontario and of the neighboring states south of the border, where public systems sought to limit religious and cultural differences; on the other, there was the growing tendency of the Roman Catholic hierarchy to assert its influence on educational policy. Rivalry and misunderstanding were deepened by the controversy over the settlement of the Jesuit Estates and even more over the unfortunate career of Louis Riel. Year by year for over a decade, the educational laws were amended until finally in 1890 and 1891 the whole system was drastically revised.

The new laws struck at the rights of religious and cultural minority, closely as it was linked with Quebec and with the Roman Catholic hierarchy. External forces were thus involved and the stormy disputes of the next few years were as bitter in Quebec or Montreal or Ottawa and even London, as in Manitoba itself. The new laws were challenged; the Supreme Court declared them constitutional; the Privy Council reversed this decision; the Federal government instructed the provincial authorities to reinstate the rights of the minority; the provincial premier refused; a Remedial Bill was introduced in the House of Commons; a general election was fought in 1896 almost entirely on this issue. The Liberal party under Wilfrid Laurier was the victor, in the face of strong opposition of the Roman Catholic hierarchy of Quebec and it stood firmly against the interference of the federal authorities in all matters relating to education. This policy established, Laurier secured the cooperation of the provincial government in extending a measure of redress but the provincial authorities remained adamant in their opposition to separate public schools. At the time this solution may have appeared acceptable and final but it has left a long shadow over the later educational history not only of Manitoba but of other provinces as well.

Within a decade a new dispute arose in the provinces of Saskatchewan and Alberta, which were fashioned out of the Northwest Territories in 1905. There, also, the population was sparse. Government services were organized under the Northwest Territories Act of 1875, which Henri Bourassa claimed bore some resemblance to the Quebec Act of a century earlier. Among other things it provided for a council or assembly to govern the territories and it also recognized the right of a minority of taxpayers, whether Protestant or Roman Catholic, to establish separate schools. Ordinances adopted in 1892 and 1901 curtailed these privileges by establishing, first a Council of Public Instruction and then a Department of Education, with the power to prescribe curricula and textbooks and the qualifications of teachers. These actions drew protests again from the Roman Catholic hierarchy, who demanded that two systems should be established on the pattern of Quebec. When the issue was finally raised in 1905 one of the chief protagonists was Henri Bourassa whose opinions were forcefully expressed both in and out of Parliament, as well as in a pamphlet "Les Ecoles du Nord-Ouest" which is a carefully documented statement of the French-Canadian position.

A cabinet crisis developed, involving Laurier and Sifton, the influential member from Manitoba. There were discussions also with Mgr. Sbarretti, the Apostolic Delegate at Ottawa. A compromise was reached, giving recognition to separate schools but denying them autonomy in the control of teacher certification and authorization of curricula. As had happened in Manitoba, the claims of the religious minority had obscured the problems of language and culture. Moreover the presence of other minority groups recently immigrated from Europe confused the issues between the original French- and English-speaking settlers.

The first of these crises occurred within the framework of Confederation and the government clearly rejected the solutions adopted in Quebec and Ontario as unsatisfactory in New Brunswick. The other two developed in new provinces where the social structure was still undetermined and in each instance the French-speaking and Roman Catholic minority, on language as well as on religious grounds, sought to have the Quebec system adopted. This was judged unacceptable because it did not give sufficient security to the common school and minority needs were provided, in Manitoba, by limiting religious teaching to special weekly periods as authorized by the school trustees, and, in Saskatchewan and Alberta, by the recognition of separate schools in certain areas. As in the older provinces, these solutions have not been considered entirely acceptable by the minority groups and there have been repeated demands for improvement, especially in the provisions for French-language schools.

●

We live in a period of rapid and relentless change, yet many of us continue to think of educational principles and patterns which prevailed a century ago. In those days education was still considered a luxury in most countries. Even where school attendance had been made compulsory, as in Prussia, these laws applied only to primary school, secondary and higher education being reserved for an elite, which was usually masculine and wealthy. Moreover, while the Mechanics Institutes in Britain and the Folk High Schools in Denmark had developed some programs for adults, it was generally considered that education was completed in childhood and anything beyond that was unconventional and unnecessary. The responsibility of a government was fully discharged by encouraging private and local agencies to carry most of the burden, to coordinate rather than to initiate, to correct deficiencies rather than to maintain general services. Naturally, under these circumstances, education was far down the list of policy and financial priorities of most governments.

The situation is very different now. Public elementary education is universal and it is one of the first concerns of any government. Responsibility has also gone far beyond this level and we expect public services to carry on through secondary school, offering the general education necessary for productive citizenship for all our youth to the age of sixteen or even eighteen. Higher education is also a public responsibility, and it now covers advanced professional and technical preparation, cultural development, as well as the informal adult education which may keep the citizen actively interested in the world about him. Education nowadays has a greater unity and continuity than it ever had before, and, at the same time, it must be provided on a vast scale that will place it within reach of every child and adult. Obviously the dimensions and the seriousness of this responsibility have changed tremendously since 1867.

How does the modern state provide such services for its citizens? Until recently, it might be said that the United States had gone further than most countries in educational development. It has developed a vast system of public common schools, of public and private colleges and universities which have served as a "melting pot" for a large immigrant population of mixed national origin and varied religious affiliation. During the past decade serious inequalities have come to light in various regions and the concept of secular public education has been challenged by Roman Catholic leaders who have organized competing systems of parochial schools and colleges. Nevertheless, public education in the United States is farther advanced than in most western countries. Rapid and significant progress has also been made in Russia, where over half a century an effective system of public education has been created. There, the common core of the curriculum is essentially the same, particularly in its historical and ideological content, but language differences are effectively recognized through the administration of the sixteen constituent republics, each of which has its own national language. Thus there is provision for certain types of minorities. In other European countries, having a smaller area but a larger population, practice varies a good deal, from Norway, where there are few private institutions, to the Netherlands, where a liberal confessional system has been in operation for many years. Clearly, the new responsibilities in education may be discharged in many ways and each government must be expected to choose a pattern that will serve the common good, making reasonable provision for minority groups.

Canadians deserve and, from many indications, they desire the best standards of educational services. During the past fifteen years public enquiries have been conducted in most of the provinces into various aspects of educational policy and administration; two national conferences have been organized for the discussion of educational problems; and expenditures have risen steadily. As in most countries, there is every indication of an awakened interest and a deeper appreciation of education based on the realization that future prosperity and even survival will depend largely on the development of our human resources.

Our acceptance of this challenge, however, is tempered by the determination to protect individual freedom and, particularly, to extend whatever rights may be reasonable to linguistic and religious minorities. The Canadian identity has been described by one of our historians as an attempt "to develop in particular North American environment a civilization European in origin and American in evolution." This is something quite different from the cultural pattern accepted in the United States, where European traditions have been rejected or refashioned under the heavy pressure of a new environment. It was to preserve the integrity of our Canadian pattern that the British North America Act was adopted in 1867 and the federal system has been extended in succeeding years.

Our provincial governments have usually assumed the responsibility for protecting minorities, but until very recently these intentions have never been clearly expressed. We have only now begun to distinguish between biculturalism and multi-culturalism, between minority rights based on language and those based on religion, between the operation of separate schools and the establishment of separate systems of school administration. It must be obvious that such distinctions are important if we are to provide justice for certain minority groups. It is obvious, also, that these concessions may be costly and that our financial resources are limited. As a consequence, for financial and even more for social and economic reasons, we must reject the claims of some groups and compromise in the demands of others in the interests of the progress and welfare of the individual provinces and of the country as a whole. No single formula can possibly be devised to serve everywhere and no formula, once adopted, can be accepted as infallible or permanent. Minority groups and educational needs are constantly changing. The confessional formula, adopted in 1867 for Quebec, was unsuitable in Ontario and within a decade was radically altered in Quebec. Further changes are in progress today because the minority groupings have altered and the demand for educational services [has] greatly increased. The same is true of the separate school pattern of Ontario or the complex confessional system of Newfoundland.

Instead of searching for a standard formula, we should be spending our effort on devising some machinery whereby the necessary and desirable compromises may be effected, and an agency through which we may spread a spirit of tolerance and understanding. In the past each provincial authority has defended its autonomy in education in a manner that prevented any continuing dialogue either between provinces or with the federal government. The result has been two-fold. Serious injustices have developed arising from financial, instructional or administrative inequalities; and the action of the federal government in the fields of technical and higher education has threatened the essential unity of educational plans and services. Both these results weigh heavily upon the majority in each province but they are likely to produce injustices to the minorities which are even more serious. These and other dangers must surely compel us to create a recognized channel of communication between all our governments, so that the rights and the needs of all Canadians can be placed under continuous review. The establishment of such an agency and the development of a better understanding both of the place of minorities in a democracy and of the broad problems of education are perhaps our most urgent needs.

II-5

Value Differences, Absolute or Relative: The English-Speaking Democracies*

SEYMOUR MARTIN LIPSET

•

To compare nations or societies which are highly similar in basic values may be even more fruitful analytically than to contrast those which are very different. As an illustration of this mode of inquiry, I will briefly expand the analysis of the stable democracies to include Australia and Canada, nations which like the United States are former colonies of Great Britain, which settled a relatively open continental frontier, and are today continent-spanning federal states. There is general agreement that, on a world-wide comparative scale, these two large, predominantly English-speaking states resemble the United States in stressing equalitarianism, achievement, universalism, and specificity. But if Canada and Australia share these basic values with the United States, they differ from it also, and it is these differences which sharply illustrate the way in which even relatively slight variations in value patterns help account for important differences among the stable and highly developed democracies.

The very tentative rankings which may be given to the positions of the four major, predominantly English-speaking democracies on the four pattern-variable dimensions are presented in Table 5:1 below. It is obviously extremely difficult to be precise about such variations, and these should be considered as at best an informed guess.

According to my estimates, Australia differs from the United States in being slightly more equalitarian, but less achievement oriented, universalistic, and specific. It also seems less universalistic and more equalitarian than Canada, but it is difficult to estimate the differences on the other two polarities. Canada differs somewhat from the United States on all four dimensions of equalitarianism, achievement, universalism, and specificity, while Britain in turn is less oriented toward these values than Canada.

To demonstrate that such differences really exist would involve a

---

* Reprinted with permission from *The First New Nation*, © 1963 by Seymour Martin Lipset, Basic Books, Inc., Publishers, New York. Abridged with special permission of the author.

Table 5:1

TENTATIVE ESTIMATES OF RELATIVE RANKINGS OF THE FOUR
ENGLISH-SPEAKING DEMOCRACIES ACCORDING TO STRENGTH
OF CERTAIN PATTERN VARIABLES

(Rankings according to first term in polarity)

	United States	Australia	Canada	Great Britain
Elitism-Equalitarianism	3	4	2	1
Ascription-Achievement	4	2.5	2.5	1
Particularism-Universalism	4	2	3	1
Diffuseness-Specificity	4	2.5	2.5	1

considerable research program. However, I have drawn on a considerable number of writings which have argued and given some evidence that these differences are as they are presented here and, for the time being, we must depend on such impressionistic evidence to support the discussion to follow. In this chapter, I will first seek to account for the differences by indicating variations in the social development of these countries which presumably created and sustained structures carrying these values, and then "derive" differences in their political systems which seem related to value patterns.

The Canadian pattern, as has been noted earlier, seems to reflect the fact that Canada always has been more conservative than the United States, that its early political history from 1776 on involved the defeat of radical reform, and that consequently some of the traditionalist "Tory" values which declined in the United States continued in Canada. The Canadian historian Frank Underhill has described the situation in the following terms:

> *The mental climate of English Canada in its early formative years was determined by men who were fleeing from the practical application of the doctrines that all men are born equal and are endowed by their creator with certain inalienable rights amongst which are life, liberty and the pursuit of happiness.... In Canada we have no revolutionary tradition; and our historians, political scientists, and philosophers have assiduously tried to educate us to be proud of this fact....*[1]

It is true, of course, that Canadian frontier conditions were just as destructive of traditional social relations as were those on the American frontier. "Distinctions of social class found little recognition in the pioneer communities where the demands of neighborhood association pressed so heavily upon the inhabitants."[2] Pressures toward egalitarianism and individualism resulted; but there were counter forces which prevented individualism of the American type from becoming the accepted way of life on the Canadian frontier.

Canada had to be constantly on its guard against the expansionist tendencies of the United States. It could not leave its frontier communities unprotected, or autonomous. Law and order in the form of the centrally controlled North West Mounted Police moved into frontier settlements along with the settlers. This contributed to the establishment of a greater tradition of respect for the *institutions* of law and order on the Canadian as compared to the American frontier. At the same time, frontier egalitarianism and individualism were played down in Canada because they were linked to American values and might conceivably undermine national integrity:

> *Efforts to strengthen the political ties of Empire or of nation led to deliberate attempts, through land grants and political preferments, to create and strengthen an aristocracy in the colonies ... and later in a less obvious fashion, in the Canadian nation. The democratic movement it was felt was liable to draw Canadian people closer to their neighbors to the south; and a privileged upper class was a bulwark of loyalty and conservatism.*[3]

One consequence of the value system which emerged is that Canadians have always been less intolerant of economic inequality and social stratification. Horatio Alger has never been a Canadian hero. As the Canadian sociologist Kaspar Naegele put it in his excellent discussion of his society:

> *There is less emphasis in Canada on equality than there is in the United States.... In Canada there seems to be a greater acceptance of* limitation *of hierarchical patterns. There seems to be less optimism, less faith in the future, less willingness to risk capital or reputation. In contrast to America, Canada is a country of greater caution, reserve, and restraint.*[4]

Canadians—as Frank Underhill, the eminent elder statesman of Canadian historians, put it recently in a public lecture—are the world's oldest and continuing "anti-Americans." The Canadian sense of nationality has always felt itself threatened by the United States, physically in earlier days, and culturally and economically in more recent years. Not only have Canadians found it necessary to protect themselves against American expansion, they have also found it necessary to define why they are not and should not become Americans, and they have done so by disparaging various elements in American life, mainly those which seemingly are an outgrowth of mass democracy and an excessive emphasis

---

[1] Frank H. Underhill, *In Search of Canadian Liberalism* (Toronto: The Macmillan Co. of Canada, 1960), p. 12.
[2] S. D. Clark, *The Canadian Community* (Toronto: University of Toronto Press, 1962), p. 65.
[3] *Ibid.*, p. 194.
[4] Kaspar Naegele, "Canadian Society: Some Reflections," in Bernard Blishen, et al., eds., *Canadian Society* (Toronto: The Macmillan Co. of Canada, 1961), p. 27. (Emphases in original.)

on equalitarianism.[5] For example, the president of the University of Toronto, Claude T. Bissell, has attempted to explain why the image of America has generally had a negative impact on Canadian writers in this way:

> *The Canadian political heritage and development created an atmosphere that was inimical to much of American literature. There was no revolutionary tradition in Canada, no glorification of force as a means of winning freedom and release. Moreover, the Canadian nation had been fashioned in a spirit of cautious defensiveness as a means of preserving what might at any moment be snatched away. All of this led to an innate suspicion of violence, and a tendency to equate the exuberant and the expansive with the empty and the vulgar. Here, I think, we have the source of the assumption on the part of Canadians of a quiet moral superiority to their more splendid and affluent neighbors.*[6]

The "assumption of a quiet moral superiority" as a means of distinguishing Canada from the United States may be seen in the first literary attempts to comment upon the Canadian scene. John Pengwerne Matthews points out that Thomas Chandler Haliburton, an eighteenth-century Canadian writer, created a "figure of the irrepressible Yankee [peddler], Sam Slick," as a "goad he could apply to the inert elements of Nova Scotia life: Sam Slick represented all those traits of bumptiousness which Haliburton so detested, and while his self-confidence and ingenuity are characteristics that Nova Scotians would do well to copy, he is the caricature of a national prototype that Haliburton did not admire."[7] Haliburton was using Sam Slick as a moral lesson to make Nova Scotians better Canadians, but this was largely ignored, because in their distaste for the American emphasis upon equality and achievement, Canadian writers could not see the difference between "the synthesis that Haliburton had created and the unadulterated American slick humor south of the border. As a result, Canadian writers and critics drew back in well-bred horror from the distasteful crudities of the frontier, and looked, more resolutely than ever, eastward across the Atlantic to the source of all good things."[8]

Insofar as elements that distinguished it from Britain, such as a frontier experience and virgin land, were also shared by the United States, Canadians turned away from them as a source of defining themselves. As a result, whereas the frontier experience in both Australia and the United States, though quite different, brought equalitarian values into the nation's image of itself, it did not do so in Canada.

Canadian intellectuals attempted to overcome their sense of colonial inferiority by trying to be as good as the British in their own medium rather than trying to find a medium that suited the attributes of their native land. Thus, whereas Canadian critics praised the poet Charles Sangster because "he may be regarded as the Canadian Wordsworth,"

Australian critics praised Charles Harpur for those poems in which he "was *not* the Australian Wordsworth."[9] Such attitudes kept Canadian intellectuals from supporting the populist doctrines espoused by many intellectuals in both Australia and the United States.

Australian nationalism, in contrast, inspired efforts to dissociate Australia from Britain, first politically, and later in terms of social values.[10] Britain was perceived antagonistically as the stronghold of rigid inequality. Australian writers romanticized the virtues of the gold rush experience or the nomadic life of the sheep-shearers. R.M. Crawford has pointed out that the self-image forged for that nation by Australian writers drawing on this local heritage was always more radical than actual social conditions, precisely because of these writers' efforts to differentiate Australia from Britain.[11] Thus where Canada retained a more elitist attitude in reaction to American equalitarianism, Australia emulated various American equalitarian patterns in reaction to British elitism.[12]

American literature, particularly that growing out of a vaguely populist intellectual tradition, has found resonance among Australian writers but has been largely ignored by Canadian writers:

> *In the field of literature, one could argue that Canadian writers have been less responsive than the Australian to American influences. As between English and American influences, they have preferred the English.... Canadian writers found it more difficult than the Australian to absorb the exuberant realism that went with the expansion of American democracy. Whitman excited only feeblest discipleship in Canada but he was a political bible and a literary inspiration to Bernard O'Dowd, perhaps the best of*

---

5 Frank H. Underhill, "The Image of Canada," address given at the University of New Brunswick Founders' Day, March 8, 1962.

6 Claude T. Bissell, "The Image of America in Canada," address delivered at the Canadian Studies Seminar, University of Rochester, March 16, 1962.

7 John Pengwerne Matthews, *Tradition in Exile* (Toronto: University of Toronto Press, 1962), p. 38.

8 *Ibid.*, p. 40.

9 *Ibid.*, pp. 58–59.

10 James Bryce was struck by these attitudes before World War I. Thus he reports, "I was amazed to find in 1912 how many Australians believed Britain to be a declining and almost decadent country." *Modern Democracies* (London: Macmillan, 1921), Vol. I, p. 268.

11 R. M. Crawford, "The Australian National Character: Myth and Reality," *Cahiers d'histoire mondiale*, No. 2 (1955), p. 715.

12 See Robin Gollan, *Radical and Working Class Politics: A Study of Eastern Australia* (Melbourne: Melbourne University Press, 1960), especially pp. 113–115. In drawing up their constitution, the Australians consciously modeled it "upon the American rather than the Canadian model." See Rev. Alexander Brady, *Democracy in the Dominions* (Toronto: University of Toronto Press, 1958), p. 153.

> *premodern Australian poets. American Utopian and protest literature found eager readers in Australia, comparatively few in Canada.*[13]

Some quantitative indicators for the value differences among the four major English-speaking nations, particularly as they pertain to achievement, may be deduced from variations in the numbers securing higher education. Perhaps the most striking evidence of the difference between American and British values is the variation in such opportunities. In the United States, the strong and successful efforts to extend the opportunities to attend colleges and universities have, to some considerable degree, reflected both pressures by those in lower status positions to secure the means to succeed, and recognition on the part of the privileged that American values of equality and achievement require giving the means to take part in the "race for success" to all those who are qualified.

> *Students enrolled in institutions of higher learning as per cent of age group 20–24, by country, about 1956, was 27.2 in United States, 12.05 in Australia, 8.0 in Canada, 3.7 in England and Wales, 5.1 in Scotland, 14.5 in Philippines, 0.7 in Jamaica, 11.9 in Puerto Rico, 4.5 in Western Europe, 6.6 in Denmark, 5.8 in France, 4.1 in West Germany, and 11.1 in U.S.S.R.*[14]

We find that almost seven times as large a group was atending such schools in the United States as in England and Wales. Some proof that these differences reflect variation in values, and not simply differences in wealth or occupational structures, may be deduced from the fact that the one major former American colony, the Philippines, has a much larger proportion enrolled in colleges and universities than any country in Europe or the British Commonwealth, a phenomenon which seemingly reflects the successful effort of Americans to export their belief that "everyone" should be given a chance at college education. A comparison of the variation in enrollment in such institutions in the two major Caribbean nations long under the hegemony of Britain and the United States, Jamaica and Puerto Rico, is also instructive. Thus Jamaica, like many other former British colonies in Africa and Asia, has a higher education system which seems premised on the belief that only a tiny elite should receive such training; while the system in Puerto Rico, like the one in the Philippines, clearly reflects the continued impact of American assumptions concerning widespread educational opportunity. Canada, though it appears to many American tourists to be so similar to the United States, has apparently not accepted its commitments to spreading educational advantages as much; it has less than one-third the United States' proportion in colleges and universities, twice that of the English but—amazingly—less than the Filipinos or Puerto Ricans. Australia is closer to the United States in this respect, particularly since the percentage reported for it is probably not based on as complete an estimate of those in higher education as the North American data. The assumptions made by various observers of the Australian scene that achievement values are gaining there would seem to be congruent with the evidence that a much larger proportion of Australians than Canadians are enrolled in institutions of higher learning.

---

[13] Claude T. Bissell, "A Common Ancestry: Literature in Australia and Canada," *University of Toronto Quarterly*, No. 25 (1955–56), pp. 133–134.

[14] The educational data for the first eight countries and the U.S.S.R. are calculated from materials in UNESCO, *Basic Facts and Figures, 1958* (Paris: 1959), and the Demographic Yearbook 1960 (New York: Statistical Office of the United Nations, 1960). The data for the Western European countries other than Britain are taken from J. F. Dewhurst, *et al.*, *Europe's Needs and Resources* (New York: Twentieth Century Fund, 1961), p. 315.

II-6

Social Class and Educational Opportunity*

JOHN PORTER

•

With the complex division of labour of modern industrial societies, education has come to be one of the most important social functions. Both the quantity and quality of education will determine a society's creative potential.... No society can move into an industrial epoch with much of its creative potential incarcerated in ignorance.

Educational systems and industrialization have grown together. Industrialization affects the content and the distribution of education, while at the same time the distribution and content of education establishes boundaries for industrial growth. The content of education is affected by the emphasis in industrial societies on the marketability of skills. In terms of its social function, education should be thus affected, because an educational system fails when it does not train people in sufficient quality and quantity for occupational roles. Knowledge for its own sake, so prized by the educational purists, is something which could perhaps come at a later stage of social development. Canadian education is sometimes criticized for presenting so little for the mind, but it would be wrong to think that in this respect Canada has fallen from some pinnacle. There never has been, in any society, knowledge for its own sake on a democratic scale. At the most, that kind of education was confined to the leisure classes of earlier historical periods, or it was a monopoly of priestly castes, such as the Brahmins of India, where societies based on agrarian economies were organized on the sacred principle. Although modern mass education up to now has been little more than the transmission of know-how of varying complexity it could be a stage in the development of a system in which there is more for the mind and less for the market.

The market, however, is always with us. A high standard of living and leisure depends on the industrial system being supplied with trained workers. In the periods of its industrial development Canada, as we have seen, has imported large numbers of skilled and professional workers, while many of its own people have remained untrained for

---

* Reprinted with permission from *The Vertical Mosaic* (Toronto: University of Toronto Press, 1965), pp. 165–173.

technical roles. It can scarcely be said in a country where in 1951 only two-fifths of those between fifteen and nineteen years of age were still in school, and where less than one in twelve of the collge age group were in college, that the demands of an industrial society were being met.

The dependence on external recruitment has created the illusion of adequacy. It has also permitted the continuity of class-bound education as exemplified by the classical college system in Quebec and the academic collegiate system in Ontario. There has, too, been the upper class institution of the private school which ... has been important in the background of Canadian elites. When these systems are threatened by educational reforms the educational purists come strongly to their defence. Often the democratic extension of education is equated with the dilution of education.

Appearing with industrialization and also having an effect on education is the egalitarian ideology. An industrial economy requires a free labour force rather than one which is legally tied, as in a caste or estate system, to specific kinds of occupations inherited from kin. Consequently industrial societies have "open" class systems consisting of a hierarchy of skills ranging from the casually employed unskilled labourer to the highly trained professional worker. Education is an important determinant of one's ultimate position in this system of skill classes. Theoretically an industrial system sorts and sifts masses of people according to their interests and talents into the multifarious range of tasks which have to be performed. Social development based on industry means constantly emerging possibilities for innovation for which new skills are required. The richness of its educational system will determine an industrial society's chances of growth and survival.

The egalitarian ideology holds that individuals should be able to move through this hierarchy of skill classes according to their inclinations and abilities. Such an ideology reinforces the needs of an industrial economic system. A society with a rigid class structure of occupational inheritance could not become heavily industrialized. On the other hand the industrial society which has the greatest flexibility is the one in which the egalitarian ideology has affected the educational system to the extent that education is available equally to all, and careers are truly open to the talented.

At some point in social development industrialization with its attendant egalitarian ideology comes into conflict with the structure of class. Up to a certain level of development a society can get along by improving for each class the kind of education available to it without interfering with class continuities. The children of former unskilled classes are given a few more years in school, and at the various levels upwards the content of education changes to meet occupational demands. This process has been referred to earlier as the upgrading of the labour force. This general upgrading can, of course, take place with only the minimum of interchange between classes. In time, with industrial development, the demands of the occupational system become so great that nothing short of a transformation in the educational system is sufficient to meet these demands which are reinforced by the demands of social equality. The changes made in the English educational system in 1944, providing free education through to the completion of university, mark a point of transformation in that country. In the United States there has always been a strong force making for equality of educational opportunity.

Modern education should be examined against the kind of model which is here being suggested—that is, a society in which the allocation of individuals to social tasks and access to educational resources is determined by ability. Thus two ends are served: the occupational structure will reflect a more rational allocation of ability; and individuals will have the greatest opportunity to develop their talents and make their contribution to the social good. Where those who survive to the upper levels of the educational system are less able than many who drop out of it, the investment in educational plant is being wasted and the most valuable resource of human talent is being squandered. A society which refuses to remove barriers to educational opportunity is falling short of the democratic ideal. The principle of equality and the principle of the rational use of economic resources thus have a mutually reinforcing function. Now, more than ever, education means opportunity. A system which does not provide equal opportunity is also inefficient. It is wrong to speak of the "Canadian" educational system because within the country there are eleven systems, one for each province and one for those territories still under the control of the federal government. Although there are many similarities between these systems there are also important differences in the availability of education.

The barriers to equal opportunity are both social and psychological. Although it is analytically useful at times to keep the social and the psychological separate, they are in fact intricately interwoven. Social barriers have been built into Canadian social structure as it has developed. None of them is beyond the control of social policy. Psychological barriers are the attitudes and values which individuals have and the motives with which they are either endowed or inculcated to become educated. The removal of the psychological barriers raises practical and ethical problems which are not so easy to solve.

•

SOCIAL BARRIERS

Of the social barriers the most obvious is the inequality of income and wealth. Education costs money and regardless of how free it may be, lower income families tend to take their children out of school at an earlier age and put them to work. Lower income families are obviously penalized when it comes to higher education, which in Canada, with the exception of the veterans' schemes, has always been prohibitively expensive. A second social barrier is family size. The larger the family the more difficult it becomes for parents to keep their children in school, or to make choices about which of their children should remain in school as far as university, if that should be a realistic choice for them. In the large family, children are put to work early to help meet the heavier expenses of child-rearing. Here there is a doubly depressing process at work because invariably in industrial societies lower income groups have larger families. The child, therefore, born into a lower income family has almost automatically a greatly reduced horizon of opportunity.

A third social barrier to equality of education lies in the regional differences in educational facilities in Canada, in part the result of our federal system. Some persons are fortunate enough to be reared in areas where educational facilities and the quality of teaching are good; others are brought up where educational standards are low. For many the institutions of higher learning are a long way from home and for them the costs of going into residence must be added to the cost of fees. Accident of birthplace thus limits a person's opportunity by determining the education available to him. The argument that education must at all levels be a provincial matter begins to fall away with inter-provincial migration and provincial variations in economic development. There is no reason to assume, as is often done, that the desire of French Canadians for cultural survival can be achieved only if education is kept a provincial "right." ... Often the claims made on behalf of provincial rights are reflections of existing structures of power developed within Canadian federalism. Associated with regional differences is the occupational and ethnic homogeneity of some regions. The social milieu created by differences in geography and ethnic composition determines to some extent the kind of educational facilities which are available. Thus it becomes more difficult to relate talent to training.

A fourth source of inequality arises from the great influence that religion has had on educational policies. The least adequate educational facilities for an industrial society ... have been those of Quebec where education for French Catholics has been not only costly but at the secondary level concentrated within the tradition of the classical college. A variety of studies have shown that, in Quebec, Catholic boys leave school much earlier than Protestant boys. In a 1956 study Professor Tremblay found that even as early as twelve years of age there was a greater proportion of Protestant than Catholic boys in school, and, although for each age beyond twelve there were fewer of both groups at school, the differential between Catholics and Protestants increased. At sixteen years one-quarter of Catholic boys were at school compared to one-half of Protestant boys.[1] Other investigators have established that for every 100 pupils in Grade 6, Quebec Protestants kept forty-two in school

---

[1] Arthur Tremblay, "Quelques Aspects de notre problème scolaire," *Bulletin de la Fédération des Collèges Classiques*, I, 5 (avril, 1956).

until Grade 11, but Quebec Catholics kept only eighteen.[2] Similarly a Quebec Royal Commission reporting in 1956 found that, in 1953, 61 per cent of Catholic children aged five to nineteen years were enrolled in the "Primary" Catholic schools of the province whereas 83 per cent of the Protestant children of the same ages were enrolled in Protestant schools.[3] A study by the Dominion Bureau of Statistics covering the years 1946 to 1958 showed similarly very different "retention" rates between Catholic and Protestant schools in Quebec.[4]

It may be argued that the earlier school leaving of Catholic children in Quebec can be accounted for by differences between Catholics and Protestants in socio-economic levels of living, and that the religious variable is by itself of no importance. It is true that the average French Catholic family has more children to educate than the average English Protestant family, and we have seen from our earlier analysis of ethnic affiliation and occupation that on the average the socio-economic status of French family heads is lower than that of English family heads. But Quebec Catholics have not been penalized as have Catholics in other provinces by tax and grant structures through which money is supplied for education. In Quebec, tax revenue, including that from corporations, is shared with the minority (Protestant) school board according to the number of resident children of each religion between the ages of five and sixteen in the community. In a province where 82 per cent of the population is French speaking and 88 per cent is Catholic it must be accepted that the resources made available for education are a reflection of the dominant values.

That education has been considered a function of the Church and only in a limited sense the function of the State is illustrated by the fact that Quebec, alone among the ten provinces, has never had a minister of education. Quebec has had a Department of Education administered by a superintendent of education reporting in the past to the cabinet through the provincial secretary and, more recently, the minister of youth. The superintendent is the head of the Council of Education which is made up of Roman Catholic and Protestant committees, each of which is responsible for their own school systems. For Catholics, then, public education has been entirely in the hands of the Roman Catholic committee composed *ex officio* of the bishops in charge of dioceses and an equal number of laymen appointed by the cabinet.

One official of the Department of Education in Quebec, Charles Bilodeau, said in 1958: "The presence of the bishops adds considerable prestige to the Roman Catholic Committee: all are eminent men who thoroughly understand the school situation in their diocese, and several are in addition experienced educators. Parents are thus assured of a thoughtful and stable education policy."[5] The Catholic view that religion and education are inseparable means that the content of education must be affected by religious ideology, and for this reason clerical control of education must be maintained. The content of this education will determine its adequacy for modern occupational systems. It is likely also that the views of the Catholic hierarchy have prevailed about the distribution of education. We have earlier seen that religion is a difficult variable to separate from ethnicity, that the two are intricately interwoven in the more general phenomenon of culture. Education is an item of culture and also the social machinery for its transmission. In Quebec this machinery has been governed by an ecclesiastical elite.

Charles Bilodeau has further pointed out the differences in Quebec for Catholics and Protestants in the availability of education:

> ...*the present secondary course exists in two separate forms; one public, of five years' duration,* often free, *but leading only to certain university faculties (science, commerce, agriculture, etc.); the other private, of eight years' duration, taught by the classical colleges and* comparatively expensive, *but giving admission to all faculties. French-speaking parents have not failed to notice that English-Canadian pupils are able to take a secondary course in the public schools at no or almost no charge, and to enter all university faculties, while their own children do not have the same opportunities.*[6]

The educational system which has developed in French Canada has not conformed to the democratic industrial model. Neither has it in "Protestant" provinces. In Quebec it is simply farther away from the model, a fact which we are here attributing to religion as a social variable. It may be true, as it is so often claimed, that the Christian humanism which pervades French-Canadian education is to be highly valued, but on the other hand its classical orientation has prevented French Canadians from making their full contribution to Canadian society.

The need for reform in the Quebec educational system has been recognized by French-Canadian educationalists, and by 1961 some important reforms had been started. The election of 1960, which saw the end of the regime of the Union Nationale party of Maurice Duplessis, brought in a Liberal government headed by Premier Jean Lesage. It was pledged to widespread reform of Quebec social structure, particularly education. Its most important change was to pay the fees of all students in the classical colleges. More fundamental changes had to wait

---

[2] "The First Report of the Canadian Research Committee on Practical Education," *Canadian Education*, IV, 2 (March, 1949), Table 2, p. 42.

[3] *Report of the Royal Commission of Inquiry on Constitutional Problems* (Quebec, 1956), IV, p. 158. The "primary" Catholic schools are all the schools excluding the classical colleges. About 2 per cent of Catholic children of the age group are thus excluded from the calculations.

[4] Canada, D.B.S., *Student Progress through the Schools by Grade* (Ottawa: 1960), p. 28.

[5] Charles Bilodeau, "Education in Quebec," *University of Toronto Quarterly*, XXVII, 3 (April, 1958), p. 402. Emphases, in Roman type, added.

[6] *Ibid.*, p. 410.

upon the report of a royal commission set up to examine the educational system in the province. In 1964 after much controversy and negotiation with the Catholic hierarchy and important Catholic lay organizations, Bill 60 was passed, for the first time making provision for a minister of education. There also appeared at this time a movement, mainly on the part of intellectuals, to have a lay system of schools for the French along with the confessional schools. Concurrently the Church was beginning to retreat from its close control of education, a development attributed in part to the liberal views of Cardinal Leger. In any case the time had arrived when the Church could no longer from its own resources supply the educational needs of an industrial society. How much the Church will ultimately relinquish its hold on education cannot be said. Belatedly it seems to have been recognized that the old system denied to French Canadians the opportunities for social mobility that came with industrialization.

In other provinces, too, religion has led to the bifurcation of education at the elementary level. Catholic "separate" schools have suffered impoverishment through tax and grant structures.[7] Where separate school education is an established right it is a costly one for which Catholics suffer more than Protestants, although both suffer. Catholic children are at an educational disadvantage—a fact which accounts in part for the concentration of Catholics in lower occupational groups. Religion, then, along with socio-economic status, ethnicity, size of family, and region, is an important variable affecting the availability of education. The inter-relatedness of these variables must be kept in mind. It is mainly the socio-economic variable which this chapter seeks to examine.

•

PSYCHOLOGICAL BARRIERS

The psychological barrriers to equality in education are much more vague. If suddenly education became as free as the air, many would not choose it. In a free society such a choice is everyone's right, but there is a great deal of evidence that the desire to stay in school and continue to university is related principally to the position which the family occupies in the general social structure, particularly its class position. In a depressed environment the appropriate motives are not forthcoming, and if they were they would probably lead to frustration. Those who are reared in a milieu indifferent to education are not likely to acquire a high evaluation of it, a situation which, although difficult, is not impossible to correct through social policy. It is for these psychological reasons, in addition to social and economic reasons, that we can speak of a class-determined educational system. If that system is based on the assumption that the motives exhibited by middle and upper class children are "natural" and are thus distributed through all classes it is a class-determined system. Until educational systems are constructed to break down those psychological barriers they are not fully democratized. There is evidence also that intelligence, as measured by the standard type of intelligence tests, is closely associated with social class position, size of family, and size of community. There is no convincing evidence, however, that motivation and intelligence are a genetic endowment of the middle and upper classes, of particular ethnic groups, or of those living in middle size cities. What is more likely, and here we see the interweaving of the psychological and the social, is that there is an appropriate social milieu through which these psychological qualities are acquired. It would, of course, be foolish to assert that all are born with an equal intellectual capacity. It is more reasonable to assume that in any given human population there is a wide range of general ability depending for its development on the appropriate social environment. Educational policy could remove from the social environment those conditions which smother ability.

The relationship between the principle of equality and educational opportunity now becomes more clear. Educational methods by which all children are encouraged to overcome their particular environments, and to pursue the educational career which best suits their talents, can be devised. In this respect much more research into the problems of selection is necessary. The general criticisms levelled at the "eleven plus" examinations in the United Kingdom would suggest that techniques are not yet adequate, but the principles underlying the British reforms of 1944 are sound. In Canada little has been done to remove the barriers imposed by social conditions on the individual's educational opportunity.

---

[7] For an account of the effect of Catholic immigration on the resources of the Separate School Board in Toronto see James Senter, "Separate Schools Wake to a Suffocating Nightmare," *Globe Magazine*, September 3, 1960.

II-7

Eskimo Education, Danish and Canadian: A Comparison*

C. W. HOBART AND C. S. BRANT

•

In this paper we attempt to compare, in terms of histories and cultural dynamics, the system of Eskimo education in Greenland with that of the Canadian Arctic. The data derive from six months of fieldwork in the Canadian Arctic, particularly in the Mackenzie District of the western Arctic, by Hobart in 1963 and 1964, and one and a half months of fieldwork in Greenland by both authors in 1965.[1] In addition an extensive survey of the literature on education for both regions has been made.

During the course of the field trips over 200 interviews were held. One hundred and fifty-nine were held in the Canadian Arctic, 105 of these with Eskimos, 54 with white missionaries, traders, Royal Canadian Mounted Police, teachers, and government officials. Forty-six were held in Copenhagen and in various communities in Greenland with both Danes and Greenlanders, including education officials, teachers, a few students, police, storekeepers, Greenland parliament members, and other government officials.

We shall not here present statistical information based on these interviews even for the Canadian Eskimos, because to do so would be to imply a precision in the available data which is not warranted. As anyone familiar with problems in interviewing native peoples will appreciate, formal interview procedures could not usually be used in talking with informants. To reduce the qualified answers of the native peoples to the "yes" or "no" dichotomies of tables would be misleading. Moreover, there are differences in the responses of men and women, of older and younger people, of Nunamiut or people living on the land and Kabloonamiut or people living on wage income. It is impossible to go into these differences within the limits of the present paper. Since to present statistics without examining differences between subgroups would only

---

* Reprinted with permission from *The Canadian Review of Sociology and Anthropology*, III, 2 (May, 1966), pp. 47–66. This paper is a revised and expanded version of "Sociocultural Conditions and Consequences of Native Education in the Arctic: A Cross-National Comparison," read at the 64th annual meeting of the American Anthropological Association, Denver, Colorado, November 20, 1965.

further misinform, we have restricted ourselves to gross description of the interview results.

We start by suggesting a provisional typology, historically framed, upon which we amplify later. The Greenland system of education, under Danish administration, has been one of cultural continuity, shifting very recently in the direction of cultural synthesis. The Canadian system has been, and continues to be—in effect if not in expressed intention—one of cultural replacement, with only a few recent and scattered tendencies towards cultural synthesis. By cultural replacement is meant the attempt, in undeveloped areas, to replace the traditional culture with a modern one in a short period—a generation or two—through the introduction of modern technological means, organizational forms, and ideological orientations, on a more or less massive basis, without thoughtfully considering the articulation and interactive effects of such introductions. Cultural continuity, on the other hand, refers to the attempt to preserve all basic features of the traditional culture, on the assumption that the conditions of life are changing sufficiently slowly to enable the old way of life to evolve; there is no need for explicit manipulation. Between these opposites lies cultural synthesis: the thoughtfully conceived, carefully implemented introduction of change on a continuing, planned basis, informed by periodic assessment of effects and modified by required corrective measures. Cultural replacement may be illustrated by the pre-Collier administration of Indian Affairs in the United States, in which provision of land, agricultural implements, and farming instructors was expected to result quickly and effectively in the transformation of migratory hunting and gathering tribes to settled communities of farmers. The outcome, for the most part, was varying degrees of sociocultural disorganization and failure to achieve the objectives.[2] Cultural synthesis may be exemplified by the special education program recently established by the U.S. Bureau of Indian Affairs among the Navajo.[3]

---

[1] In Greenland, the work was conducted in the villages of Angmagssalik, Kulusuq (Kap Dan) and Kungmuit in East Greenland, and in the West Greenland communities of Godthab, Egedesminde, Kutdligssat, Umanak, Upernavik and Augpilagtok. In Canada, research was done in Aklavik, Inuvik, Tuktoyaktuk, Fort McPherson, Gjoa Haven, Spence Bay, Coppermine, Cambridge Bay and Cape Parry. For support of the field research, we express appreciation to the Boreal Institute, University of Alberta, the University of Alberta General Research Fund, and the Department of Northern Affairs and National Resources, Ottawa. We are grateful to the many individuals, private and governmental agencies and departments, in Ottawa, Copenhagen, the Canadian Arctic, and Greenland, for their cooperation and assistance. The opinions and interpretations expressed in this paper are, of course, solely our own.

[2] See, for example, Charles S. Brant, "White Contact and Cultural Breakdown Among the Kiowa Apache," *Plains Anthropologist*, IX, 23 (1964).

[3] See Madison L. Coombs, *Doorway Toward the Light, the Story of the Special Navajo Education Program* (Lawrence: University of Kansas, 1962).

GREENLAND

From the outset, the Danish administrative and economic policies toward Greenland have been protective and non-exploitative.

"The basic principle of Danish rule since Egede (in 1721) has been to assist the people of Greenland to achieve the fullest possible life, protected as far as possible from the disadvantages which might accrue from connection with the outside world."[4]

Trade, both within Greenland and between it and other countries, was a monopoly of the Royal Greenland Trading Company which acted in terms of two cardinal principles. (1) The Company was operated for the benefit of the populace, on a "break even" policy such that Greenlanders were able to buy and sell goods as advantageously as possible short of outright subsidy, and (2) in general only those new goods were introduced which would contribute to the ease of survival and the comfort of the people: luxury goods, trinkets, sweets, and liquor were largely excluded. In order to minimize the introduction of disease and the possibility of disruptively rapid acculturation, entry into Greenland was barred to all save those making a contribution to the welfare of the area. The judicial system which the Danes gradually introduced depended heavily on the moralities, judicial concepts, and sanctions of the native inhabitants. The educational policies of the Danes have been similarly gradualistic and synthetic.

For more than 200 years the Danes followed a policy which fostered the continuation of traditional Eskimo culture in Greenland in all major respects save religion. Schools were established widely in local communities, with teachers recruited from the local population, usually individuals trained as Lutheran catechists, knowledgeable in the three R's and in religion, but often untrained as teachers. The language of instruction and of the textbooks was Eskimo. The content of the curriculum had local relevance, and book learning was supplemented by practical training in traditional skills and crafts, given by such figures as the leading kayak builder, seal hunter, or sealskin seamstress. The purpose of education was to assist people to make their living where they were, utilizing local resources and established techniques, not to train them for, or induce aspirations toward, occupations and lifeways unlikely to be available in an isolated and non-Europeanized society. Least of all was there any inducement toward emigration to Denmark.

The results of this system are impressive. Illiteracy was abolished a century ago. Provision was first made for education beyond the elementary level at the same time, and there has been further expansion of new secondary and continuation schools during the past generation.[5] The result has been not only a literate people but one able to supply trained leadership as well: throughout Greenland the clergy is almost everywhere recruited from the native populace. Until 1955 the teachers were all

Greenlanders,[6] and currently Greenlanders head the school system, the Police Department, and the broadcasting system in Greenland.

But Greenland's long isolation was broken sharply and permanently by World War II, and further by the post-War change from the status of colony to that of a province of Denmark. Since the middle 1950's changes in education have included: importation of significant numbers of Danish teachers, increasing from one in 1955 to 300 in 1965; growing emphasis upon the Danish language, but with Eskimo retaining parity in the curriculum; establishment of a few small, cottage-hostel type of residential schools for advanced grades and in some cases for gifted pupils; diversification of curricular materials to include more Denmark-oriented content, but continuing emphasis on Greenlandic literature, history, geography, art, and music; instruction in those European-derived practical skills which are becoming increasingly relevant in Greenlandic life, through advanced vocational training; establishment in Greenland of post-primary educational facilities, particularly a *Realskole* (grades 8 to 10) and a Teacher Training College; and provision of manifold opportunities for technical, university, and professional education in Denmark, and for brief periods of exposure to Danish life, such as a summer or a year for grade school children.

These changes have come about as a result of the demand of the populace and the attempts of the Greenland Administration to meet the changing personnel needs of the area. The Greenlanders became aware during and after World War II that there were imminent opportunities and developments which they were not trained to implement. And rapid changes in the post-war economy of Greenland made it clear that the system of education and training was unable to meet requirements for personnel with particular—often elemental—qualifications. The importation of Danish technical personnel was seen as creating "an upper class consisting chiefly of Danes and... a socially worse-situated lower class consisting mainly of Greenlanders."[7] We shall see however that the attempt to solve this problem has tended to some extent to exacerbate it.

The key figures in the process of educational change which has been taking place in Greenland for the last decade have been the Danish teachers. We shall comment both on the sources of their effectiveness and some of the negative consequences of their arrival on the Greenland scene.

---

4 Royal Danish Ministry for Foreign Affairs, *Greenland* (Ringkjøbing: n.d.), p. 35.
5 *Ibid.*, p. 37.
6 The term "Greenlander" refers to the inhabitants of Greenland, whether of Eskimo or mixed Eskimo and European ancestry. In fact, the majority today are of such mixed ancestry. In Greenland, the term "Greenlander" in reference to people, and the designation "Greenlandic" for the indigenous language, are customary usages both in speech and written communication.
7 Udvalget for Samfundsforskning i Grønland, *Uddannelsessituationen i Vestgrønland I* (København: 1961), p. 69.

The significant contributions of the Danish teachers derive from two sources. The obvious one is the greater pedagogic skills, enlarged educational goals, and the higher performance standards which they brought, and which were often in sharp contrast to the more casual, even apathetic performances of the native teachers. But the crucial source of their effectiveness is a *style* of educational leadership and community activity that tends to maximize their impact on the communities in which they teach. A very large measure of freedom is granted to teachers to select and flexibly to adapt curricular materials to the interests, backgrounds, needs, and prevailing educational handicaps of pupils and native communities. Each teacher chooses his own textbooks, completely free of formal or informal pressures; if he wishes he may write and reproduce his own text materials, and a number do so. As a resident in the local community, the Danish teacher does not possess such privileges or perquisites as are likely to shut him off from significant interaction with the local population and segregate him socially amongst fellow Danes, if any.[8] He does not receive a special annual shipment of foodstuffs, as do most teachers in the Canadian Arctic. Instead, teachers' requirements in Greenland communities are largely supplied through local, and largely native-staffed, stores of the Royal Greenland Trade Department which provide for all customers on a cash and carry basis. The Danish teacher is thus on a footing of equality with all others, as simply another customer, with all the opportunities—indeed, they are unavoidable—for informal social interaction with parents and pupils which this provides in small communities.

The Danish teacher must frequently use native modes of travel, such as dog-sleighing, and engage in such subsistence activities as seal-hunting and fishing, learned from native people. In these, he is coached, and sometimes ridiculed for his errors and initial ineptitude, by local people. Social separation of Danes and Greenlanders is minimal, and with the exception of a single nearly defunct Danish social club, in the Angmagssalik District, something of a survival from the colonial past, we could find no evidences of social discrimination. This does not mean that both groups do not engage in some forms of interaction largely amongst themselves, but it does mean that there are no institutional or attitudinal barriers to intergroup activity, and that a great deal does prevail on a plane of equality. Intermarriage amongst Danish and Greenlandic teachers in Greenland is not uncommon. Marriages of Danish women to Greenlandic men, as well as Danish men to Greenlandic women, occur in upper as well as lower class groups.

The greatest barrier between the Danes and the Greenlanders is linguistic. Relatively few Greenlanders know Danish well, and Danish teachers, as yet inadequately trained in Greenlandic, operate under a language handicap. However, many Danish educators in Greenland make genuine efforts to acquire knowledge of Greenlandic. They are spurred on both by their real desire to interact more meaningfully with

Greenlanders, in the community as well as in the school, and by the availability of lessons in Greenlandic free of costs. With growing bilingualism of both Danes and Greenlanders, the language gulf should in time be bridged.

There is a growing emphasis upon instruction in Danish. Much of the demand for instituting such instruction in the earlier grades has come from the better-educated levels of Greenlandic society, notably from members of the Greenlandic Council, an elected quasi-legislative body currently composed of fourteen Greenlanders and one Dane, a 20-year resident of Greenland. They recognize that, as interaction and synthesis of the two cultures progresses, a more thorough knowledge of Danish is essential as preparation for higher education, which is not available in Greenland and is most naturally obtained in Denmark. But there is no discernible tendency for Greenlanders at any social level to downgrade their image of the mother tongue nor to anticipate its replacement as the language of daily life.

Residential schools in Greenland have been established in a few places on a small scale to make a richer and more rounded program of instruction for the ablest pupils. By personal contact and persuasion, Danish educators at the district level obtain the consent of a few Greenlandic parents of apparently gifted children in outlying areas for these pupils to attend residential schools in the larger settlements of the district. Here the children, aged ten and older, live in small, unpretentious cottage hostels, supervised by a Greenlandic housemother. Life in this home-away-from-home is thoroughly Greenlandic—in foods, disciplinary attitudes, speech. Parents are within one day or less of travelling distance by dog-team, and such pupil-parent contacts are encouraged by the teachers. As at home in the remote community children in the cottage hostel are expected to participate in the daily chores. Searching interviews disclosed virtually no symptoms of maladjustment in the children—bedwetting, nightmares, sleep withdrawal, chronic crying—which might be attributable to separation from family and home community.

One focus of our study has been the socio-psychological impact of education. Among Greenlanders, there appears to us to be a high degree of maintenance of feelings of group self-esteem and a positive valuation of most aspects of traditional culture. Danes and things Danish are not accepted wholesale, mechanically, slavishly. Ways of doing, attitudes and motivational patterns are not, in a blanket manner, regarded as good by Greenlanders because of their association with the Danish way of life. In all of the sealing and fishing areas of Greenland there is extensive

---

[8] Danish teachers, along with other types of Danish personnel in Greenland, receive subsidized housing and are paid on a higher salary scale than Greenlanders. The view of the Danes is that this is justified because they are subject, upon return to Denmark, to income tax on their earnings in Greenland, while Greenlanders pay no income tax. There is some ill feeling, in this connection, on the part of many Greenlanders.

survival of traditional ways and practices, surprising to one familiar with the Canadian Arctic. Kayaks and dog sleds are still widely built and used: one does not find signs of their repudiation in favour of Kabloona substitutes such as canoes, jolly boats, and skidoos, so common in the Canadian Arctic.

In every place visited, especially in the less acculturated districts, we found evidences of considerable independence of outlook, and of overt resistance when Danish teachers or other officials were regarded as tactless or overbearing in their behaviour.[9] One interesting symbol of the emerging synthesis is the general insistence by many on the usage "Greenlander" rather than the disjunctive labels "Eskimo" and "Dane."

However, there appears to be reason to fear that this situation may be somewhat short-lived, a result of past educational arrangements which are being presently changed. In particular there are three interrelated and serious problems currently apparent in the Greenland school system, all a result of the recent massive importation of Danish teachers into the system. These are the high turnover in Danish teachers, the extent to which the arrival of a Danish teacher in a small community undermines the authority and prestige structure of the community, and the qualifications being established for teachers of Eskimo background in Greenland.

Until a decade ago there was no teacher turnover problem because there were no Danish teachers in Greenland. However, as we have noted, the rate of importation of Danish teachers has increased very rapidly in recent years, and the end is not in sight. A certain proportion of these teachers, higher than in the Canadian Arctic or on the Alaskan Arctic Coast, settle down to make a career of teaching in Greenland, some of them marrying Greenlanders. But about 60 per cent stay only for the minimal term of their two-year contract: many expressed an interest in staying longer, but felt that it was not fair to their children, wives, and families at home to remain. The result is that in any one year many of the Danish teachers, although formally well prepared, are very poorly qualified in experience for their work, since they are teaching Greenlanders for the first time. Their ineptitude is apparent in a number of ways. They are not familiar with examples which will be meaningful to the children. They are strangers to parents who cultivate acquaintanceships much more slowly than do highly mobile Westerners. They are unfamiliar with the psychology of Greenlanders: accordingly, their dependence on sternness of manner and liberal use of punishment—which are common and effective classroom strategies in Denmark—tends to bewilder Greenlandic children, unused to this kind of treatment by adults, to destroy rapport, and to hinder the educational process. The availability of excellent instructional materials designed for Greenland tends to mitigate the effects of nonfamiliarity with Greenlandic examples,[10] but only time and experience bring the understanding of Greenlandic motivation which is a prerequisite to good teaching. About the time that many teachers have come to this understanding they return to Denmark.

There are two further conditions which aggravate this problem. The first is that the more insecure or unsure of himself a teacher is, the more authoritarian his classroom manner tends to be. Since this tends merely to frighten the children and so decrease his effectiveness the situation is viciously circular. The second is that it is usually the least experienced teachers who are sent to the smallest and the most remote settlements. Those who stay long enough to become experienced and who elect to remain in Greenland for an extended period are usually promoted to principalships of larger schools in larger and more Danicized communities. The result is that pupils and parents in small settlements who have had the least contact with Danes, have frequently to adjust to Danish teachers who have no experience with Greenlandic values and motivations and are largely cut off from others who might advise them.

The situation just described is intensified by the practice, where a Danish teacher is sent to a small community, of placing him in authority over the native teacher who has taught there all of his life. As a result it commonly happens that an extremely young and professionally immature Danish teacher, perhaps only twenty-one years old and newly graduated from teacher training, is placed over a Greenlander, forty or fifty years of age, who has taught in this community for two or three decades. The effect of this situation, which has been common during the last ten years, is that the experienced native person who, as teacher and catechist, has been one of the most respected men in the community, loses prestige sharply as he is reduced to following the instructions of one half his age. The policies and procedures of the native teacher are modified by the Dane, which implies that the native teacher is incompetent. Inevitably the native teacher's morale and self-respect suffer drastically. In a number of communities we heard of native teachers who in this circumstance had become listless, uncaring, and often increasingly given to alcoholism. There were stories of native teachers who sat reading magazines while the class was left to its own devices, teachers who were drunk on the job—and in most cases these men had been good, effective

---

9 Serious instances of tactless, overbearing behaviour appear to occur infrequently. Danish teachers receive a broadly humanistic education, with a modest amount of training in pedagogy. The orientation course on Greenlandic life and society prior to taking up positions in Greenland is very short. In our observation, Danish teachers are non-ethnocentric and flexible in attitudes. District school administrators are alert to check any tendency of teachers with experience in Denmark but none in Greenland to play the unmodified authoritarian role traditional in Danish education.
10 Perhaps the most impressive aspect of the Greenland school system to a North American is the amount of instructional material relevant to Greenland and written in Greenlandic which has been painstakingly prepared, and is beautifully illustrated and published. Several dozen such volumes have been prepared which cover a wide range of fields, including reading, history, geography, arithmetic, music, religion, etc.

teachers, as measured by the prevailing standards, before their sudden subordination.

The most obvious consequence of this is its implication to the Greenlanders affected, that it is the Danish origin, the magic of the white skin, which justifies the superordination of the Dane, and the subordination of the Greenlander. Although the Danes have expended a great deal of effort and money during the last decade in bringing Danish teachers to Greenland, they have done very little during this period to upgrade the native teachers so that they would be able to teach the same curriculum as Danish teachers. Only within the last two years have there been pilot programs of intensive summer school workshops and of training in Denmark for native teachers, and these have enrolled only a few dozen Greenlanders. The extent to which the absence of a massive effort to upgrade the qualifications of native teachers may result, in the long run, of a denigration of things Greenlandic—and a corresponding over-valuation of things Danish—can scarcely be foreseen.

One consequence was clearly apparent during the summer of 1965. The Greenland Council was in the process of formulating recommendations for changes in the educational system. One important area had to do with specification of the qualifications of Greenlanders for certification to teach in Greenland. The unanimous decision of the Council was that the certification requirements should be exactly the same as in the rest of Denmark: the Council members were decidedly hostile to any suggestions which might imply the lowering of these standards for Greenland—no matter how irrelevant or unrealistic these standards might be. The Danish requirement prescribes that qualified teachers be fluent in English, and have a reading knowledge of German. Thus, following the recommendation of the Council, to qualify for certification as a teacher a Greenlander will have to be fluent in three languages—Greenlandic, Danish, and English—and have a reading knowledge of a fourth—German. A likely consequence of this policy will be to increase the proportion of teachers in Greenland who are Danish. This in turn will have three further consequences. It will strengthen the tendency, already strong in other occupational spheres, for high status jobs to be held by Danes and low status jobs to be held by Greenlanders, thus increasing the significance of racial and ethnic differences in Greenland. It will tend sharply to impede the mobility of Greenlanders into white collar occupations, since numbers of studies have shown that for upwardly mobile members of acculturating groups, the teacher's certificate is often used as a springboard into training for the higher professions. And it will tend powerfully toward the increased Danicization of the area, and probably toward the polarization of the populace into a more wealthy and powerful Danish acculturated group, and a rather improverished, relatively powerless, distinctly apathetic, more traditionally Greenlandic group.

It should be emphasized that these anticipated developments are not primarily the fault of the Danish Administration: they will be the result of decisions made by a democratically elected Greenland Council. However, if the Danish Administration had had the foresight to attempt to improve the Greenland educational system primarily through intensive efforts to upgrade the skills and training of the catechist teachers, who constitute some of the most intelligent elements of the populace, using Danish teachers only on a very limited basis, the course of developments would certainly have been different. As it is, the Danish teacher has become a symbol of educational excellence, for reasons which are often mistaken or irrelevant, and it was the policy decisions of the Administration which have brought this to pass. The Council appears to feel that Danish teachers have a "white magic" which is necessary for the adequate education of Greenlandic children, and if Greenlanders are to be equally competent they must have the training which will confer upon them this same mysterious quality. To the suggestion that only a very few Greenlandic young people will be able to attain such polylingual fluency, Council members only gave the grim and unrealistic answer, "They must and they will."

Nevertheless, discussion of these current developments should not be permitted to obscure the fact that education in Greenland is genuinely integrative and synthetic: students are taught to read and write in both Greenlandic and Danish; they study both Greenlandic and Western European geography, history, literature, art, and music; vocational training includes both traditional Greenlandic and modern industrial skills; and instruction takes place in both languages. Thus in terms of language, attitudes, and skills, the education seeks to make available to the student two alternatives and two possible identities, the Greenlandic and the Danish. No doubt few are able to actualize both very fully, but the significant point is that the school does not prejudge the alternatives. In so far as possible it makes both available to the student.

●

THE WESTERN CANADIAN ARCTIC

The Western Canadian Arctic contrasts rather sharply in many ways with Greenland. In the first place it is not so rich in fish and sea mammal resources as Greenland, although during earlier times this difference was counterbalanced by the greater abundance of caribou. The depletion of the caribou herds in the Canadian Arctic is without parallel in Greenland.

The most dramatic contrast is between the provisions made by the Canadian and the Danish governments for the Arctic areas under their jurisdictions. The chapter titles which Jenness uses in his study of Eskimo Administration in the Canadian Arctic testify eloquently to the extent to which the Canadian government—preoccupied with other problems—has almost completely ignored the Arctic during most of the twentieth century: "Government Myopia (Pre-1903)," "Wards of the Police (1903–1921)," "A Shackled Administration (1921–1931)," "Bureaucracy in Inaction (1931–1940)," "Laying the New Foundations (1945–1950)," "Steering without a Compass."[11] During this period "the three empires"—the R.C.M.P., the missions, and the Hudson's Bay Company—along with a sprinkling of free traders made such provision for Eskimos as their interests suggested and their often meagre resources allowed. Governmental guidance was virtually non-existent. There were no restrictions on travel to the Arctic, with the result that epidemics periodically swept through the Arctic, decimating the populace again and again. There was neither a check on the condition of the caribou herds, nor control of their slaughter, with the result that the herds have shown a precipitous and, for some Eskimos, a disastrous decline. There was no systematic provision of education for Eskimos until 1959. There were no regular efforts made, in the face of the disasters noted above, to check on Eskimo welfare, with the result that as recently as 1957 and 1959, Eskimo bands suffered starvations in each of which a number of people died.

The educational system which has come into existence in the Western Arctic, at first under Mission auspices, and, since 1952, increasingly under Federal auspices, contrasts as sharply with the Greenland system as have the Danish and the Canadian Arctic administrative philosophies. The educational system in the Western Arctic is characterized by these features: continuous use of non-native teachers, in the past dominantly clergy, changing to lay teachers today; throughout its history, instruction given wholly in English; establishment and heavy utilization, from the beginnings, of residential schools, with latter-day emphasis upon large units; curriculum almost entirely oriented to the southern Canadian culture and value system; and minimal attempts to produce text materials appropriate to the Arctic.

The history of Eskimo education in Canada has throughout involved confrontation of generations of pupils by wholly non-native teachers. The earliest schools in the western Canadian Arctic were established by the Oblate Fathers at Fort Providence in 1867, by Anglican missionaries at Hay River in 1918 and at the mouth of the Mackenzie Delta in 1929, later by both groups at Aklavik on the Mackenzie river. The white teachers who staffed these schools maintained, to quote Diamond Jenness, "religious kindergartens that hardly deserve the name of schools," and provided an education that "taught nothing and explained nothing."[12] Some had little appreciation of Eskimo psychology and discipline was frequently maintained by the liberal use of corporal punishment. The traumatic effects of this were yet evident in the way our adult informants recalled their school experiences, thirty and more years later, when we interviewed them.

The last decade and a half has seen the retrieval of educational responsibility by government from the missions and a vast increase in school facilities and in percentage of school-age children in attendance. But the "new look" in Eskimo education is in major respects only an upgraded and extended replication of the mission program, with religious aspects suitably played down.

We will comment especially on (1) exclusive use of Southern Canadian teachers, (2) English language instruction, (3) Southern Canadian curriculum materials, and (4) use of very large boarding schools. All of these features were characteristic of the mission organized schools: their perpetuation under the federally administered educational system justifies the designation of this as an upgraded mission-type educational program.

(1) Both the mission and the federal schools have made exclusive use of Southern Canadian trained teachers, who in virtually all cases have been whites. Under the federal program there has been an upgrading of these teachers in terms of their formal qualifications. However, it can be argued that the net effect of this changeover has been negative as far as education is concerned. The mission teachers, although formally less well qualified, were characterized by a missionary commitment, which meant that their period of Arctic teaching tended to be relatively lengthy. As a result they came to know the Eskimo children quite well, far more frequently than do lay teachers today. Thus, despite the criticism of them made earlier, they more often came to discover which motivational and teaching procedures were most effective with Eskimo children. By contrast, the federally employed teachers sign a two-year contract to teach in the North, and they may resign after one year if they are willing to pay their return fare to their Southern Canadian homes. The rate of contract renewal is so low that the teacher turnover rate is about 30 per cent annually; a teacher who has more than two years of Arctic teaching experience is considered a veteran. The result is that a sizeable proportion of Eskimo children are taught by "green" teachers, and this seriously affects the educational process.

It takes the average teacher from the South, suffering from culture shock, isolation in an unusual environment, and the handicap of overtraining in the culture-bound precepts of professional pedagogy, at least one year to discern the particular problems in teaching his shy and unsophisticated Eskimo pupils and to devise ways of coping with them. The arrangements of teachers' housing and provisioning characteristically tend to seal them off socially from the native communities. In Inuvik they live in the "serviced" white area of town, and teachers all over the Arctic annually receive a large shipment of provisions from southern Canada to last them all year. Thus they are independent of the people

---

[11] Diamond Jenness, *Eskimo Administration: II, Canada* (Montreal: Arctic Institute, 1964).
[12] *Ibid.*, pp. 43, 47.

and the land as far as food is concerned. Their life outside the classrooms is overwhelmingly that of participation with other resident whites—fellow teachers, Hudson's Bay Company and Department of Northern Affairs personnel, policemen—in a caste-like situation.

A variety of consequences of this teacher staffing situation were encountered during the fieldwork. In one remote community Eskimo informants were plainly still shocked, two years after the original events, at the fact that a teacher had frequently shouted or screamed at the children. In some communities, despite the esteem in which education was held, the rapport between teachers and pupils, and between teachers and families, had so broken down that families made little effort to get their children to school, and teachers complained of the regularity with which they had to go out and "round up the children."

(2) The exclusive use of English as the language of instruction among children understanding little or none of this language, by teachers knowing nothing of Eskimo language—who thus cannot explain any difficult English concepts, or grammatical usages in Eskimo—creates a number of difficulties. The first year or two of classes must, of course, be given over almost entirely to the teaching of English, with the result that two years of grade retardation is usual. The retardation is aggravated by the fact that many of the children are over-age when they enter school, miss a year during the course of their schooling, or both. It was precisely to minimize an unnecessary increase in this kind of retardation that the Special Navajo Education Program, devised in the United States, made provision for teaching a number of subjects in the Navajo language. This was done in order to avoid tying educational advancement in all spheres to mastery of English, and also to provide children in new and strange educational situations with the emotional support of some "official" use of their native tongue.[13]

Not only is instruction exclusively in English, but the tendency of children to use Eskimo among themselves is so effectively discouraged that it is virtually never heard among children on boarding school premises. For boarding school children two negative consequences of this situation deserve mention. The first is that during the summer vacation periods at home the child's communication with parents and kinsmen is hampered by a growing value and attitude gap resulting from his tendency to view everything Eskimo, language included, as being of little worth, since it is not worth recognition in the school curriculum. The second is that the exclusively English nature of the school situation and the almost exclusively Eskimo nature of the home situation tends to increase the child's problems of integrating these overwhelmingly dissimilar facets of his life, and to give to the school an air of unreality and irrelevance to life as he and his family experience it. The school situation appears to be a kind of unique "game" to the child, which he learns to play when he is in the appropriate situation, but does not play elsewhere. As a result there is little carryover from the school to the home situation. For example, when children past grade three are instructed in school to draw a house, they portray a two-storey house, surrounded by trees, with a flagstone walk leading up to the door: in short, a "schoolbook" house which they have never directly seen and which is unrelated to the houses they know.

(3) All of the text materials used by Eskimo children in the Western Canadian Arctic were devised for southern Canadian children. The only progress which has been made toward the production of Arctic-related material consists of two experimental Curriculum Guides, one a Social Studies Program, and the other a Language Arts Program, produced in the Mackenzie District. For neither is there specially prepared accompanying textbook material. The most obvious consequence of the use of Southern Canadian material is that many of the objects and concepts with which southern children are familiar, such as fences and farm life and city life, are completely strange to the Eskimo child. Teachers who were interviewed frequently complained of the problem they encountered in trying to explain these irrelevancies to their classes. Thus valuable time is wasted in trying to explain things to the Eskimo child which are useless for him to know. The fact that much of the content is meaningless to him increases the irrelevance and the "never-never-land" game aspect of the education process for the child. Furthermore, since education as such is seen as important, and since the distinctive aspects of Eskimo life and culture are completely ignored, the only possible conclusion must be that there is nothing in native lore or tradition which is worth learning. Thus this curriculum tends to be destructive of respect for Eskimo values and for father, mother, and others highly able in native skills but not formally educated. Moreover, when the child is removed from home, from the age of six or seven to fifteen years, for education in a hostel school where none of the native skills are taught, it is clear that the consequence of this education is to render him unable to return to his home community, since he has not had the opportunity to learn the values and the skills which are prerequisite to living there.

(4) Some idea of the emphasis upon residential schools in the Mackenzie District of the Canadian Arctic is provided by figures for the 1963–64 school year. There were then 818 Eskimo children between ages 6 and 18 attending schools operated by the government in the area between Pelly Bay and the Alaskan border. Three hundred and fifty-three, or 43 per cent, attended residential schools, and 300 of the 353 were in one large institution, the Sir Alexander Mackenzie School, at Inuvik.

The large present-day residential school, in material terms, presents an enormous contrast to those of the past. In construction, equipment, furnishings and comfort, it ranks with the best schools of Southern Canada. In the Inuvik school, Eskimo children experience a standard of living superior in every respect to that in their home settings.

---

[13] Coombs, *Doorway Towards the Light*, pp. 19, 20.

The social and cultural environment of the large residential school is something else, however. From the age of six, children are annually air-lifted from the little communities along the Arctic coast, with their warm, kinship-based, inter-personal environments, to the large efficiency-oriented, under-staffed,[14] strange, impersonal surroundings of the residential school hostels.

The large turnout at departure time in late summer is not to be explained by any wholesale or unqualified enthusiasm on the part of the parents for sending children away. In most settlements the choice is between residential school education and none at all, and Canadian Northern Service Officers have done a persuasive job of selling the importance of education. Teachers reported that there was relatively little crying and complaining by pupils in their presence, but this should not be taken at face value. Parents commonly reported that in accord with Eskimo tradition, they counselled their children to contain their emotions lest they make the white people at school feel unhappy. Most of the school personnel mistake the rather mask-like smiling faces surrounding them as evidence of good adjustment on the part of the children of a supposedly innately cheerful and happy people. Most of the children do appear to cope with the separation experience very well, probably because their early childhood training is nearly ideal, and thus they do not react neurotically to the separation. But significant symptoms of trauma of separation from family and familiar surroundings, such as bed-wetting, nightmares, and quiet crying in bed, are not uncommon.[15] Many of these go unremarked by the overloaded staff; others are explained away in folk-commonsense terms. The emotional deprivation which is suffered by the Eskimo mothers of young children, out in the settlements,[16] is entirely beyond the field of perception of the school personnel.

The modern residential facilities of the boarding school provide the Eskimo child with an experience of physical comfort and convenience which is commonly dysfunctional for the intersession periods and the post-school life of the pupil back in his home community. The demands of the school for participation in the tasks of maintenance are minimal and light. Everything is provided and life is rather effortless: plentiful and well-prepared food is automatically ready at mealtimes; hot water is at hand for the turning of a faucet; clean clothes return from the laundry at regular intervals; clean warm bedding is provided; and the interior environment is always at a constant warm temperature comfortable to whites. For the Eskimo child, accustomed from an early age to taking part in the constant, arduous tasks of household maintenance, and hardened to the rigours of the Arctic climate, residential school life is experienced as a very "soft" life indeed. And, as might be expected, he tends to develop a marked distaste for conditions at home after experiencing the sharp contrast between the two environments.

What are the consequences of this residential schooling experience for Eskimo children? Particularly among the less acculturated Eskimo children from communities such as Gjoa Haven, Spence Bay, Coppermine, Holman Island in the central Arctic, and the bush areas of the Delta, our interviews show that a coherent pattern of problem behaviour emerges in children as a result of experience in residential schools. It is the picture of an unhappy, dissatisfied, unadjusted child—almost always described by the word "cranky" by informants who could speak any English. In contrast to the obedience, respectfulness, and helpfulness typical of Eskimo children in "unspoiled" communities, such children were disobedient, complaining, disrespectful, and reluctant to undertake chores spontaneously or at the indirect hinting of parents in the way which is traditional among Eskimos. They were unable to amuse themselves in a self-contained manner or be contented.

Especially marked was the children's loss of respect for parents, which has several sources. For one thing, they discover that there are many good things in life which are apparently taken for granted in the white world. They come to appreciate some of these luxuries while at school, and to disdain parents who may never have heard of them and in any case cannot provide them. This loss is also rooted in the school curriculum, which is almost exclusively oriented to the white man's culture, with no distinctly Eskimo content at all, as noted earlier.

Other behavioural consequences of schooling include jealousy and fighting. The returned child, deprived at the age of 6 or 7 of his mother's love and care for 10 months of the year, becomes greedily demanding of it and resentful of another child's becoming the object of her attention. The traditional Eskimo internalized controls on aggressive behaviour tend to break down in the competition-oriented school subculture, and this is aggravated by the experience of frustrating physical privations to which children are suddenly returned at home. Other consequences mentioned by Eskimo parents are lying, stealing and sneaky behaviour, all of them offenses against traditional Eskimo morality and virtually unheard of in the more remote settlements.

---

[14] The ratio of Eskimo children to dormitory staff in the residential school at Inuvik in 1963–64 was more than three times as large as that in the residential school at Wrangell, Alaska.
[15] By far the most common of these is bed-wetting, according to adult informants. One Catholic sister who has served as a Junior Boys Supervisor for 13 years in hostels in part housing Eskimo children, estimated that about one-third of the Eskimo boys she has known during this period wet their beds at times. It should be emphasized that this is virtually completely unknown in unbroken Nunamiut families.
[16] The most extreme example encountered was of a woman from Coppermine who, following the departure of two of her children for school in Aklavik, reported that she woke up crying every morning, all fall and winter. Her misery eventually forced her husband to move the entire family to Aklavik the following spring. Many other indications of the depth of emotional distress of Eskimo mothers at the loss of their children might be mentioned.

To be sure, Eskimo children learn much of the material they are taught in the schools, and even if there is no one else in camp to whom the child might speak English except himself—and such an instance was observed of a child carrying on an English conversation with himself—his abilities are prized by his parents. Should a white man turn up in the community, he will be quickly and proudly summoned to act as interpreter. But it can well be asked: to what extent do children generalize what they learn? Girls do well in Home Economics at the expensively and modernly equipped vocational school at Yellowknife. Put such a girl into a job such as housekeeper at a nursing station and she will apply her skills excellently, preparing fine meals for the patients and keeping a spotless kitchen. But look inside her own home and you will get the impression she learned nothing at school. Such a two-response or "two-game" pattern is what one would expect of the children in these circumstances. Writing of the *day* school at Baker Lake in the Eastern Arctic Vallee notes: "For the most part, the day school is a purely Canadian agency, an envelope of Kabloona society and culture in which the child is sealed off from the traditional Eskimo milieu. If the child were put on board a rocket each morning and whisked within minutes to some school in the South, then whisked back to Baker Lake again in the afternoon, the contrast between his school milieu and that of his home would not be much greater than it is at present."[17] This separation between education and environment is even more sharp where the child's living arrangements during the period of the school year are purely Canadian. Thus residential school children experience completely different worlds in their home communities and in the residential school. About the only tie between the two is an airplane ride. In the two worlds, they speak different languages, wear different clothes, eat different foods, live in different facilities, have different associates, follow different schedules, experience different disciplines, enjoy different recreations. The parents of children from outlying regions know nothing of the children's life in the school, and the school personnel know almost nothing of life in the camps from which the children come.

Obviously, much of contemporary Eskimo education in the Western Canadian Arctic is inappropriate, and perhaps even dis-educative from the standpoint of preparation for the life children will lead as adults. But educational and other officials are often quite candid in stating one of their goals to be the weaning of children away from traditional Eskimo community and culture. They justify this in terms of the high rate of Eskimo population growth and the increasing availability of more advanced types of employment in Arctic industrial centers for well-trained, sophisticated Eskimos—employment which will enable them to live richer, more interesting lives.

In response to this position, several replies may be made. First, the assumption of great increase in advanced types of employment is open to serious question, indeed has been questioned by experts in economic development and even by the Deputy Minister of Northern Affairs himself in a 1961 publication.[18] The second would challenge the right of planners to decide what kind of communities and cultures should survive and what kind should become extinct. Articulate Eskimos in Alaska have expressed themselves rather eloquently on this point.[19] The third is that there is evidence that often it does not work. Where the effort is one of cultural replacement there is always the possibility that the product may "fall between two stools," may be unfitted to return to the traditional life of his father, having experienced a softer, "better" way, but may not acquire the motivations and internalized disciplines which are presumed in contemporary wage employment. Most Arctic settlements have examples of this wastage, drifters who are unable to adapt to the loneliness or the employment conditions of the town, but who despise traditional employments, and live parasitically off the sharing patterns of the community. Claremont has documented the widespread existence of this pattern among young Eskimos aged 20 to 35 in the Mackenzie Delta, most of whom were products of church residential schools.[20]

We do not wish to imply that the education of Eskimos should be primarily oriented to fitting them to continue living the current pattern of life of the settlements from which they come: clearly the rapidly increasing size of the Eskimo populace and the speed of change of life in these communities as well as the broadening range of opportunities in the world today make that both impossible and undesirable. However, we do maintain that the regimen and the diet in the hostel, and the curriculum in the school, which are oriented only toward the Southern Canadian way of life, are equally unrealistic, and often tragic in their consequences. The ideal would be an educational program similar to that in Greenland, which would keep open two possibilities—fitness for training for southern type wage or salary employment, and for returning to the life of hunting and trapping on the land—just as long as possible. We advocate this for two reasons. The first is that there are some who will never acquire the skills and the motivations to make a very successful adjustment to wage employment. If they are able to return to life in the settlements their lives will be happier, more productive, and more law-abiding than if they are condemned to a "hanger-on" way of life around some community like Inuvik, Aklavik, or Cambridge Bay. The second is that if young people are not early alienated from either way of life, their chances will be maximized for integrating both ways to some extent

---

[17] Frank Vallee, *Kabloona and Eskimo in the Central Keewatin*, Ottawa: Northern Affairs and National Resources, 1962, p. 162 (mimeographed).

[18] R. G. Robinson, "The Future of the North," *North*, VII, 2 (March-April, 1961).

[19] "Dying on the Vine," *Tundra Times* (Fairbanks, Alaska), editorial, II, 21 (August, 1964).

[20] D. H. J. Clairmont, *Deviance Among Indians and Eskimos in Aklavik, N. W. T.* (Ottawa: Queen's Printer, 1963).

within their own personalities. Only thus can they avoid the confusion of identity, and the covert but endless seeking for home that is characteristic of those taken too early from home and weaned to a boarding school way of life lacking the warmth and the relationship satisfactions which only home can provide.

●

CONCLUSION

At the outset, we suggested that the contrasting conceptual models of cultural continuity and cultural replacement, as defined, were applicable to the Danish and Canadian systems of Eskimo education, respectively, when they are viewed in long-term historical perspective. The purport of our data and interpretations for both systems have been that, while the direction of change has been towards cultural synthesis, the magnitude of such change has been very great in the Danish case and very slight in the Canadian one. The transition to a synthetic system in Greenland, greatly accelerated in the past decade, has not occurred without seriously disruptive effects, some of which might have been avoided or minimized by different policy decisions. Such decisions might have been indicated by a more carefully considered forecast of probable effects of alternatives.

However, it is evident that the administration in Greenland is non-ethnocentric, planning-minded, and self-critical; moreover, that it has seriously encouraged and utilized social research as an aid in the formulation and periodic modification of policies and programs.[21] In

---

21 The evidence for this assertion, apart from our interviews with officials in Copenhagen and Greenland, may be found in the following government publications: Udvalget for Samfundsforskning i Grønland, *Uddannelsessituationen i Vestgrønland* (The Educational Situation in West Greenland), Vol. I: *Generelle uddannelsesproblemer* (General Educational Problems), 1961; Vol. II: *Skoleuddannelsen* (School Education), 1961; Vol. III: *De unges valg af erhverv* (The Young People's Choice of Vocation), 1963; *Familie og Ægteskab i Vestgrønland* (Family and Marriage in West Greenland), Vol. I: *Opløsning af ægteskab* (Dissolution of Marriage), 1961; *Alkoholsituationen i Vestgrønland* (The Alcohol Situation in West Greenland), 1961; *Kriminalloven og de vestgrønlandske samfund* (Criminal Law and West Greenland Society), Vol. I: *Samfundsvidenskabelige undersøgelser* (Social Scientific Inquiry), 1962; Vol. II: *Kriminallov for Grønland af 5. marts 1954 med kommentarer* (Criminal Law for Greenland of March 5, 1954, with Commentary), 1962; *Befolkningssituationen i Vestgrønland* (The Population Situation in West Greenland): *Bebyggelsespolitik og befolkningsudvikling* (Settlement Policy and the Growth of Population), 1963; *Samarbejdsproblemer mellem grønlaendere og danskere i Vestgrønland* (Problems of Cooperation Between Greenlanders and Danes in West Greenland), 1963. All of these monographs, published by Andreassen and Co., Copenhagen, contain summaries in Greenlandic, and English, excepting Vol. II on Criminal Law, which has a Greenlandic summary only.

Canada, while there are occasional signs of development of such orientations in northern education and administration, the emergence of a policy of cultural synthesis, as we have defined the concept, seems very problematic. The main thrust of the program remains directed towards cultural replacement.

The differential effects of the two systems of Eskimo education, in terms of cultural and personal integrity, are marked. The future development of these systems will have profound consequences for the cultural and economic evolution of Greenland and Arctic Canada.

PART THREE

Social and Economic Change

III

Introduction

•

Today, social change in Canada is taking place much faster than ever before. The independence found in rural society is disappearing, and urbanization and suburbanization are occurring at an unprecedented rate. The increase in technological change in industry and agriculture is producing specialization in vocations and professions. Communications media have had an impact on all spheres of human thought and action. However, some factors still contribute to resistance to change: cultural inertia and satisfaction with the status quo, and vested interests of individuals and institutions.

Though in practice the school has been an agency for conserving and perpetuating the existing social order, educational theory has not lacked proponents of the school as a creator of new social orders. The ideals of Plato were reflected by the French revolutionary the Marquis de Condorcet (1743–1794), who believed that the State and its schools should work for the social regeneration of man. The German philosopher Immanuel Kant (1724–1804) thought that a child should be educated, not with reference to present conditions, but according to "the *idea* of humanity and its entire destiny." The French romanticist Jean Jacques Rousseau (1712–1778) decried the injustice of the *ancien régime* and postulated that education according to nature would bring about a better man and a better society. The Swiss educator Johann Pestalozzi (1746–1827) and the German educator Friedrich Froebel (1782–1852) both wished to use education to ameliorate working-class conditions. In the United States, Horace Mann (1796–1859) dedicated his life to the belief that a common school for all children would create a better society and would minimize social and economic class distinctions. John Dewey (1859–1952) worked to destroy the false dichotomy between liberal education and vocational education that had helped perpetuate class distinctions on the European continent.

The Depression brought about a new group of social reformers led by George S. Counts who contended in his *Dare the School Build a New Social Order?* (1932) that it is the responsibility of the school to lead the way out of social and economic stagnation. He believed that the just society could be achieved with educational planning.

In Canada, expenditure on education increased from 2.6 per cent of the gross national product in the late 1920's to over 5 per cent in the late 1960's. In 1966, expenditure on academic and vocational education accounted for 2.3 per cent of the national budget, 27.8 per cent of provincial expenditures, and 30.4 per cent of municipal expenditures.

The Massey Commission (1951) insisted that the case for education was good in itself and did not have to be tied in with its economic yield. The Gordon Commission (1957), although agreeing with the value of education per se, put emphasis on the productivity of investment in higher education. The Economic Council of Canada, in its *First Annual Review* (1964), put still more emphasis on highly skilled manpower: "During the post-war period it has become increasingly apparent that the future prosperity of a nation will depend in large measure on its success in creating and maintaining an adequate supply of professional, technical, managerial and other highly skilled manpower."[1] The Bladen Commission in its report, *Financing Higher Education in Canada* (1965), went further in relating education to economic growth: "... there is good reason to argue that we may ten years hence have more for other things because we spend so much more on our universities."[2]

Canadian educators fully realize that education must assume responsibility in effecting change. But, as Floyd G. Robinson pointed out:

One current manifestation of the emergence of a somewhat limited leadership view resides in our present preoccupation with educational planning. Where it has been developed in some detail (e.g. in Europe), educational planning attempts to do such things as predict the number of engineers required by the economy ten years hence, and to select and direct the appropriate number of students into this field to ensure that this need will be met. While such planning is both laudatory and necessary, it by no means represents the full implementation of a leadership role for education, since the needs which it anticipates are usually based upon a simple extrapolation of present economic trends (e.g. the assumption that the gross national product will continue to increase by 5% annually). In other words, the basis for planning has tended to be some simple assumption about future material needs, rather than some postulation of future human requirements. To plan for the delivery of 20,000 engineers by the end of the next decade does not, it seems to me, pose a problem of the same order of complexity as planning for the elimination of racial prejudice, or for the emergence of a world citizenship view. But the full meaning of a leadership role for education can only be glimpsed when such larger goals are contemplated.[3]

---

[1] Economic Council of Canada, *Economic Goals for Canada to 1970, First Annual Review* (Ottawa: Queen's Printer, 1964), p. 160.
[2] Bladen Commission, *Financing Higher Education in Canada* (Toronto and Quebec: University of Toronto Press and Les Presses de l'Université Laval, 1965), p. 58.
[3] Floyd G. Robinson, "Relationship Between Educational and Societal Change," *The Canadian College of Teachers*, Vol. VII (1964), p. 11.

The individual is not forgotten in the growing concern for social change. Much is being written about the need for wisdom in the technological age, as opposed to intellectual training devoid of any values. As Clarence E. Smith put it:

> *It is, I know, unfashionable to speak of the soul, but we cannot substitute intellect for it. There is a logic of the deeper human experience which is different from the logic of the intellect alone. The latter leads to cleverness, the former to wisdom. What the world of the future will need is people wise of soul rather than people skilled and clever in the use of the artifacts of the future.*[4]

B. R. Clark, in *Educating the Expert Society*, warns us that education for technology alone can easily lead to an era of "technical barbarism" and hopes that modern youth, while educating itself for technical competence, will keep this warning in mind.[5]

Another area of significance for social change and education is the development of communications media. The use of new technological aids such as educational television is widening the dimensions of educative experience. The *Telescuola* in Italy provides educational television seven hours a day, six days a week, from October to June. In France, eight thousand schools are fully equipped to receive telecast lessons meticulously prepared by the French government and closely integrated with the national school curriculum. Only through experimentation with new media can their full potentials be discovered. Marshall McLuhan suggests, in his *Understanding Media*, that the only defence against the new technologies is to understand their powers and to use them constructively.

There are three readings in this section. In the first, John Porter puts forward the thesis that Canada no longer has an agricultural economy and must use education to become a productive and modern industrial society. The second selection, from the *Second Annual Review* of the Economic Council of Canada, examines the average education of the working population, the relationship between educational background and income, and the effect on the Canadian economy of an increase in education. This study underlines the potential benefits for Canada that will result from increased emphasis on education. The third selection, by John M. Culkin, is a summary and an interpretation of the philosophy of Canada's internationally known writer on communications, Marshall McLuhan. If the schools are to meet the challenges of the electronic age, they must try to understand the deep social and psychological impact of the modern means of communication.

---

[4] Clarence E. Smith, "The Nature of Educational Change," *Journal of Education*, No. 8 (Vancouver: March, 1963), p. 39.

[5] B. R. Clark, *Educating the Expert Society* (San Francisco: Chandler Publications, 1962), pp. 288–289.

III - 8

Social Change and the Aims and Problems of Education in Canada*

JOHN PORTER

•

In many ways, Canada is like the United States, in that it is trying to create a new nation in the North American continent; but it is very different in that, unlike the United States, it has no charter values. It did not begin, as the United States did, with a revolution, a revolution in which there were clearly articulated aims—aims which became embodied in the Constitution and the Bill of Rights. Canada has no such charter instruments, and consequently, it has no charter values, in the sense that the United States has them. If there are Canadian values, they tend to be counter-revolutionary, colonialist, conservative and monarchial (rejection of republicanism, for example).

If there is any basic, positive value expressed about the character of Canadian society and what it ought to be, it is to be found in the notion of a pluralist society. If there is any recurring article of faith in Canadian literature, it tends to be this: that Canada is attempting an experiment in which the principle of ethnic differentiation is the most important. That is to say, it is creating a society in which various groups retain their identity, and in which most individuals are almost required to retain an identity with a European group.

This principle of ethnic differentiation in Canada serves class differentiation. That is to say, it is the means by which people are marked off as being different from one another. Such a principle is incompatible with the idea of equality, because the notion of ethnic differentiation emphasizes the particular attributes and characteristics of individuals, rather than general and universal principles, such as their common humanity. Thus the Canadian notion that the good society is served by ethnic differentiation is a factor preventing the implementation of thoroughgoing democratic institutions.

There is also a lingering image of Canada as a rural society, an image which is frequently reinforced by the official symbolism in Canada,

---

* Reprinted with permission from *Education 6:15* (Scarborough: W. J. Gage, Ltd., 1967), pp. 101–105. This paper is an abridgment of the opening address given to the CTF Seminar on Teacher Education and Certification, May 9, 1966.

as found on postage stamps and the backs of money notes. All have pictures and engravings of forests, streams, Canada geese, and other such outdoor scenes. These symbols tend to be misleading, because Canada is basically now an industrialized and urbanized society, and must cope with the problems of this type of society. In 1961, only one-tenth of Canadians lived on farms. One striking measure of urbanization is that in 1961 one-half of the people lived within the seventeen metropolitan areas, including Montreal, with its 2.1 million, and Toronto, with its 1.8 million. Two-thirds of the people of Canada live within the provinces of Ontario and Quebec, and three-quarters of all post-war immigrants have gone to those provinces. There is thus a trend to urbanization and metropolitan growths to which educational systems must give some thought.

The drop in the agricultural labor force is particularly striking. In 1931 farming accounted for 29 per cent of the whole labor force; in 1941, 26 per cent; in 1951, 16 per cent; and in the last census, in 1961, 10 per cent. Between 1951 and 1961 there was a loss of 142,000 occupied farms and the off-farm migration through the 1950's was about 40,000 per year. Thus Canada is no longer a rural society or a society based on primary occupations, although some Canadians occasionally look back with nostalgia to the society that they once knew.

There has been a similar shift in the occupational structure—a shift out of manual into non-manual occupations. At the turn of the century less than a quarter of the labor force were in the non-manual occupations. By the middle 1960's, over half the labor force were engaged in white-collar and personal-service types of work. And particularly striking has been the increase in professional, managerial, and clerical occupations. But while there has been this great shift out of manual into non-manual occupations, there has been at the same time an increase in the skill content of the remaining manual occupations. This up-grading into higher-level occupations and to higher skill levels within occupations represents, or could represent for the people in the society, upward social mobility, in that people are able to be in higher-level occupations than their parents were. The reason, of course, is that as the higher-level occupations are expanding rapidly, the recruits for these occupations must come from lower down in the class structure, because of differential fertility, which means: the higher the social class, the lower the birth rate.

Thus one of the most important things to remember in looking at the demands on educational systems in emerging and developing industrial societies is the degree of education and training which must be given to those in social classes that have formerly had low levels of education. Unless this problem is successfully solved, industrial societies are not likely to develop to their potential, and they are also likely to lose out in the competitive processes. Thus to some extent one can regard twentieth-century industrial competition between societies as a test of educational systems.

If a society, as it is becoming industrialized, fails to up-grade its labor force in the way suggested, there is an alternative open to it, and that is to go and get the skills some place else; and this is what Canada has done, to a great extent. It is quite fair to say that the high level of industrialization which Canada enjoys today rests not only on the importation of foreign capital, but also on the importation of skills and professions which Canadian educational systems have failed to produce. This, I think, reflects a low evaluation of education in Canadian society.

Unfortunately, what has happened in Canada is that we have failed in the past to invest nearly enough in educational facilities and in educational plants. We have failed to transmit positive values about education to those classes which did not formerly have a high educational level. When one realizes, for example, that over half of the parental generation in this country has no more than Grade 8 education, one sees something of the tremendous job of transmitting educational values to the younger generation. Thus, if the labor force demands of the future are to be met, it is necessary for state educational systems and public policy to break down the family and cultural resistances to education.

By any measure, Canadian educational systems are seriously inadequate for the great industrial development of the post-Second-World-War period. In 1951, at the threshold of this development, more than half the men in the labor force, 55 per cent, that is, had no more than elementary school education. Another third had some high-school, and less than a tenth had some university or other tertiary-level training. In the 20-24 age group at least half had no more than elementary-school. This, in 1951, was the labor force of the future.

One of the problems of having such a large uneducated segment of the labor force is that it tends to perpetuate itself. It produces large families and early school-leavers. In 1961, for example, in families where the male wage-earner earned more than $7,000 a year, half the children 19-24 years old were in school, but where the male wage-earner's income was less than $4,000, less than one-eighth were in school. Since 1961 in Canada there seems to have been some improvement in the high-school retention rates. But it is only in the last few years that Canadian high schools have become social institutions serving more than half of their possible membership. In 1951, for example, something like 40 per cent of the 15–19 year age group were still in school. The high-school systems, in fact, have tended to be institutions for the middle classes.

Nowhere are the value systems of the United States and Canada more sharply contrasted than in those values which relate to education and lead to the democratization of educational institutions. Both at the level of the society, and at the level of the family where values are transmitted, the value system of Canada has been largely hostile to the extension of education on any scale. Unlike the United States, Canada does not have, running through its history, a social philosophy stressing the importance of education for the pursuit of happiness and the provision of opportunity. In the United States these values are reflected in the land-grant colleges, in court decisions upholding the right to use public funds to establish high schools, and in the constitutions of some states which prohibit public institutions from charging fees. This strong articulation of positive values about education is stressed in terms of what education can do for individuals. But it is also consistent with the basic values of American society.

Here in Canada there is some increasing awareness of the importance of post-secondary education. Politicians talk about it a lot, and there is a great deal of discussion about it in the press, but mighty little has been done about it, in terms of the scale upon which investments are required in tertiary-level education and the research which goes along with it. It is this slowness of educational policies to emerge from the political system that leads me to assert the low evaluation of education in Canadian culture. It seems to me that the need to train youngsters and to keep them in school long enough to get to university, is one of the principal tasks facing Canadian educational systems. Students must be kept in the educational streams for much longer than they have been in the past. This is perhaps the most important problem facing Canada today, considering the international competition for skills.

One of the problems is the misuse of teachers, or the tendency not to utilize fully the skills and the training of teachers, by having them do all sorts of things which are not related to their principal task of teaching—all the clerical and custodial duties which they perform in the schools. We would get much more out of teachers if we kept them to their professional roles. Sub-professional groups are needed, such as teachers' aides, or teachers' assistants. Most other professions have tiers of occupations behind them. Dentists have dental hygienists and dental assistants and dental technicians. There are graduate nurses and registered nurses and nurses' aides. This tiering of occupations behind a profession enables the profession to get on with its particular work.

One major problem, as already suggested, is to transmit positive values to the social classes that formerly have not benefited from education; and here it is necessary to consider the teacher's role in transmitting educational values, since the family has failed in this task and will probably continue to fail in it. It is possible, for example, for teachers to have a much greater exposure to the social sciences, which might alert them to this phenomenon, this problem of transmitting educational values. It seems that teachers have often thought of education as something which people can have if they work hard enough, so that they can proceed up to the level of being educated Brahmans if they take the opportunities that are available to them. But the task is more one of positively searching out talent, of encouraging and not discouraging. Teachers too often speak about "weeding out" people who for some reason should not be there, or who they think should not be there. Teachers have to think much more of encouraging and keeping in, rather than of operating on the principle that large numbers of students are contaminating the chosen few who really should be educated.

There are two possible ways of alerting the teacher to these problems. One is a greater exposure to social science; but another one, and perhaps the better one, is the creating of a new occupation, which might be called an educational social worker. We have medical social workers, psychiatric social workers, and it seems to me that there would be some point in staffing schools with social workers specifically trained in ensuring that the hostile attitudes to education that are embedded in some of our subcultures are overcome by direct therapy, by going into the homes and encouraging students to stay in the educational stream. This second alternative would at least leave teachers free to teach, and get on with their own work, rather than having to telephone parents about children who have not turned up for days, and so on.

If one of the aims of Canadian society is the progress into higher levels of industrialization, it is essential to transmit and to reinforce positive values about education which will keep more and more people in the educational stream through to the tertiary level of education. These values must be transmitted much lower in the class structure than formerly. We have for too long accepted social barriers which have prevented the acquisition of education and which have tended to reduce the opportunities in Canadian society.

III-9

Education and Economic Growth*

ECONOMIC COUNCIL OF CANADA

•

Education is a crucially important factor contributing to economic growth and to rising living standards. This has been the conclusion of a growing body of economic analysis in a number of countries. This is the conclusion also reached in our exploratory analysis of the contribution of education to the growth of the Canadian economy and to the welfare of its people.

It has long been recognized that education possesses intrinsic value as a factor enhancing the quality and enjoyment of life of individuals, as well as the quality and energy of a whole society. We fully appreciate this fundamental value of education and we would not wish to detract in any way from the basic view that education is a means of enlarging man's understanding, stimulating his creative talents, ennobling his aspirations, and enriching human experience. But education also has economic aspects whose character and dimensions have only more recently become a matter of interest and careful study, and it is primarily certain *economic* aspects of education which are the special focus of attention in this Chapter.

We are, of course, fully aware of the constitutional responsibilities of the provinces in the field of education. Our concern relates to the role of education in the growth of the national economy. The economic importance of education has already been stressed in our *First Annual Review,* especially in our discussion of the vital need for creating and maintaining an adequate supply of professional, technical, managerial and other highly skilled manpower as a basis for future growth of the Canadian economy. We also placed "increased investment in human resources to improve knowledge and skills" at the head of our list of essential ingredients for attaining the goal of faster and better sustained productivity growth....

Three central questions are examined in this Chapter:

1. To what extent did the average education of the working popula-

---

* Reprinted with permission from the Economic Council of Canada, *Towards Sustained and Balanced Economic Growth, Second Annual Review* (Ottawa: Queen's Printer, 1965), pp. 71–95.

tion increase over the half century from 1911 to 1961, and how does this compare with the increases which took place in the United States over the same period?

2. What relationships are there between levels of educational attainments and levels of income for various groups in the Canadian economy?

3. What contribution has rising education made to the over-all growth of the Canadian economy?

The Chapter concludes with a more general discussion of the medium- and longer-term tasks to be faced in providing for an adequate expansion of educated and skilled manpower, together with an adequate expansion of appropriate educational facilities.

At the outset it should be emphasized that our work in examining the significance of education for Canadian economic growth is very much in the nature of a pioneering venture. Many practical difficulties beset explorations in this area—conceptual problems in defining education in measurable terms, inadequacies of information, the complexities of many of the techniques of analysis and the imprecision of many of the particular statistical estimates and results. But we consider it to be useful to make some initial findings and conclusions generally available in this Review, even though these must be considered approximate and incomplete.[1]

Illustrative of the difficulties encountered are the problems arising in the key estimates of the "stock" of education in the labour force— that is, the average level of education of the entire working population: employees, farmers, managers, professional workers and all others. The educational attainment of the labour force, according to these estimates, is calculated from the average years of formal schooling, subsequently adjusted for changes in the average numbers of days of attendance per school year. However, the basic data exclude certain minor parts of the formal education system. Also, the available data do not take account of various forms of training after formal education— for example, vocational, technical and apprenticeship training as well as worker and management training received on the job, and other training. Although such types of education are of growing importance, especially with a view to keeping worker and management training up to date in the context of rapid scientific and technological change, the changes which have occurred in these categories over the past three or four decades have not greatly affected the total stock of

---

[1] The principal findings and conclusions in this Chapter are largely based on two analytical studies which have examined in considerable detail various economic aspects of increased education in Canada: Gordon W. Bertram, *The Contribution of Education to Economic Growth*, Staff Study No. 12, Economic Council of Canada (Ottawa: Queen's Printer, 1965); and J. R. Podoluk, *Earnings and Education* (Dominion Bureau of Statistics: 1965).

education in the labour force. Particular difficulties also arise in connection with the development of estimates for gains and losses in the educational attainments of the labour force in respect of immigration and emigration.

A further major question concerns the subject of differences in the quality of education. Even the most casual survey of educational institutions and facilities, curricula, qualifications of teachers and other aspects of the highly decentralized educational systems in North America readily suggests that there are major differences in the quality of education—not only over time, but also at any given point of time between different regions and localities within Canada, within the United States, and between these two countries. Such differences are, of course, virtually impossible to quantify in any meaningful over-all terms. Even among those who are most competent to judge various elements of such quality factors, there does not appear to be a consensus as to whether the over-all quality of education in Canada is higher or lower than in the United States. The picture is so obviously a mixed one. Outstanding examples of high quality educational standards at all levels of education can be found within each country which compare in highly favourable terms with lower quality standards in various parts of the other country. After careful consideration of these matters it has been concluded, as a working assumption for our analysis, that the *average* quality of education is roughly similar in the two countries—in short, that these differences largely cancel out, and that one year of education in Canada is, on the whole, roughly the equivalent of one year of education in the United States.

Another working assumption underlying the following analysis is that the quality of an average day's education around 1960 can be roughly equated with the quality of an average day's education fifty years earlier. A considerable improvement in the quality of Canadian education has undoubtedly taken place during this period, but no satisfactory basis appears to exist for estimating such a quality improvement in quantitative terms. The implication is, as is emphasized in the latter part of the analysis, that this and other factors have made education an even more important factor contributing to the nation's economic growth than is suggested by available statistics.

Many questions in this large and important field require further examination and analysis, including particularly some of the reasons for the marked differences in Canadian and United States education performances and trends over recent decades. We intend to develop our work further in this field.

Despite the many difficulties underlying any appraisal of education as a factor in economic growth, we believe that the estimates shown in this Chapter are valid as general orders of magnitude, and provide an adequate basis for six basic conclusions:

1. There has been a substantial long-term rise in the educational attainments of the Canadian labour force. But the average level of such attainments has been considerably below that of the United States, and has increased more slowly than in the United States. There has thus been a widening "educational gap" between the two countries.

2. This gap appears to have widened particularly at the secondary school level in the inter-war years, and particularly at the university level in the post-war period.

3. The income of individuals is generally closely related to the extent of formal schooling. In fact, available data show that differences in lifetime earnings of individuals classified by occupational groups appear to be directly associated with differences in levels of schooling. Moreover, the additional income benefits derived from obtaining a high school or university education, in relation to the costs of such education, appear to be somewhat higher in Canada than in the United States, and the rates of return from increased investment in education would appear to compare very favourably with the returns available from other types of investment.

4. The benefits of increased education, according to certain calculations and assumptions, are estimated to have accounted for a share in the general order of one quarter of the *increase* both in the average standard of living and in the productivity of Canadians from 1911 to 1961. Although this is a large contribution, it is apparently substantially lower than that indicated in comparable estimates for the United States.

5. Differences in the average educational attainments appear to be an important element in the difference in living standards between Canada and the United States.

6. The potential future economic benefits to Canadians and to the Canadian economy generally from increased educational attainments are very large, but they can only be fully realized over extended periods of time.

●

EDUCATION OF THE LABOUR FORCE

The Canadian economy has benefited greatly during this century from the improved quality of its labour force as reflected in enhanced educational attainments. But this improvement has been uneven, and has fallen well short of what could have been achieved.

A careful historical appraisal of the development of education in Canada suggests that spectacular advances were made in education from the latter part of the nineteenth century to the early 1920's. In this

Table 9:1

EDUCATIONAL ATTAINMENT OF THE MALE LABOUR FORCE BY AGE GROUPS, 1911 AND 1961[2]

(Percentage distribution)

Age Group	Total	0–4 Years Elementary School 1911	0–4 Years Elementary School 1961	5–7 Years Elementary School 1911	5–7 Years Elementary School 1961	8 Years Elementary School 1911	8 Years Elementary School 1961	1–3 Years High School 1911	1–3 Years High School 1961	4 Years High School 1911	4 Years High School 1961	Some University Education 1911	Some University Education 1961[3]	Complete University Education 1911	Complete University Education 1961
Total	100.0	24.2	7.5	34.5	20.8	16.1	17.6	18.1	29.7	3.2	8.7	1.5	10.1	2.4	5.6
25–34	100.0	18.4	3.9	33.2	14.6	18.3	19.5	21.3	33.8	4.3	8.7	1.8	13.5	2.7	6.0
35–44	100.0	23.4	6.1	34.9	21.4	16.1	15.0	18.2	31.6	3.2	9.5	1.6	10.1	2.5	6.3
45–54	100.0	28.7	9.5	35.8	23.4	14.2	17.8	15.7	27.3	2.3	8.5	1.3	8.4	2.0	5.0
55–64	100.0	34.6	15.3	35.7	29.1	12.4	18.3	12.7	20.3	1.7	7.4	1.1	5.3	1.7	4.2

---

[2] Gordon W. Bertram, *The Contribution of Education to Economic Growth*, Staff Study No. 12, Economic Council of Canada (Ottawa: Queen's Printer, 1965).

[3] Includes Grade 13 for provinces in which Grade 13 is given.

Table 9 : 2

PERCENTAGE INCREASES IN AVERAGE YEARS OF SCHOOLING
OF MALE LABOUR FORCE AGED 25-64, 1911-61[4]

1911-21	7.0
1921-31	5.2
1931-41	7.9
1941-51	7.5
1951-61	6.1
1911-61	38.6

period, literacy and elementary education for all citizens were strongly promoted. Particularly noteworthy was the record of educational achievement in Ontario in the later decades of the last century, under the spur of a vigorous, dedicated and well-informed Department of Education. But Canadian educational advances appear to have tapered off by 1920; the earlier momentum at the primary school was not maintained and there were only limited advances at the secondary school level.

Renewed dynamism has clearly characterized major segments of Canadian education in the post-war years. This is perhaps especially true of the years since the 1961 census date which, for practical reasons, has had to be the terminal point in our initial analysis in this field. Yet, having regard to the very large numbers of people already in the labour force who received only limited formal education in earlier years, it will take many, many years to bring about a substantial rise in the average level of education—even up to the level, say, which has already been achieved in the United States. And it would clearly take large and sustained efforts over a period of many decades to close the gap with the United States.

The general pattern of increases in the educational attainments of the Canadian labour force from 1911 to 1961 is indicated in Table 9:1. Over this period, the proportion of persons with *only* elementary education in the male labour force has declined from 75 to 46 per cent while, at the other end of the educational scale, the share of those with university degrees has risen from 2.4 to 5.6 per cent. Moreover, the proportion of those completing four years high school has moved up to 8.7 per cent in 1961 from 3.2 per cent in 1911. In addition, it is important to note that the younger age groups generally have more formal education than the older groups, especially in 1961.

Between 1911 and 1961, the average number of years of formal schooling of the male labour force increased by close to two-fifths (Table 9:2).

---

[4] Gordon W. Bertram, *op. cit.*

Education Stocks and Flows

Changes in the average number of years of schooling, or in the *stock* of education in the labour force, are very largely determined by the combined effects of three *flows*—the inflows of younger people into the labour force after leaving school, the outflows resulting from retirements and mortality, and the net flows associated with immigration and emigration. The inflows of younger people tend to increase the average stock of education, since they generally have more schooling than their parents. Similarly the outflows, especially those arising from retirement of older persons, also generally tend to raise the average level of schooling of the remaining labour force, since the older age groups typically have relatively less schooling than the over-all average. Net migration, which may obviously add to or detract from the stock of education, is discussed below.

Over any one year, the net flow of people into or out of the labour force is generally very small in relation to the over-all size of the labour force. Even over a decade, the new entrants or the departures do not constitute a dominant proportion of the labour force. Consequently, the net change in the average educational level in the labour force is not greatly affected in any one year or decade. This will be true even during the coming ten years when there will be an extraordinarily large influx of younger people with educational attainments far above those who will be departing. Thus, the average educational level in the labour force tends to change relatively slowly over short or even medium-term periods. In fact, the historical record shows only a rather gradual trend of improvement in this average over a period of many decades. For example, the average numbers of years of schooling among the Canadian male labour force, which had been slightly less than seven years in 1911, had risen to slightly over nine years by 1961—an increase of only about two and a half years over half a century, or less than 7 per cent per decade and about one-half of one per cent per year (Table 9:2).

Many factors may, of course, tend to accelerate or retard the long-term rising trend in educational levels of the labour force—changing age distribution patterns in the total population resulting in temporary bulges or dips in the numbers of new entrants to the labour force; stepped-up or lagging efforts to promote higher educational attainments; changes in legal school-leaving ages, legislation limiting the employment of children and other such institutional factors; marked changes in the availability of new job opportunities; the movement of population from rural to urban areas (children of urban families generally spend more years in school than children of farm families); and a host of additional influences.

The dominating fact about changes in the education stock is that an extremely powerful combination of factors is probably required to bring about any substantial short-term or medium-term change in this stock. At the same time, basic factors may have prolonged and cumulative effects stretching over many decades. For example, the above-mentioned vigour and dynamism in Canadian education in the early part of this century, even though it was not maintained after the early 1920's, appears to have had important effects stretching at least through to the Second World War. Conversely, the lagging educational efforts after the early 1920's appear to have been a factor in the slow advances in the educational stock through the 1940's and 1950's. The rate of improvement was also restricted by the relatively low number of new entrants to the labour force coming from the domestic educational system. Further, the higher school retention rates and the increased enrolment ratios in the 1950's did not have much effect in that decade, but will tend to have longer term effects on the rising stock of education in the 1960's and 1970's and beyond.

The Effects of Immigration and Emigration on the Stock of Education

Canda has experienced substantial flows of immigration and emigration in the course of its history. In particular, immigration has at times been an important factor contributing new vigour and new cultural dimensions in the Canadian society. In the context of this Chapter, the question naturally arises as to what effects such flows —both of immigrants and emigrants—may have had on the stock of education in the labour force.

Information about the educational attainments of immigrants, and even more especially of emigrants, entering or leaving the Canadian labour force, is unfortunately very limited. On the basis of available knowledge, however, it would appear that these flows have not produced any major or decisive shifts in the stock of education in Canada over the past half century. This would appear to be so partly because net migration even when large in relation to the current growth of the labour force, has never been large in relation to the existing total labour force. But it would also appear to be so because the average level of education of migrating labour has probably not been dramatically different from the average level of education of the labour force.

This has been true, for example, even in the decade of the 1950's when migration flows were relatively large. The median years of schooling of both male immigrants coming into the labour force and male emigrants leaving the labour force in 1951–61 was about 9.6 years. This compares with the median years of schooling of the total Canadian labour force of 8.7 years in 1951 and 9.4 years in 1961.

At the higher levels of educational attainment, the net movement showed some gain for the Canadian education stock in the 1950's. As already noted in Table 9:1, 5.6 per cent of the Canadian male labour force had university degrees in 1961. But it is estimated that 6.3 per cent of male immigrants coming into the labour force in 1951–61 had university degrees, while only 5.8 per cent of male emigrants had

Chart 9:1

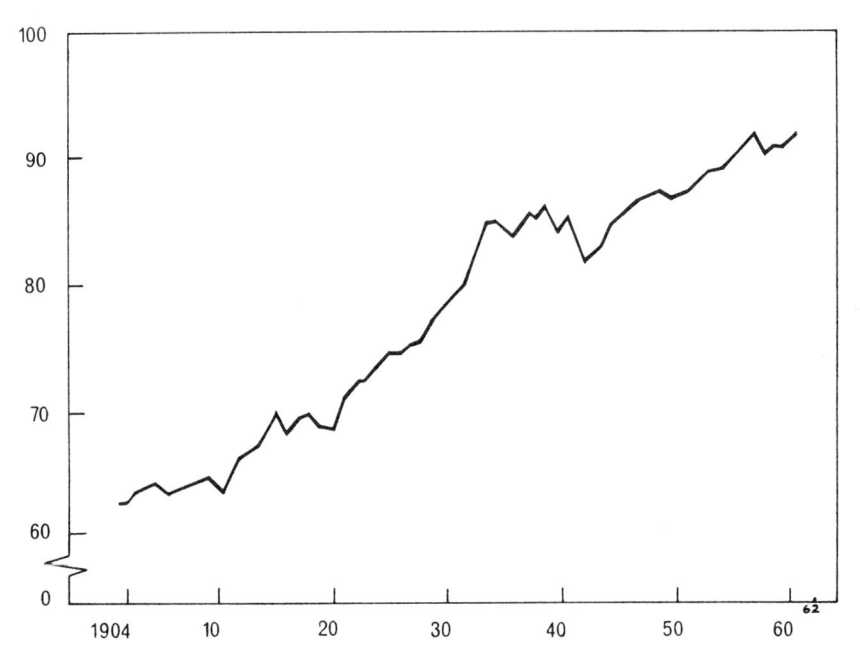

AVERAGE DAILY ATTENDANCE AS A PERCENTAGE OF ENROLMENT, CANADIAN PUBLIC SCHOOLS[5]

university degrees. Moreover, the number of male labour force immigrants with university degrees was over four times larger than the number of male emigrants with degrees. Even this immigrant flow was, however, not a dominating factor in relation to the total stock of the male labour force with university degrees in Canada. But the over-all effect of this migration was to bring about some increase in the average educational level of the male labour force in Canada.

School Attendance

Another important characteristic of Canada's increased educational attainments over this century has been that the increase in average years of schooling per person has also been accompanied by an increase in the average daily attendance per school year. That such attendance has risen substantially since the turn of the century, is shown in Chart 9:1. Many factors have contributed to this. Two deserve special emphasis. One is the large-scale shift of population from rural to urban areas. Especially in earlier decades, the employment of children—particularly boys—in farm work was a powerful factor tending to reduce school attendance. The other factor was legislation affecting compulsory school attendance, school-leaving ages, and the employment of children.

Table 9:3

MEDIAN YEARS OF SCHOOLING OF MALE LABOUR FORCE, BY AGE GROUPS, CANADA 1961 AND UNITED STATES 1962[6]

Age Group	Canada (1961)	United States (1962)
25–34	10.0	12.4
35–44	9.6	12.2
45–54	9.0	11.1
55–64	8.3	9.0

The influence of such legislation, together with its stricter enforcement, appears to have had an important bearing on this matter. Regulations governing family allowances have also been a factor contributing to increased school attendance over the past two decades.

The increase in average daily attendance has a significant bearing on the quality of an average year's education, and consequently on the real educational stock of the labour force. Moreover, as in the case of years of schooling, a significant rise in attendance, even if it were only maintained at the new level and not further increased, produces a prolonged and cumulative effect over several decades, as younger people with higher average attendance come into the labour force and older people with lower attendance withdraw. Thus, the rising attendance shown in Chart 9:1 will still be producing some cumulative effects over the 1960's, 1970's and beyond.

Canadian-United States Comparisons

Average years of education per person in the male labour force rose rapidly and fairly steadily from 1910 to 1960 in the United States, with gains of approximately 9 to 10 per cent in each decade over this half century. The Canadian increases were somewhat more uneven (Table 9:2) and also were consistently below those in the United States. As a consequence, it is estimated that while average years of schooling increased by less than two-fifths in Canada, the comparable increase in the United States was about three-fifths. Thus, a widening education gap has developed between the two countries over these fifty years.

An indication of the recent gap is provided in Table 9:3, showing median years of schooling. The United States medians by age groups are approximately in the range of one-fifth to one-quarter higher than the Canadian medians for the 25–54 age groups in 1961–62.

---

[5] Gordon W. Bertram, *op. cit.*
[6] Gordon W. Bertram, *op. cit.*

This gap between the two countries is further indicated in Table 9:4. Perhaps the most notable figures in this Table are the substantially higher proportions of the male labour force at the university degree level and at the 4-year high school level in the United States.

Moreover, the gaps between the two countries at these higher levels of education are particularly pronounced for the younger age groups, again indicating the relatively more rapid pace of educational attainments in the United States during the post-war period. For example, in 1960 about 45 per cent of the United States male labour force had four years of high school or more education, compared with 24 per cent in Canada in 1961. It might also be noted that in the 35–44 age group in Canada there is a slightly higher proportion of persons with university degrees than in the younger 25–34 age group. This reflects the post-war upsurge of war veterans who completed university degrees. But in the United States, where there was a similar post-war upsurge of university enrolment of war veterans, enrolments were maintained at high levels resulting in a further expansion in the proportion of the younger age groups obtaining university degrees.

Another important indicator of educational developments and differences in Canada and United States can be derived from the records of enrolment in each country. The proportion of males attending school is shown by various age groups in Chart 9:2 covering a period of four decades. The United States percentages are above the Canadian percentages for all years and for all age groups. Although there has been considerable variation in these differences over time, the relative size of differences is consistently and for some periods dramatically larger for persons at the high school and university levels. For example, while the Canadian record is very close to that of the Unites States for the 10–14 age group (mainly in elementary school), the 15–19 age group showed substantially lower enrolment ratios in Canada than in the United States —32 versus 50 per cent in 1931, and 41 versus 62 per cent in 1951. Even after a very sharp rise in this ratio in Canada between 1951 and 1961, the 1961 Canadian ratio was still about 10 percentage points lower than the comparable United States ratio.

These enrolment comparisons indicate that student retention in Canadian schools has been much lower than in the United States over the past few decades, especially at the high school and university levels. This is also indicated in Table 9:5 which shows the percentage of the Canadian and United States male labour force in the 25–34 and 55–64 age groups by various levels of minimum educational attainment. These data indicate not only that the United States has consistently achieved higher retention rates for students, but also that there was a wider gap in retention rates between the two countries in the early post-war period than four decades earlier, at least at the high school and university levels. In the 55–64 age group, for example—the group which would have largely completed elementary education prior

Table 9:4

EDUCATIONAL ATTAINMENT OF THE MALE LABOUR FORCE BY AGE GROUPS, CANADA 1961 AND UNITED STATES 1960[7]

(Percentage distribution)

Age Group	Total	0–4 Years Elementary School Can.	U.S.	5–7 Years Elementary School Can.	U.S.	8 Years Elementary School Can.	U.S.	1–3 Years High School Can.	U.S.	4 Years High School Can.	U.S.	Some University Education Can.[8]	U.S.	Complete University Education Can.	U.S.
Total 25–64	100.0	7.5	5.8	20.8	12.4	17.6	16.0	29.7	20.5	8.7	24.6	10.1	9.5	5.6	11.1
25–34	100.0	3.9	3.2	14.6	7.9	19.5	9.8	33.8	21.9	8.7	30.8	13.5	11.7	6.0	14.7
35–44	100.0	6.1	4.5	21.4	9.9	15.0	12.9	31.6	21.4	9.5	29.5	10.1	9.9	6.3	11.9
45–54	100.0	9.5	6.9	23.4	15.3	17.8	20.1	27.3	20.7	8.5	20.0	8.4	3.3	5.0	8.8
55–64	100.0	15.3	11.1	29.1	20.1	18.3	26.1	20.3	16.6	7.4	12.2	5.3	6.9	4.2	7.0

[7] Canada—Gordon W. Bertram, *op. cit.*; United States—*United States Census of Population 1960*.
[8] Includes Grade 13 for provinces in which Grade 13 is given.

Chart 9:2

MALE ENROLMENT IN SCHOOL AS A PERCENTAGE OF TOTAL MALE POPULATION IN AGE GROUP, CANADA AND UNITED STATES[9]

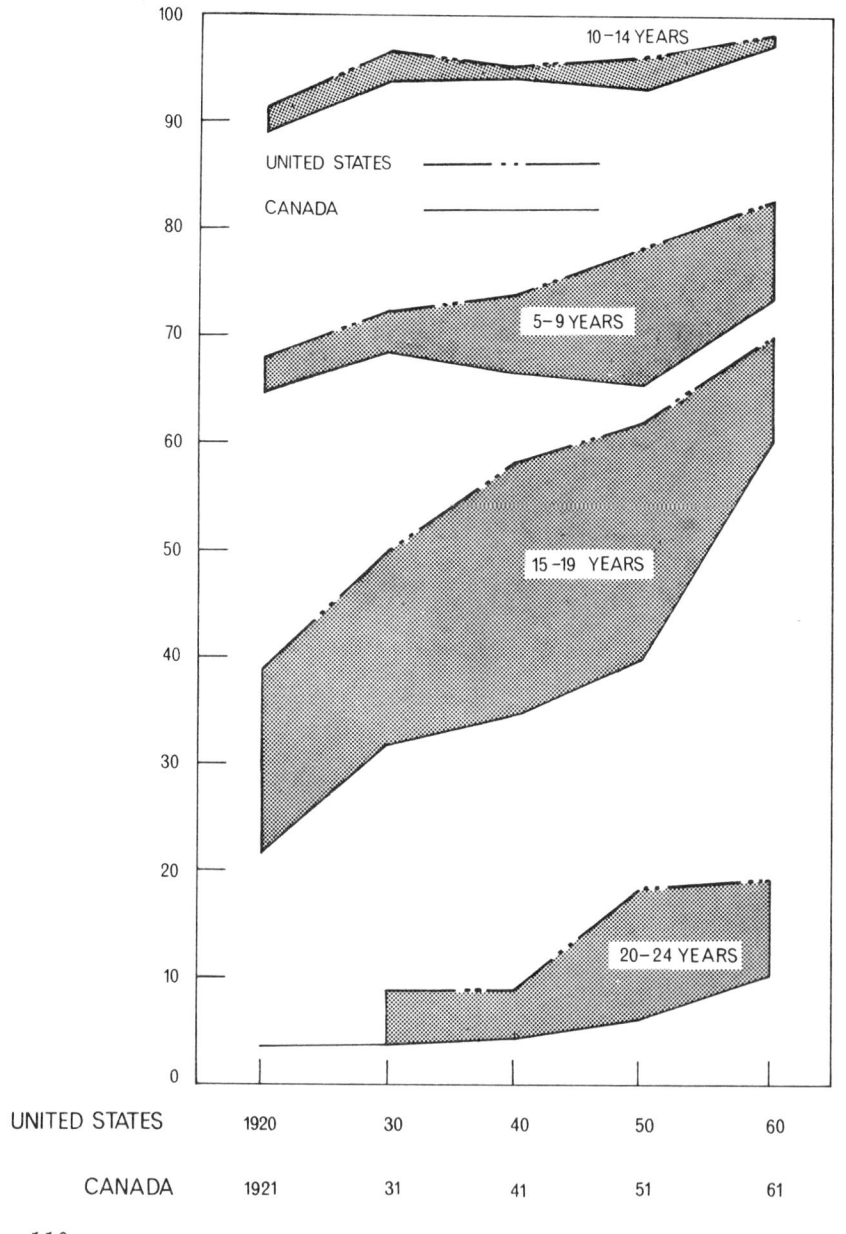

Table 9:5

MINIMUM YEARS OF EDUCATIONAL ATTAINMENT OF MALE LABOUR FORCE, AGED 25–34 AND 55–64, CANADA 1961 AND UNITED STATES 1960[10]

Minimum Educational Attainment	Age Group	Per Cent of Male Labour Force — Canada	Per Cent of Male Labour Force — United States	Percentage by Which U.S. Exceeds Canada
8 Years Elementary School	25–34	81.5	88.9	9
	55–64	55.5	68.8	24
4 Years High School	25–34	28.2	57.2	103
	55–64	16.9	26.1	54
University Degree	25–34	6.0	14.7	145
	55–64	4.2	7.0	67

to 1920—the percentage of those completing elementary school, 4 years high school and a university degree in the United States were, respectively, 24, 54 and 67 per cent higher than the percentage of those reaching similar education levels in Canada. In the 25–34 age group—the group which would have largely completed elementary education in the earlier part of the post-war period—the comparable percentage margins of United States attainments over Canadian attainments were 9, 103 and 145 per cent. It is clear, however, that after 1951, Canada's retention performance improved very dramatically, not only absolutely but also in relation to the United States. This has been especially the case at the high school level as suggested by the change in the enrolment ratio in the 1951–61 period for the 15–19 age group (Chart 9:2).

In terms of the average number of days of attendance per year of school, there also appears to have been a somewhat greater rise in the United States than in Canada over the past half century—an increase of about 50 per cent in Canada, compared with over 55 per cent in the United States per person in the male labour force (Table 9:6). When this is combined with the relatively greater rise in the average number of years of school attended, it is estimated that the total number of days of school attended per person in the male labour force has risen by 147 per cent in the United States over the period 1910–60, compared with 107 per cent in Canada in 1911–61. In other words, the total stock of education in the male labour force, taking account of changes both in years of schooling and in average daily attendance, has risen by well over one-third more in the United States than in Canada over this fifty-year period.

---

[9] Gordon W. Betram, *op. cit.*

[10] Canada—Gordon W. Bertram, *op. cit.*; United States—*United States Census of Population 1960.*

Table 9:6

PERCENTAGE INCREASE IN AVERAGE YEARS AND DAYS OF SCHOOL ATTENDED PER PERSON IN THE MALE LABOUR FORCE, CANADA 1911–61, UNITED STATES, 1910–60[11]

	Average Years of School Attended	*Average Days Attended per Year*	*Average Total Days Attended*
Canada	39	50	107
United States	59	56	147

•

EDUCATION AND INCOME

Many factors besides education may play an important role in differences in earnings between individuals—for example, differences in ability, intelligence, family background, experience, physical energy, health, personality, and even chance. But accumulating evidence and analysis point more and more to education as a pervasive and basic element contributing to the income potential of people, and therefore also of a whole economy or society, or of particular regions or localities....

The average level of annual income from employment, by levels of education for the male nonfarm labour force, is shown in Table 9:7.[12] A very strong relationship is indicated between income levels and educational attainments. For example, the average income of those who have completed four to five years of high school is more than one and a half times the average of those who have only elementary school education; and those who have university degrees have an average income which is not only more than two and a half times the average of those with only elementary school education but also more than twice the average of those who have only one to three years of high school.

In addition, the higher the level of education, the greater are the

Table 9:7

AVERAGE ANNUAL INCOME FROM EMPLOYMENT BY LEVELS OF EDUCATION, MALE NONFARM LABOUR FORCE, 1960[13]

	Dollars	*Index (0–8 years = 100)*
0–8 Years Elementary	3,526	100
1–3 Years High School	4,478	127
4–5 Years High School	5,493	156
Some University	6,130	174
University Degree	9,188	261
Total	4,602	

Chart 9:3

INCOMES BY AGE GROUP AND EDUCATION LEVEL, MALE NONFARM LABOUR FORCE, 1961[14]

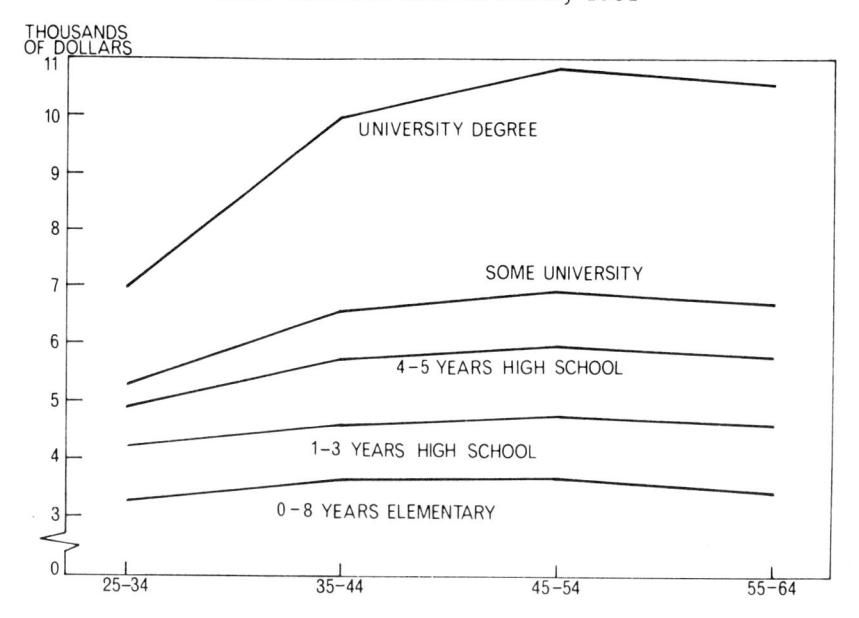

earnings differences between younger and older age groups. The earnings curves shown in Chart 9:3 indicate that for those with relatively little education, earnings tend to be rather flat for all age groups, while for those with the highest educational attainments, earnings are substantially greater at higher age levels.

Chart 9:3 suggests that higher education not only helps to account for higher initial earnings, but also that subsequent experience and performance is also influenced by the degree of initial formal training. In other words, advances in an individual's earnings potential are more

---

[11] Gordon W. Bertram, *op. cit.*, and Edward F. Denison, *The Sources of Economic Growth in the United States and the Alternatives Before Us*, Supplementary Paper No. 13, Committee for Economic Development (January, 1962). Note: Canadian data refers to 25-64 age group, U.S. data to 25 years and over.

[12] This section of the Chapter is based on data relating to all male income earners, except farm operators. This data covers only the income received from employment. The 1961 Census did not collect information of farm income. Also excluded in the basic statistics in this section are nonfarm individuals in the labour force who reported no income in the 1961 Census; these individuals consisted mainly of unpaid family workers.

[13] Based on data from *1961 Census of Canada*.

[14] Based on data from *1961 Census of Canada*.

Table 9 : 8

AVERAGE LIFETIME EARNINGS BY OCCUPATIONAL GROUP AND LEVEL OF EDUCATION, MALE NONFARM LABOUR FORCE, AGED 25–64, 1961[15]
(Thousands of dollars)

	0–8 Years Elementary	1–3 Years High School	4–5 Years High School	Some University	University Degree
Labourers	114	112	118	—	—
Craftsmen	135	157	171	170	194
Miners and Quarrymen	150	172	185	—	—
Transportation and Communication Occupations	136	161	183	196	—
Service and Recreation	112	142	164	191	245
Sales	142	175	210	217	256
Clerical	135	150	161	160	173
Professional Occupations	171	196	224	225	354
Managerial Occupations	201	233	284	316	423
All Occupations	131	168	209	234	354

pronounced and prolonged in professional, managerial and other occupations requiring relatively high degrees of education, skill and flexibility. They are less pronounced and declines set in earlier for those in unskilled or semi-skilled occupations requiring relatively lower educational attainments.

A closer look at average lifetime earnings by occupational groups and by levels of schooling reveals that there is an almost universal pattern for such earnings *within* each occupational group to be higher, the higher the levels of educational attainment. Illustrating this relationship between earnings and education, Table 9:8 indicates that extremely wide income disparities exist within most occupational categories as between those with high levels of education and those with relatively little. For example, in managerial occupations and in the professional and technical occupations, those with university degrees have lifetime earnings more than twice as large as those with only elementary education. Table 9:8 is based on the income, occupational, educational distribution at the time of the 1961 Census. Over time, there tends to be a general upward shift in lifetime earnings, and the figures shown in Table 9:8 thus tend generally to understate the lifetime earnings which may be expected for the future.

One other important factor regarding the occupational patterns of incomes is that, at least under post-war conditions of general scarcity of many of the more highly educated occupational groups, the average incomes for individuals in these groups have been rising more rapidly than the average of all incomes, and much more rapidly than the

Chart 9:4

PERCENTAGE INCREASES IN AVERAGE INCOME DECLARED FOR TAX PURPOSES, 1948–62[16]

(*Income adjusted to a constant [1949] dollar basis*)

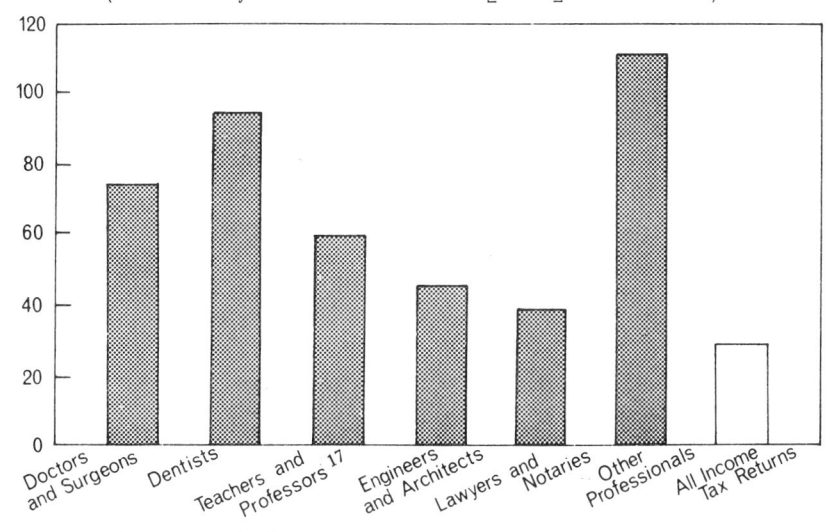

[Bar chart showing approximate values: Doctors and Surgeons ~74; Dentists ~94; Teachers and Professors[17] ~59; Engineers and Architects ~45; Lawyers and Notaries ~38; Other Professionals ~112; All Income Tax Returns ~29]

average incomes of the groups of individuals with generally lower educational attainments. This is indicated, for example, in Chart 9:4 which draws information from Canadian taxation statistics.

Canada-United States Comparisons

The United States Census of 1960, like the Canadian Census of 1961, bears out the well-known fact that levels of education and levels of income are closely correlated (Table 9:9). In addition, as in Canada, the average incomes of the more highly educated occupational groups have been increasing more rapidly in recent years than the average incomes of the less-educated groups.

One of the most interesting features shown in Table 9:9 is that the median income of Canadians with university degrees is somewhat higher than the comparable median in the United States. Two factors help to explain this rather surprising fact. First, the United States has a relatively much larger proportion of university graduates in its labour force

---

[15] J. R. Podoluk, *op. cit.*
[16] Based on *Taxation Statistics*, Department of National Revenue.
[17] Professional categories relate to individuals in independent practice, except for teachers and professors. This latter category covers all employees of educational institutions in 1948 but teachers and professors only in 1962. The average increase in income actually obtained by this group in 1948–62 is thus probably somewhat less than indicated in this Chart.

Table 9:9

MEDIAN INCOMES OF MALE NONFARM LABOUR FORCE AGED 25 AND OVER, BY LEVEL OF EDUCATION, CANADA, 1960 AND UNITED STATES, 1959[18]

	Canada 1960 (Canadian dollars)	United States 1959 (U.S. dollars)	United States as a Percentage of Canada
0–8 Years Elementary	3,074	3,262	106
1–3 Years High School	4,233	4,936	117
4–5 Years High School	4,941	5,520	112
Some University	5,368	6,045	113
University Degree	7,956	7,693	97

—for example, the proportion of the male nonfarm labour force having university degrees in 1960 was very substantially higher in the United States than in Canada (Table 9:4). There is consequently a much greater relative scarcity of such highly educated individuals in Canada. One of the results has been that there is proportionately heavier concentration of university graduates in the higher-income managerial, professional and technical occupational groups in Canada than in the United States—87 per cent versus 76 per cent, according to their respective censuses—and, conversely, a relatively considerably smaller proportion in some of the lower income occupations, such as the clerical and sales groups.

Second, the strong United States educational efforts at the university level in recent decades has produced a very sharply accentuated flow of university graduates. Consequently there is a relatively much heavier concentration of university graduates among the younger groups in the United States than in Canada, especially in the 25–34 age category. At the same time, the pattern of income growth among university graduates in the United States is very similar to that in Canada (Chart 9:3), with very large increases in income between the ages of 25 and 65. Thus, the relatively very much larger recent influx into the United States labour force of young university graduates, whose incomes are still low in relation to older university graduates, has undoubtedly been an important factor depressing the statistical measurement of the median income of this group in the United States as compared with Canada.

●

THE ECONOMIC VALUE OF EDUCATION

The preceding discussion of income-education relationships leads to the question of the economic value of expenditures on education as an investment which yields increased future income benefits. A rough estimate of the "profitability" of higher education for individuals, in terms of the estimated rate of return upon increased investment in education, can be calculated by measuring the extra income which, on the average, is associated with a higher level of education, against the extra outlays and costs involved in obtaining such education. In other words, for some particular level of schooling—for example, the completion of a university degree—the benefits from extra education can be calculated as the difference between the average lifetime earnings per person with a university degree less the average lifetime earnings, say, of persons who have only completed high school, after a deduction for the extra costs involved. The extra costs for higher education should, of course, take account not only of money expenses for such items as books, tuition, transportation—but also of income foregone—that is, the average income which could have been earned during the years while a person was gaining more education. On the basis of such calculations which have recently been made, it has been estimated that the returns on the "human investment" in high school and university education in Canada are in the range of 15 to 20 per cent per year, with slightly higher rates for an investment in a university education than in a high school education.[19] Moreover, it might be noted that the above calculations treat all costs of education as investment; if some part of these costs were to be treated as consumption rather than investment, the rates of return would be higher.

Such calculations suggest that there appear to be somewhat higher returns to education for individuals in Canada than in the United States.[20] This difference is partly a reflection of the relatively greater scarcity of more highly educated persons in Canada. In any event, it suggests that there is somewhat greater scope in Canada than in the United States for future gains from increased investment in our human resources.

These rates of return, it has been noted, are rates of return to individuals. The calculations have not taken public costs of education into account—either capital or operating costs. These costs, however, are probably small in relation to the private costs to individuals, including foregone income. This would imply that even the over-all rates of return to the economy for total investment in education would be relatively high—perhaps in the range of 10 to 15 per cent. Indeed, such rates would appear to compare favourably with the rates of return (even

---

[18] Based on data from *1961 Census of Canada* and *United States Census of Population 1960*.

[19] See J. R. Podoluk, *op. cit.*

[20] See Gary Becker, *Human Capital*, National Bureau of Economic Research (New York and London: Columbia University Press, 1964); and W. Lee Hansen, "Total and Private Rates of Return to Investment in Schooling," *Journal of Political Economy* (April, 1963).

on a pre-tax basis) which typically accrue to total capital investment in physical and financial assets. This would have an important implication for Canadian economic policy—suggesting that relatively greater emphasis should be placed on facilitating expanding investment in education in relation to expanding investment in other assets. In fact, this conclusion would appear to be in general accordance with the growing concern in many parts of the Canadian economy that the shortage of skilled and trained technical, professional and managerial manpower is even more critical than the problem of enlarging the physical facilities required for increasing output.

•

THE CONTRIBUTION OF EDUCATION TO ECONOMIC GROWTH

A combination of many factors is required for the long-term growth of real income and productivity. As suggested in the preceding Chapter, education is one of the most important of these factors, especially when viewed as a form of investment which enhances the quality and productive capabilities of any nation's most important resource—its people.

An attempt to make an approximate calculation of the contribution which increased education has made to the growth of the real income of Canadians, and a comparison with similar calculations for the United States, has been undertaken in a special study.[21] The essence of this approach is to determine, on the basis of available information and of certain assumptions, what the real income per person would have been in 1961 if the quality of the labour force, as measured by its educational attainment, had not changed since 1911. A key assumption in this calculation is that three-fifths of the differences in incomes of individuals is attributable to differences in educational attainments, with the other two-fifths being attributable to differences in ability, intelligence, effort, family background, chance, and various other factors. The conclusion of this calculation is that the average real income per person in the male labour force is estimated to have been roughly one-quarter higher in 1961 than it would have been if the average educational attainment had remained at the 1911 level. In other words, these calculations suggest that in the neighbourhood of one-quarter of the increase in real per capita income over this period is attributable to the increased educational stock in the labour force. Moreover, this should be regarded as a minimum estimate. It is based only on the preceding estimates of increased average years of formal schooling, together with increased average daily school attendance. It takes no account, for example, of increased education and training outside the elementary and secondary schools and universities, or of the increased quality of education over time. Nor does it, of course, reflect the indirect impact of higher education on such factors as the development of improved research and technology, better organization for production, and the general advance of knowledge.

A comparable calculation for the United States suggests that increased educational attainment was a relatively much more important factor, accounting for more than two-fifths of the growth of real per capita income of the male labour force in the United States over the same period.[22] This contribution of education to economic growth has been recognized at the highest levels in the United States. In his message to Congress on Education on January 29, 1963, President Kennedy stated:

> *This nation is committed to greater investment in economic growth; and recent research has shown that one of the most beneficial of all such investments is education, accounting for some 40 per cent of the nation's growth in productivity in recent years. It is an investment which yields a substantial return in the higher wages and purchasing power of trained workers, in the new products and techniques which come from skilled minds, and in the constant expansion of this nation's storehouse of useful knowledge.*

Thus, while education has made an important contribution to the growth of real income and productivity in Canada over the past half century, the even greater contribution of education to growth in the United States indicates that education has apparently been a factor tending to widen rather than narrow differences in income and productivity between the two countries over this period.

Very considerable scope would appear to exist in Canada to promote the growth of average per capita income by improving the educational stock of the labour force. The accumulating evidence and analysis suggest that the benefits from such improvements can be substantial for both the individuals and the economy as a whole. The revitalization of education in Canada in the 1950's and 1960's is laying the basis for enlarging the contribution of education to Canada's future growth. This will be accentuated by a very much larger number of better educated young people who will enter the labour force in the remainder of this decade and in the 1970's. As already emphasized, these developments will not bring about a quick and substantial rise in the educational stock of the labour force. Much of the benefit will be experienced in a prolonged and cumulative way over a period of several decades. But the benefits ultimately will be large. This reinforces the need for sustained and unflagging efforts to strengthen and extend the educational base for

---

[21] Gordon W. Bertram, *op. cit.*
[22] *Ibid.* The calculations are similar to those undertaken by Edward F. Denison in *The Sources of Economic Growth in the United States and the Alternatives Before Us*, Supplementary Paper No. 13, Committee for Economic Development (January, 1962).

long-term future growth of the economy and the living standards of Canadians.

•

TASKS FOR THE FUTURE

The principal short- and medium-term tasks for the future in raising the average educational attainment in the Canadian labour force are now very different than those which our society faced three or four decades ago. A high rate of enrolment throughout the elementary school level, and even through the earlier years of high school, has been achieved along with a high level of average daily attendance. At the same time, following the very high birth rates during the latter part of the 1940's, there has been an enormous expansion of both elementary and secondary school facilities to accommodate a vastly increased flow of children through the lower levels of the educational system.

To advance educational levels through the formal education system, attention currently needs to be focused on five particular areas:

1. The closing of the remaining gaps in secondary school facilities. Although these facilities are now widely available, there are still some parts of Canada and some parts of the population for which secondary school facilities and opportunities are seriously inadequate. There is an urgent need to remedy these deficiencies so that education at the secondary level is a real and practical possibility for all Canadian children.

2. The reduction of drop-outs in high school and the increase of retention rates to achieve a much higher rate of high school completions.

3. The tremendous expansion required especially at the university and post-secondary technical school level in terms of higher enrolment ratios and retention rates for those of post-secondary school age, in the circumstances of an unprecedented upsurge in the numbers of young people who will be moving out of the 15–19 (mainly high school) age group into the 20–24 (post-secondary) age group over the coming decade.

4. The more rapid development of facilities for a sharply accelerating flow of professional and other highly skilled manpower at the post-graduate university level—the level at which we have made least progress to date in the Canadian educational system.

5. Vigorous efforts to improve the quality and methods of education.

Intensified efforts in these critical areas of education will require a great enlargement of resources for education. But as already emphasized, the rate of economic return to education is very high. The fact that intensified efforts can only yield substantial returns over the long run makes it all the more necessary to start immediately.

In addition, there is a general need to upgrade and bring up to date the education and skill qualifications of the existing labour force, including management and professional workers. There is also, with respect to the existing labour force, a more *urgent* need for immediate action to help to deal with manpower shortages and deficiencies in particular skills and occupations which constitute an existing or impending obstacle to the maintenance of economic growth. This implies a need for retraining and for continuing education outside the formal education system. Moreover, retraining can not only raise the income level of individuals, but also provide a high rate of return in relation to the costs involved. It will also tend to promote greater flexibility and mobility of manpower in the economy. Along with this there is an equally urgent need for intensified efforts to make the most effective use possible of the existing stock of skilled and educated manpower. Similarly, there is a need for more vigorous and well-informed manpower policies in Canadian industry, together with greater manpower mobility and flexibility, as a basis for the more effective matching of demand and supply of scarce skill capabilities and professional and managerial talents.

The urgency of such matters is reinforced, as was emphasized in our *First Annual Review*, by the fact that Canada can no longer rely to the same extent as in the first dozen years after the Second World War on improvements in the quality of our labour force in many critically important areas through substantial net immigration of highly trained manpower. Of course, we should continue to try to encourage the inflow of skilled manpower from abroad. However, in a world of great and apparently growing shortages of more highly skilled and educated manpower, we must move energetically towards a more self-reliant development of our domestic manpower resources to meet our pressing needs.

III-10

A Schoolman's Guide to Marshall McLuhan*

JOHN M. CULKIN

•

Education, a seven-year-old assures me, is "how kids learn stuff." Few definitions are as satisfying. It includes all that is essential—a who, a what, and a process. It excludes all the people, places, and things which are only sometimes involved in learning. The economy and accuracy of the definition, however, are more useful in locating the problem than in solving it. We know little enough about *kids*, less about *learning*, and considerably more than we would like to know about *stuff*.

In addition, the whole process of formal schooling is now wrapped inside an environment of speeded-up technological change which is constantly influencing kids and learning and stuff. The jet-speed of this technological revolution, especially in the area of communications, has left us with more reactions to it than reflections about it. Meanwhile back at the school, the student, whose psyche is being programed for tempo, information, and relevance by his electronic environment, is still being processed in classrooms operating on the postulates of another day. The cold war existing between these two worlds is upsetting for both the student and the schools. One thing is certain: It is hardly a time for educators to plan with nostalgia, timidity, or old formulas. Enter Marshall McLuhan.

He enters from the North, from the University of Toronto where he teaches English and is director of the Center for Culture and Technology. He enters with the reputation as "the oracle of the electric age" and as "the most provocative and controversial writer of this generation." More importantly for the schools, he enters as a man with fresh eyes, with new ways of looking at old problems. He is a man who gets his ideas first and judges them later. Most of these ideas are summed up in his book, *Understanding Media*. His critics tried him for not delivering these insights in their most lucid and practical form. It isn't always cricket, however, to ask the same man to crush the grapes and serve the wine. Not all of McLu is nu or tru, but then again neither is *all* of anybody else. This article is an attempt to select and order those elements of

---

* Reprinted with permission from the *Saturday Review* (March 18, 1967).

McLuhanism which are most relevant to the schools and to provide the schoolman with some new ways of thinking about the schools.

McLuhan's promise is modest enough: "All I have to offer is an enterprise of investigation into a world that's quite unusual and quite unlike any previous world and for which no models of perception will serve." This unexplored world happens to be the present. McLuhan feels that very few men look at the present with a present eye, that they tend to miss the present by translating it into the past, seeing it through a rear-view mirror. The unnoticed fact of our present is the electronic environment created by the new communications media. It is as pervasive as the air we breathe (and some would add that it is just as polluted), yet its full import eludes the judgments of commonsense or content-oriented perception. The environments set up by different media are not just containers for people; they are processes which shape people. Such influence is deterministic only if ignored. There is no inevitability as long as there is a willingness to contemplate what is happening.

Theorists can keep reality at arm's length for long periods of time. Teachers and administrators can't. They are closeted with reality all day long. In many instances they are co-prisoners with electronic-age students in the old pencil box cell. And it is the best teachers and the best students who are in the most trouble because they are challenging the system constantly. It is the system which has to come under scrutiny. Teachers and students can say, in the words of the Late Late Show, "Baby, this thing is bigger than both of us." It won't be ameliorated by a few dashes of good will or a little more hard work. It is a question of understanding these new kids and these new media and of getting the schools to deal with the new electronic environment. It's not easy. And the defenders of the old may prove to be the ones least able to defend and preserve the values of the old.

For some people, analysis of these newer technologies automatically implies approbation of them. Their world is so full of *shoulds* that it is hard to squeeze in an *is*. McLuhan suggests a more positive line of exploration:

> *At the moment, it is important that we understand cause and process. The aim is to develop an awareness about print and the newer technologies of communication so that we can orchestrate them, minimize their mutual frustrations and clashes, and get the best out of each in the educational process. The present conflict leads to elimination of the motive to learn and to diminution of interest in all previous achievement: It leads to loss of the sense of relevance. Without an understanding of media grammars, we cannot hope to achieve a contemporary awareness of the world in which we live.*

We have been told that it is the property of true genius to disturb all settled ideas. McLuhan is disturbing in both his medium and his message. His ideas challenge the normal way in which people perceive reality.

They can create a very deep and personal threat since they touch on everything in a person's experience. They are just as threatening to the establishment whose way of life is predicated on the postulates he is questioning. The establishment has no history of organizing parades to greet its disturbers.

His medium is perhaps more disturbing than his message. From his earliest work he has described his enterprise as "explorations in communication." The word he uses most frequently today is "probe." His books demand a high degree of involvement from the reader. They are poetic and intuitive rather than logical and analytic. Structurally, his unit is the sentence. Most of them are topic sentences—which are left undeveloped. The style is oral and breathless and frequently obscure. It's a different kind of medium.

"The medium is the message," announced McLuhan a dozen years ago in a cryptic and uncompromising aphorism whose meaning is still being explored. The title of his latest book, an illustrated popular paperback treatment of his theories, playfully proclaims that *The Medium Is the Massage*—a title calculated to drive typesetters and critics to hashish and beyond. The original dictum can be looked at in four ways, the third of which includes a massage of importance.

The first meaning would be better communicated orally—"The *medium* is the message." The *medium* is the thing to study. The *medium* is the thing you're missing. Everybody's hooked on content; pay attention to form, structure, framework, *medium*. The play's the thing. The medium's the thing. McLuhan makes the truth stand on its head to attract attention. Why the medium is worthy of attention derives from its other three meanings.

Meaning number two stresses the relation of the medium to the content. The form of communication not only alters the content, but each form also has preferences for certain kinds of messages. Content always exists in some form and is, therefore, to some degree governed by the dynamics of that form. If you don't know the medium, you don't know the message. The insight is neatly summed up by Dr. Edmund Carpenter: "English is a mass medium. All languages are mass media. The new mass media—film, radio, TV—are new languages, their grammars as yet unknown. Each codifies reality differently; each conceals a unique metaphysics. Linguists tell us it's possible to say anything in any language if you use enough words or images, but there's rarely time; the natural course is for a culture to exploit its media biases. . . ."

It is always content-in-form which is mediated. In this sense, the medium is co-message. The third meaning for the M-M formula emphasizes the relation of the medium to the individual psyche. The medium alters the perceptual habits of its users. Independent of the content, the medium itself gets through. Pre-literate, literate, and post-literate cultures see the world through different-colored glasses. In the process of delivering content the medium also works over the sensorium of the consumer. To get this subtle insight across, McLuhan punned on *message* and came up with *massage*. The switch is intended to draw attention to the fact that a medium is not something neutral—it does something to people. It takes hold of them, it jostles them, it bumps them around, it massages them. It opens and closes windows in their sensorium. Proof? Look out the window at the TV generation. They are rediscovering texture, movement, color, and sound as they retribalize the race. TV is a real grabber; it really massages those lazy, unused senses.

The fourth meaning underscores the relation of the medium to society. Whitehead said, "The major advances in civilization are processes that all but wreck the societies in which they occur." The media massage the society as well as the individual. The results pass unnoticed for long periods of time because people tend to view the new as just a little bit more of the old. Whitehead again: "The greatest invention of the nineteenth century was the invention of the method of invention. A new method entered into life. In order to understand our epoch, we can neglect all details of change, such as railways, telegraphs, radios, spinning machines, synthetic dyes. We must concentrate on the method in itself: That is the real novelty which has broken up the foundations of the old civilization." Understanding the medium or process involved is the key to control.

The media shape both content and consumer and do so practically undetected. We recall the story of the Russian worker whose wheelbarrow was searched every day as he left the factory grounds. He was, of course, stealing wheelbarrows. When your medium is your message and they're only investigating content, you can get away with a lot of things—like wheelbarrows, for instance. It's not the picture but the frame. Not the contents but the box. The blank page is not neutral; nor is the classroom.

McLuhan's writings abound with aphorisms, insights, for-instances, and irrelevancies which float loosely around recurring themes. They provide the raw materials of a do-it-yourself kit for tidier types who prefer to do their exploring with clearer charts. What follows is one man's McLuhan served up in barbarously brief form. Five postulates, spanning nearly 4,000 years, will serve as the fingers in this endeavor to grasp McLuhan:

1. 1967 B.C.—*All the senses get into the act.* A conveniently symmetrical year for a thesis which is partially cyclic. It gets us back to man before the Phoenician alphabet. We know from our contemporary ancestors in the jungles of New Guinea and the wastes of the Arctic that preliterate man lives in an all-at-once sense world. The reality which bombards him from all directions is picked up with the omni-directional antennae of sight, hearing, touch, smell, and taste. Films such as *The Hunters* and *Nanook of the North* depict primitive men tracking game

with an across-the-board sensitivity which mystifies Western, literate man. We mystify them too. And it is this cross-mystification which makes inter-cultural abrasions so worthwhile.

Most people presume that their way of perceiving the world is *the* way of perceiving the world. If they hang around with people like themselves, their mode of perception may never be challenged. It is at the poles (literally and figuratively) that the violent contrasts illumine our own unarticulated perceptual prejudices. Toward the North Pole, for example, live Eskimos. A typical Eskimo family consists of a father, a mother, two children, and an anthropologist. When the anthropologist goes into the igloo to study Eskimos, he learns a lot about himself. Eskimos see pictures and maps equally well from all angles. They can draw equally well on top of a table or underneath it. They have phenomenal memories. They travel without visual bearings in their white-on-white world and can sketch cartographically accurate maps of shifting shorelines. They have forty or fifty words for what we call "snow." They live in a world without linearity, a world of acoustic space. They are Eskimos. Their natural way of perceiving the world is different from our natural way of perceiving the world.

Each culture develops its own balance of the senses in response to the demands of its environment. The most generalized formulation of the theory would maintain that the individual's modes of cognition and perception are influenced by the culture he is in, the language he speaks, and the media to which he is exposed. Each culture, as it were, provides its constituents with a custom-made set of goggles. The differences in perception are a question of degree. Some cultures are close enough to each other in perceptual patterns so that the differences pass unnoticed. Other cultural groups, such as the Eskimo and the American teen-ager, are far enough away from us to provide esthetic distance.

2. *Art imitates life.* In *The Silent Language* Edward T. Hall offers the thesis that all art and technology is an extension of some physical or psychic element of man. Today man has developed extensions for practically everything he used to do with his body: stone axe for hand, wheel for foot, glasses for eyes, radio for voice and ears. Money is a way of storing energy. This externalizing of individual, specialized functions is now, by definition, at its most advanced stage. Through the electronic media of telegraph, telephone, radio, and television, man has now equipped his world with a nervous system similar to the one within his own body. President Kennedy is shot and the world instantaneously reels from the impact of the bullets. Space and time dissolve under electronic conditions. Current concern for the United Nations, the Common Market, ecumenism, reflects this organic thrust toward the new convergence and unity which is "blowing in the wind." Now in the electric age, our extended faculties and senses constitute a single instantaneous

and coexistent field of experience. It's all-at once. It's shared-by-all. McLuhan calls the world "a global village."

3. *Life imitates art.* We shape our tools and thereafter they shape us. These extensions of our senses begin to interact with our senses. These media become a massage. The new change in the environment creates a new balance among the senses. No sense operates in isolation. The full sensorium seeks fulfillment in almost every sense experience. And since there is a limited quantum of energy available for any sensory experience, the sense-ratio will differ for different media.

The nature of the sensory effect will be determined by the medium used. McLuhan divides the media according to the quality or definition of their physical signal. The content is not relevant in this kind of analysis. The same picture from the same camera can appear as a glossy photograph or as a newspaper wirephoto. The photograph is well-defined, of excellent pictorial quality, hi-fi within its own medium. McLuhan calls this kind of medium "hot." The newspaper photo is grainy, made up of little dots, low definition. McLuhan calls this kind of medium "cool." Film is hot; television is cool. Radio is hot; telephone is cool. The cool medium or person invites participation and involvement. It leaves room for the response of the consumer. A lecture is hot; all the work is done. A seminar is cool; it gets everyone into the game. Whether all the connections are causal may be debated, but it's interesting that the kids of the cool TV generation want to be so involved and so much a part of what's happening.

4. *We shaped the alphabet and it shaped us.* In keeping with the McLuhan postulate that "the medium is the message," a literate culture should be more than mildly eager to know what books do to people. Everyone is familiar enough with all the enrichment to living mediated through fine books to allow us to pass on to the subtler effects which might be attributed to the print medium, independent of the content involved. Whether one uses the medium to say that *God is dead* or that *God is love* (--- -- ----), the structure of the medium itself remains unchanged. Nine little black marks with no intrinsic meaning of their own are strung along a line with spaces left after the third and fifth marks. It is this stripping away of meaning which allows us to X-ray the form itself.

As an example, while lecturing to a large audience in a modern hotel in Chicago, a distinguished professor is bitten in the leg by a cobra. The whole experience takes three seconds. He is affected through the touch of the reptile, the gasp of the crowd, the swimming sights before his eyes. His memory, imagination, and emotions come into emergency action. A lot of things happen in three seconds. Two weeks later he is fully recovered and wants to write up the experience in a letter to a colleague. To communicate this experience through print means that it must first be broken down into parts and then mediated, eyedropper fashion, one thing at a time, in an abstract, linear, fragmented, sequential way. That is the essential structure of print. And once a culture uses such a medium for a few centuries, it begins to perceive the world in a one-thing-at-a-time, abstract, linear, fragmented, sequential way. And it shapes its organizations and schools according to the same premises. The form of print has become the form of thought. The medium has become the message.

For centuries now, according to McLuhan, the straight line has been the hidden metaphor of literate man. It was unconsciously but inexorably used as the measure of things. It went unnoticed, unquestioned. It was presumed as natural and universal. It is neither. Like everything else it is good for the things it is good for. To say that it is not everything is not to say that it is nothing. The electronic media have broken the monopoly of print; they have altered our sensory profiles by heightening our awareness of aural, tactile, and kinetic values.

5. 1967 A.D.—*All the senses want to get into the act.* Print repressed most sense-life in favor of the visual. The end of print's monopoly also marks the end of a visual monopoly. As the early warning system of art and popular culture indicates, all the senses want to get into the act. Some of the excesses in the current excursions into aural, oral, tactile, and kinetic experience may in fact be directly responsive to the sensory deprivation of the print culture. Nature abhors a vacuum. No one glories in the sight of kids totally out of control in reaction to the Beatles. Some say, "What are the Beatles doing to these kids?" Others say, "What have we done to these kids?" All the data isn't in on what it means to be a balanced human being.

Kids are what the game is all about. Given an honest game with enough equipment to go around, it is the mental, emotional, and volitional capacity of the student which most determines the outcome. The whole complicated system of formal education is in business to get through to kids, to motivate kids, to help kids learn stuff. Schools are not in business to label kids, to grade them for the job market or to babysit. They are there to communicate with them.

Communication is a funny business. There isn't as much of it going on as most people think. Many feel that it consists in saying things in the presence of others. Not so. It consists not in saying things but in having things heard. Beautiful English speeches delivered to monolingual Arabs are not beautiful speeches. You have to speak the language of the audience—of the *whom* in the "who-says-what-to-whom" communications diagram. Sometimes the language is lexical (Chinese, Japanese, Portugese), sometimes it is regional or personal (125th Street-ese, Holden Caulfield-ese, anybody ese). It has little to do with words and much to do with understanding the audience. The word for good communication is "Whom-ese"—the language of the audience, of the "whom."

All good communicators use Whom-ese. The best writers, filmmakers, advertising men, lovers, preachers, and teachers all have the knack for thinking about the hopes, fears, and capacity of the other person and of being able to translate their communication into terms which are *relevant* for that person. Whitehead called "inert ideas" the bane of education. Relevance, however, is one of those subjective words. It doesn't pertain to the object in itself but to the object as perceived by someone. The school may decide that history is *important for* the student, but the role of the teacher is to make history *relevant to* the student.

If *what* has to be tailored to the *whom*, the teacher has to be constantly engaged in audience research. It's not a question of keeping up with the latest slang or of selling out to the current mores of the kids. Neither of these tactics helps either learning or kids. But it is a question of knowing what values are strong in their world, of understanding the obstacles to communication, of sensing their style of life. Communication doesn't have to end there, but it can start nowhere else. If they are tuned in to FM and you are broadcasting on AM, there's no communication. Communication forces you to pay a lot of attention to other people.

McLuhan has been paying a great deal of attention to modern kids. Of necessity they live in the present since they have no theories to diffract or reflect what is happening. They are also the first generation to be born into a world in which there was always television. McLuhan finds them a great deal different from their counterparts at the turn of the century when the electric age was just getting up steam.

A lot of things have happened since 1900 and most of them plug into walls. Today's six-year-old has already learned a lot of stuff by the time he shows up for the first day of school. Soon after his umbilical cord was cut he was planted in front of a TV set "to keep him quiet." He liked it enough there to stay for some 3,000 to 4,000 hours before he started the first grade. By the time he graduates from high school he has clocked 15,000 hours of TV time and 10,800 hours of school time. He lives in a world which bombards him from all sides with information from radios, films, telephones, magazines, recordings, and people. He learns more things from the windows of cars, trains, and even planes. Through travel and communications he has experienced the war in Vietnam, the wide world of sports, the civil rights movement, the death of a President, thousands of commercials, a walk in space, a thousand innocuous shows, and, one may hope, plenty of Captain Kangaroo.

This is all merely descriptive, an effort to lay out what *is*, not what should be. Today's student can hardly be described by any of the old educational analogies comparing him to an empty bucket or a blank page. He comes to the information machine called school and he is already brimming over with information. As he grows his standards for relevance are determined more by what he receives outside the school than what he receives inside. A recent Canadian film tells the story of a bright, articulate middle class teen-ager who leaves school because there's "no reason to stay." He daydreams about Vietnam while his teacher drones on about the four reasons for the spread of Christianity and the five points such information is worth on the exam. Only the need for a diploma was holding him in school; learning wasn't, and he left. He decided the union ticket wasn't worth the gaff. He left. Some call him a dropout. Some call him a pushout.

The kids have one foot on the dock and one foot on the ferryboat. Living in two centuries makes for that kind of tension. The gap between the classroom and the outside world and the gap between the generations is wider than it has ever been. Those tedious people who quote Socrates on the conduct of the young are trying vainly to reassure themselves that this is just the perennial problem of communication between generations. 'Tain't so. "Today's child is growing up absurd, because he lives in two worlds, and neither of them inclines him to grow up." Says McLuhan in *The Medium Is the Massage.* "Growing up—that is our new work, and it is *total*. Mere instruction will not suffice."

Learning is something that people do for themselves. People, places, and things can facilitate or impede learning; they can't make it happen without some cooperation from the learner. The learner these days comes to school with a vast reservoir of vicarious experiences and loosely related facts; he wants to use all his senses in his learning as an active agent in the process of discovery; he knows that all the answers aren't in. The new learner is the result of the new media, says McLuhan. And a new learner calls for a new kind of learning.

Leo Irrera said, "If God had anticipated the eventual structure of the school system, surely he would have shaped man differently." Kids are being tailored to fit the Procrustean forms of schedules, classrooms, memorizing, testing, etc., which are frequently relics from an obsolete approach to learning. It is the total environment which contains the philosophy of education, not the title page in the school catalogue. And it is the total environment which is invincible because it is invisible to most people. They tend to move things around within the old boxes or to build new and cleaner boxes. They should be asking whether or not there should be a box in the first place.

The new learner, who is the product of the all-at-once electronic environment, often feels out of it in a linear, one-thing-at-a-time school environment. The total environment is now the great teacher; the student has competence models against which to measure the effectiveness of his teachers. Nuclear students in linear schools make for some tense times in education. Students with well developed interests in science, the arts and humanities, or current events need assistance to suit their pace, not that of the state syllabus. The straight line theory of development and the uniformity of performance which it so frequently encourages just don't fit many needs of the new learner. Interestingly, the one thing which most of the current educational innovations share is their break with linear or print-oriented patterns: team teaching, nongraded schools, audio-lingual language training, multi-media learning situations, seminars, student research at all levels of education, individualized learning, and the whole shift of responsibility for learning from the teacher to the student. Needless to say, these are not as widespread as they should be, nor were they brought about through any conscious attention to the premises put forward by McLuhan. Like the print-oriented and linear mentality they now modify, these premises were plagiarized from the atmosphere. McLuhan's value is in the power he gives us to predict and control these changes.

There is too much stuff to learn today. McLuhan calls it an age of "information overload." And the information levels outside the classroom are now higher than those in the classroom. Schools used to have a virtual monopoly on information; now they are part-time competitors in the electronic informational surround. And all human knowledge is expanding at computer speed.

Every choice involves a rejection. If we can't do everything, what priorities will govern our educational policies? "The medium is the message" may not be bad for openers. We can no longer teach kids all about a subject; we can teach them what a subject is all about. We have to introduce them to the form, structure, gestalt, grammar, and process of the knowledge involved. What does a math man do when a math man does do math? This approach to the formal element of a discipline can provide a channel of communication between specialists. Its focus is not on content or detail but on the postulates, ground rules, frames of reference, and premises of each discipline. It stresses the modes of cognition and perception proper to each field. Most failures in communication are based on disagreement about items which are only corollaries of a larger thesis. It happens between disciplines, individuals, media, and cultures.

The arts play a new role in education because they are explorations in perception. Formerly conceived as a curricular luxury item, they now become a dynamic way of tuning up the sensorium and of providing fresh ways of looking at familiar things. When exploration and discovery become the themes, the old lines between art and science begin to fade. We have to guide students to becoming their own data processors to operate through pattern recognition. The media themselves serve as both aids to learning and as proper objects of study in this search for an all-media literacy. Current interest in film criticism will expand to include all art and communication forms.

And since the knowledge explosion has blown out the walls between subjects, there will be a continued move toward interdisciplinary swapping and understanding. Many of the categorical walls between things are artifacts left over from the packaging days of print. The specialist's life will be even lonelier as we move further from the Gutenberg era. The trends are all toward wholeness and convergence.

These things aren't true just because Marshall McLuhan says they are. They work. They explain problems in education that nobody else is laying a glove on. When presented clearly and with all the necessary examples and footnotes added, they have proven to be a liberating force for hundreds of teachers who were living through the tension of this cultural fission without realizing that the causes for the tension lay outside themselves. McLuhan's relevance for education demands the work of teams of simultaneous translators and researchers who can both shape and substantiate the insights which are scattered through his work. McLuhan didn't invent electricity or put kids in front of TV sets; he is merely trying to describe what's happening out there so that it can be dealt with intelligently. When someone warns you of an oncoming truck, it's frightfully impolite to accuse him of driving the thing. McLuhan can help kids to learn stuff better.

PART FOUR

Levels of Education

IV

Introduction

•

Canada, now in its second century, is going through a period of vibrant growth and is becoming a more contributive force in the world. It can fulfil its promise only with a highly educated population. The needs for an educated society are so great that intensification of learning is required at all levels of formal education. In this Part, an attempt is made to present some aspects of Canadian education at the elementary, secondary, and university levels.

In the elementary schools, the most widely used book in the early nineteenth century was Murray's *English Reader* (1799). The first sentence of this book, intended for young Canadians, reads: "Diligence, industry, and proper improvement of time, are material duties of the young." The rest of the book is written in the same style and contains such fascinating readings as, "The Mortifications of Vice," "On the Immortality of the Soul," and "The Pursuit of Happiness Often Ill-Directed." Murray's *English Grammar* (1795) was also used widely for over fifty years and enlightened children by setting rules governing English "orthography," "etymology," "syntax," and "prosody."

The concept of reading has come to be progressively enlarged. Elementary education has undergone a revolutionary change with the growing impact of research in child psychology and in linguistics. Most recently, McLuhan and Fiore, stressing over-all communications rather than just the printed word, have vividly portrayed the child's world with which the teacher must deal:

> *There is a world of difference between the modern home environment of integrated electric information and the classroom. Today's television child is attuned to up-to-the-minute "adult" news—inflation, rioting, war, taxes, crime, bathing beauties—and is bewildered when he enters the nineteenth-century environment that still characterizes the educational establishment where information is scarce but ordered and structured by fragmented, classified patterns, subjects, and schedules. It is naturally an environment much like any factory set-up with its inventories and assembly lines.... Today's child is growing up absurd, because he lives in two worlds, and neither of them inclines him to grow up. Growing up—that is our new work, and it is* total. *Mere instruction will not suffice.*[1]

The significance of the elementary stage in a child's education involving the development of his linguistic perceptions and his social behaviour is being increasingly realized, but there remains an urgent need to make provision for education before the age of six. Particularly in lower income classes, there is a wasteful and unnecessary emptiness between the ages of three and five, when most children enter kindergarten. Nationwide pre-schools for children in this age group would fill a definite need. The development of children's abilities during this period would create additional pressure on the elementary school and eventually on the high school for an improvement in the quality of their programmes.

The major trend in the development of Canadian secondary education has been toward comprehensive or composite schools. However, the national pattern varies and some areas have separate vocational schools. Composite schools do not eliminate differences in the abilities of students. Provisions for the more able students are generally made through alternative subjects, as the public is not willing to accept complete social segregation based on the European pattern of different types of schools. Moreover, if there is a miscalculation, it is easier to transfer a student across the hall than across the city. Up to now, the rule of thumb has been that the brighter students take academic subjects and the others, vocational and industrial subjects. Counselling students according to their aptitudes is important, and most schools have guidance officers to help students choose from a variety of curricula. The major question is whether the Canadian composite school can enable a student to develop to the extent possible in the selective environment of the British grammar school, the French lycée, and the German gymnasium. The composite school will succeed only if it can reconcile two conflicting ideals: a selective academic education for the few and a universal education for all.

Educators now realize that adolescents should do more than read about the current civic, economic, educational, political, and social problems of their immediate community. Participation in some aspects of these problems would provide practical experience that would enable adolescents to better understand their adult roles and the skills necessary for a creative life. As Marshall McLuhan and Quentin Fiore put it in *The Medium Is the Massage*:

> *The youth of today are not permitted to approach the traditional heritage of mankind through the door of technological awareness. This only possible door for them is slammed in their faces by a rear-view-mirror society.*
>
> *The young today live mythically and in depth. But they encounter instruction in situations organized by means of classified information—subjects are unrelated, they are visually conceived in terms of a blueprint. Many of our institutions suppress all the natural direct experience of youth, who respond with untaught delight to the poetry and the beauty of the new technological*

---

[1] From *The Medium Is the Massage* by Marshall McLuhan and Quentin Fiore. © Copyright 1967 by Bantam Books, Inc., p. 18.

> *environment, the environment of popular culture. It could be their door to all past achievement if studied as an active (and not necessarily benign) force.*
>
> *The student finds no means of involvement for himself and cannot discover how the educational scheme relates to his mythic world of electronically processed data and experience that his clear and direct responses report.*
>
> *It is a matter of the greatest urgency that our educational institutions realize that we now have civil war among these environments created by media other than the printed word. The classroom is now in a vital struggle for survival with the immensely persuasive "outside" world created by new informational media. Education must shift from instruction, from imposing of stencils, to discovery—to probing and exploration and to the recognition of the language of forms.*
>
> *The young today reject goals. They want roles—R-O-L-E-S. That is, total involvement. They do not want fragmented, specialized goals or jobs.*[2]

The university picture is much more complicated today than it was even twenty years ago, when the humanities were still the most discussed issue. Now, overwhelming increases in student enrollment, growing professional, technical, and vocational demands, questions of public finance, of university government, and of student participation are all major issues. According to the projection made by E. F. Sheffield for the Canadian Universities Foundation, full-time enrollment in Canadian universities and colleges in 1970–71 will be 13.2 per cent of the population 18 to 24 years of age, and in 1975–76 15.7 per cent. (It was 4.2 per cent in 1951–52 and 7.5 per cent in 1961–62.) The number of higher education institutions has also increased.

W. G. Fleming pointed out in his study of Ontario Grade 13 students that about one-fourth of those who did not go to a university had better school records than nearly one-half of those who did go.[3] Apparently, much more could be done to encourage capable students to enter universities and strengthen Canadian professional, literary, and artistic life. One example of an attempt to encourage higher education is in Newfoundland, where, since 1966, tuition at Memorial University has been free. In addition, a plan has been introduced to pay $100 per month to students residing outside St. John's and $50 per month to those whose homes are in the city.

In recruiting staff for its universities, Canada has always drawn upon the resources of other countries. In 1957, 43 per cent of new positions were filled by non-Canadians, and in 1962 the percentage had risen to 49. The need for expansion of graduate education in Canadian universities is obvious.

In its 1967 report, the Spinks Commission, evaluating the development of graduate work and research in the provincially supported universities in Ontario, recommended the following: the formation of an

Ontario Universities Research Council, additional assistance for scholarships, fellowships, and faculty research, and a central library for Ontario universities, at Toronto. It also made various proposals for the co-ordination of graduate studies and research. As C. T. Bissell has stated: "Without research money one cannot hope to attract good staff. Unless this situation is dramatically remedied, Canadian universities will drift into a position of permanent mediocrity."[4]

This Part is divided into three sections: Elementary Education, Secondary Education, and University Education.

●

ELEMENTARY EDUCATION

W. H. Worth indicates that as much as 80 per cent of the shaping of the human mind takes place between conception and the age of eight, and that the most rapid period of school achievement occurs during nursery school, kindergarten, and primary school grades. Consequently, he argues, major emphasis in terms of time, energy, and money ought to be applied to the critical early years in the lives of our children.

●

SECONDARY EDUCATION

There are two readings in this section. In the first, H. T. Coutts discusses the philosophy and purposes of secondary education and evaluates universal education, occupational training, preparation for citizenship, and education for leisure. In the second, Lawrence W. Downey sets forth untested hypotheses in secondary education, analyses the dynamics of organizational change, and proposes guidelines for assessing the effects of change.

●

UNIVERSITY EDUCATION

This section consists of two readings. In the first, Neville V. Scarfe describes two major philosophies of higher education: one that rejects students that are thought to be not academic, and the other that believes in the power of a good teacher to modify, stimulate, and promote the potentialities of almost any high school graduate. In the second reading, Murray G. Ross expounds the view that the aim of a university should include not only hard and disciplined study, but also the freeing and nourishing of intuition and imagination.

---

[2] From *The Medium Is the Massage* by Marshall McLuhan and Quentin Fiore. © Copyright 1967 by Bantam Books, Inc., p. 100.

[3] W. G. Fleming, *Background and Personality Factors Associated With Educational and Occupational Plans and Careers of Ontario Grade 13 Students* (Toronto: O.C.E., 1957).

[4] C. T. Bissell, "The Importance of Greatness," *CAUT Bulletin*, XXXV, 4 (May, 1965), p. 8.

IV A-11 ELEMENTARY EDUCATION

The Missing Component in Education*

W. H. WORTH

●

With hindsight sharpened by desperation, some educators and laymen have finally come to recognize the real significance of the educational enterprise at the elementary level. After investing massive amounts of time, energy and money in devising new programs and instituting therapeutic procedures at the secondary level in an effort to prepare the next generation for effective urban living, they now have a very uncomfortable feeling that they may have "bet on the wrong horse." For as one writer recently pointed out: "The missing component in a program of preparation for social and educational accommodation to the rapid changes that lie ahead for our urban society is a platform of excellence in the first, second and third grades. It is this platform, not later rehabilitation, that will make fluid adjustments to a changing occupational structure possible."

Thus we have the resurgence of what might be called the critical-years hypothesis—the assertion that the kinds of experiences that a child has in the early years determine his subsequent school career. This hypothesis is not new. It has been voiced many times in many different ways. But today there is increased evidence supporting this hypothesis. Six propositions about human growth and development serve as a backdrop for the ensuing discussion of new actions and procedures at the elementary level.

1. *The most rapid growth in many stable characteristics occurs in the early years.* The validity of this proposition has been established by a recent publication by Benjamin Bloom which examines and interprets a large mass of data from hundreds of studies on the shaping of human beings from infancy to adulthood. For example, the study reveals that in terms of intelligence measured at age seventeen, about 50 per cent of the development takes places between conception and age four, about 30 per cent between ages four and eight, and about 20 per cent between ages eight and seventeen. Similarly, it is noted that approximately 50 per cent of general school achievement at grade 12 (age eighteen) has been

---

* Reprinted with permission from *Canadian School Journal*, XLIII, 3 (April, 1965), pp. 12–14.

reached by the end of grade 3 (age nine). In fact, the study indicates that about 17 per cent of the growth in school achievement takes place between ages four and six, with about another 17 per cent taking place between ages six and nine. Thus the most rapid period of growth in school achievement appears to occur during the age span encompassed by nursery school, kindergarten and the primary grades.

2. *Variations in environment have greatest effect on a characteristic during its most rapid period of growth.* The Bloom study also demonstrates that many stable human characteristics begin their growth very rapidly and then slow down. Characteristics which tend to follow this type of curve of development include intelligence, aggressiveness in males, dependence in females, and general school achievement. The effects of environments on these kinds of characteristics, especially of extreme environments, appear to be greatest in the more rapid and earlier periods of development and least in the less rapid and later periods of development. Hence pessimism is warranted about the likelihood of producing major changes in a characteristic if its curve of development approaches or reaches a virtual plateau at the secondary school level.

3. *Early learnings are difficult to alter or replace.* The power of early learning and its resistance to later alteration and extinction has long been known to experimental psychologists and personality and learning theorists. It is now generally recognized among educators as well that the first learning takes place more easily than a later one that is interfered with by an earlier learning. An illustration of this phenomenon is to be found in the development of children's language patterns. Recent studies have shown that, for many children, speaking habits are almost completely set in the early years and that permanent changes in word usage and pronunciation at later stages are difficult to effect. It would appear, therefore, that the efficiency of the total educative process can be maximized by giving careful attention to the nature of the beginning learning experiences that children have under the guidance of the school.

4. *Human development is essentially a sequential process.* A number of theoretical and empirical descriptions of human development emphasize the way in which the developments at one period are determined, at least in part, by earlier developments, and in turn influence and determine the nature of later developments. Illustrative of this later type of description is the study recently reported by Moss and Kagan. These investigators observed that achievement strivings during the early years were a good index of future achievement behavior during adolescence and adulthood. It was further noted that, for boys in particular, the period between the ages of six and ten is the crucial time for the crystallization of the desire for task mastery and intellectual competence. In view of the apparent serial order in the development of many aspects of intellectual growth, there seems to be some urgency to the task of discovering and

arranging the appropriate sequencing of learning experiences from the first day of school onward.

5. *Environment is the major determiner of school achievement.* Whatever may be the genetic potential of a child for learning, there is little doubt that his environments largely determine what is learned in school. These environments include the home, the peer group and the school itself. The latter environment is the one over which educational authorities can exercise the greatest amount of direct control through the allocation of human and material resources. This fact, when coupled with the immense power of early environments and the relative lack of influence of the peer group at this time, strongly suggests that investments in education at the elementary level are likely to pay greater dividends than those at any other level in our educational system. That this is so with respect to at least one aspect of the school environment has already been demonstrated by Cheal (*Investment in Canadian Youth*) who found that the qualifications and salaries of elementary teachers correlate more highly with retention rate in Canadian high schools than do those of secondary teachers.

6. *Future school achievement can be predicted with increasing accuracy.* This proposition reflects the increasing accuracy in prediction of an individual's characteristics with advances in age and stabilization of environment. Thus as Payne has shown, it is possible to predict with considerable accuracy grade 6 arithmetic achievement at the grade 1 level. Similarly, Alexander has demonstrated that reading comprehension at grade 8 can be predicted with a correlation of $+.73$ at grade 2 and a correlation of $+.88$ at grade 4. Early identification of the potential dropout is now also possible. The degree of accuracy and length of time interval of such predictions should increase markedly with improvements in measurement techniques and data-processing procedures within the next few years. Consequently we can look forward to having from six to ten years' advance notice of probable low achievement and premature school leaving. Given such advance notice we can hardly justify sitting idly by and watching the prophecies come true!

The six propositions underlying the critical-years hypothesis hold many implications for new actions and procedures at the elementary level. Four rather comprehensive changes are suggested by these propositions. These changes are aimed at the prevention and early adjustment of learning difficulties as alternatives to later therapy and terminal treatment.

1. *Extending school services to children under six years of age.* If the base on which much school learning flourishes is laid before the age of six, it seems reasonable to propose the downward extension of services by the regular school system to accommodate children at this earlier age. Such action would tend to counteract the impact of the deprived educa-

tional environment to which some youngsters are now exposed in their pre-school years. Moreover, it would be in accord with the time-honoured principle of equal educational opportunity. And, in fact, it would provide a measure of equalization when it can be of greatest benefit—during the formative years. Furthermore, appropriate nursery school-kindergarten programs would likely promote more effective language development, intellectual growth, and/or social-personal adjustment in many other children as well.

This suggestion is advanced even though there is not as much research evidence to support it as one would like to have. Aside from the technical difficulties of the kind of research that the situation demands there are at least three good reasons for this state of affairs.

One is that the intellectual development of the child has been of relatively little concern in nursery school-kindergarten programs in the past. Hence it has been extremely difficult to assess their influence on the cognitive aspects of a child's development. A second is that many unqualified personnel have been permitted to conduct so-called nursery schools and kindergartens. As a consequence, the outcomes have often been much less than were anticipated. A third reason for the paucity of empirical evidence about the efficacy of nursery school-kindergarten programs stems from the lack of differentiated instruction in the primary grades. In too many elementary school classrooms all children, regardless of previous experience and variations in achievement, are fed the same educational diet. Such treatment has tended to obliterate any long-term effects that might be attributable to nursery school or kindergarten attendance.

In the main, the argument for extending school services to children under six years of age rests largely on the propositions advanced earlier and the application of logic.

2. *Broadening the scope of pupil personnel services.* If pupil problems in adaptation and learning are to be identified and attacked at the point where they are apt to be most easily overcome, then there will need to be a marked expansion of pupil personnel services at the elementary level. Every large elementary school will require a resident school psychologist or guidance counsellor to aid in the identification and diagnosis of potential problem cases and to provide specialized adaptive treatment. These persons would also act as consultants to teachers in the development of individualized programs for such pupils, and maintain close liaison with their parents. Similar functions can be performed in smaller schools by visiting teachers.

Elementary school teachers should also be able to call upon the services of a central pool of specialized personnel which might include reading clinicians, social workers, psychiatrists, speech therapists, psychologists, and the like, for assistance with particularly difficult cases. In addition, some school systems will need to make provision for the collection of much more data than they are now collecting in the early grades, while others will have to arrange to analyze more effectively the data that are now available as a basis for wise curriculum decision making.

3. *Facilitating more individualized instruction.* Elementary school workers have long paid lip-service to making provisions for individual differences among pupils. But provisions for accommodating these differences have traditionally consisted of little more than a grouping together for instructional purposes of children of like age, ability, and/or achievement with few real changes in curriculum.

Even this minimum provision is relatively rare in Alberta schools, according to a recent survey of grouping practices by Arbeau ("A Survey of Pupil Grouping Practices in Grade 1 to 12 in Alberta Schools," unpublished M.Ed. thesis, University of Alberta, 1963). The survey showed that one-third of Division 1 teachers and one-half of Division 2 teachers in the province undertook no intra-classroom grouping whatsoever. Moreover, almost one-quarter of the grade 1 teachers in our schools reported that they did not regroup the pupils within their classes for instruction in any subject—not even reading. One can only infer from such findings that in a large number of elementary classrooms in Alberta we are still asking almost every child to learn the same thing, the same way, at the same time.

To facilitate more individualized instruction, we will need to discard the traditional graded system, and some of its more complex cousins, and develop a flexible form of school organization which will take into account differences in rate and kind of learning among elementary school children.

4. *Improving the quality of the teaching force.* Obviously the key figure in the child's school environment is the teacher. For it is the elementary teacher who must guide his educational development during its period of most rapid and influential growth. This is indeed a grave responsibility.

Moreover, it is a responsibility which only a truly professional person of broad education and consummate skill can effectively meet. Equally obvious, however, is the fact that relatively few members of the present teaching force employed at the elementary level may be so classified. Hence, the most significant challenge facing Alberta education today is that of providing a well-qualified teacher in every elementary school classroom in the province.

The urgency of this task demands action on at least three fronts. First, is the recruitment for teacher education of larger numbers of young women with the interest and potential ability to work effectively with children four to eight years of age. Too many children are now exposed during this crucial phase in their education to persons who are either unqualified or who, although once qualified, have slipped into the rut of obsolescence. There is also a great need to attract more men into teaching at the Division 2 level. They are essential as identification models for boys in personality formation and to help them build a desire for task mastery and intellectual competence.

A second front on which action is required is that of selection and placement. At the present time, large numbers of certificated, but relatively unqualified, teachers are being hired and placed in elementary classrooms in urban schools. These teachers are, in the main, those who elected to follow the secondary route program, but then accepted an elementary teaching post in an urban centre in preference to a secondary teaching post in a rural area. Consequently, rural high schools have encountered some difficulty in securing qualified personnel and education in urban elementary schools has tended to suffer from the lack of a specialized teaching force. To alleviate this situation, urban school systems should consider adopting and publicizing a policy of preferential hiring of elementary route graduates for elementary school positions.

A third front for action is that of preparation. A logical corollary of the propositions outlined earlier is that the elementary school teacher must be a person of status and quality. Accordingly, it would appear that the time is now at hand to increase the minimum period of teacher education required for initial certification from two to three years and to lay plans for requiring a fourth year in the near future. Experience in this province and elsewhere, indicates that this high-standards approach is unlikely to aggravate the teacher shortage. It is far more likely to lead to excellence in education in the early years.

If the critical-years hypothesis is valid, then the actions taken at the elementary level are crucial. They could mean the difference for many members of the next generation betwen a life in a mental or penal institution or a productive life in society; the difference between employment and unemployment. A society that places great emphasis on verbal learning and rational problem-solving, and which greatly needs highly skilled and well-educated individuals to carry on the economic-political-social functions in an increasingly complex world, cannot ignore the enormous consequences of educational deprivation at any level.

IV B-12 SECONDARY EDUCATION

The Loom Also*

H. T. COUTTS

●

The Second Conference on the Canadian High School was concerned with theoretical and practical problems. Through lecture and discussion many current and emerging ideas were brought into focus. Among these were the challenge of change in our complex social setting, in learning theory, in school organization, in curriculum development, and in teaching specific subjects. At the end of the conference, the writer was left asking questions about some of the persistent problems of secondary education.

1. *What should be the underlying philosophy and purposes of secondary education in this half of the twentieth century?* We have evidence enough to show that various groups within society have different expectations, aspirations, ideals, and goals in relation to many aspects of life, including education. The phenomenon is not new. Through the ages man has continued to debate whether the major purpose of education should be to develop the intellect, rectify the morals, provide occupational competence, or prepare for all aspects of living including the use of leisure. Most of us, I think, continue to accept an old generalization formulated by the Commission on the Reorganization of Secondary Education in 1918:

> ...*education in a democracy, both within and without the school, should develop in each individual the knowledge, interests, ideals, habits, and powers whereby he will find his place and use that place to shape both himself and society toward ever nobler ends.*[1]

Surely responsible groups within our society are capable of arriving at a consensus that would give acceptable educational direction at the provincial, the system, and the school levels. In doing so, those involved will be forced to reassess their own scale of values. They may find that the adult society, which subscribes in idealistic fashion to one set of objectives, is in reality worshipping false gods. One can scarcely expect teen-age youth to adhere to values that are not practised by the adult community.

---

* Reprinted with permission from *Education*, V, 20 (Scarborough: W. J. Gage, Ltd., 1965), pp. 119–123.

2. *Is the concept of universal education at the secondary school level a dream or a necessity?* Changing patterns of living and making a living, coupled with a concept of democracy that recognizes the dignity and worth of each human being and his rights, privileges, and responsibilities, have been a strong force in favor of educational opportunity for all who can profit from it. Such changes, stimulated by developing technologies and automation, are so affecting patterns of employment and use of leisure, that educational institutions have been asked to provide for the needs and interests of an increasingly wide range of abilities. The result is that a very high percentage of teen-age youth are remaining in the secondary school. While this creates a dilemma and untold problems, society has accepted universal secondary education as a reality and a necessity. If it were once a dream, it is no longer so. I am not convinced, however, that the society which demands universal education appreciates how close this goal is nor how many unsolved problems it creates. Too often the society fails to understand, largely because it has not reflected too much about the matter, that changes in organization, curriculum, and instructional procedures are complementary to changes in the composition of the student body. Nor have professional educators succeeded well as communicators.

3. *Have changes in the structure of secondary education lagged behind changes in its form?* It seems to me that we have been doing a great deal to vary the form of secondary education. For example, much that is new in mathematics and physics programs is in the method of teaching rather than the content. Yet there does remain for consideration the matter of the substance of education. It is true that some curricular changes have been made. But it is really for a more fundamental look at the matter of education that I make a plea. We need to question some of our long-established priorities in the light of the many changes that are taking place. We need to ask what we mean by matriculation for university entrance. We ought to consider whether our use of academic, vocational, and general are really desirable distinctions to make. It may be that such distinctions, and the organizational forms that have been developed in association with them would be unnecessary, or at least modified, were we to consider more penetratingly the question of substance.

4. *Can the comprehensive or composite school provide best for educational needs of teen-age youth in our society?* If the composite school is more than a name, if in fact its philosophy supports the concept of comprehensiveness, it can offer a wide variety of programs to meet all of the purposes suggested above. What matters is, as Harold Baker said

---

[1] *Cardinal Principles of Secondary Education,* Bulletin No. 35 (Washington, D.C.: Department of Interior, Bureau of Education, 1918).

last year in another context, "not the organization, but what is done within it." Much depends on the spirit of the school as developed and accepted by staff, students, and community.

It seems essential that the composite school should serve a variety of purposes. One serious danger is that these purposes are not kept in their proper proportion. An even greater danger is that one purpose is stressed to the exclusion of others. I need not tell you that one composite high school differs from another for this reason.

The future of the composite school must be re-examined in face of the expenditure of large sums on so-called vocational and technical education. There is no general acceptance in Canada of the comprehensive school idea. Evidently British Columbia has accepted it in modified form, Alberta even more completely, and some provinces scarcely at all.

5. *Is the secondary school really developing the potential of its students? Does it continue to operate, consciously or unconsciously, on educational myths?* What I am still doubtful about is whether, in an effort to provide variety and certain kinds of specialization, we develop the potential of our students in any one of many directions. It seems to me, for example, that there are a few fundamentals from which all students may profit to some degree. For this reason I have the hope that we may provide sequential experiences in mathematical concepts for *all* pupils as part of general education. Basic understandings and generalizations in this subject would seem to be of primary importance and, I hope, will not have to be sacrificed to courses in adding for accountants, mensuration for carpenters, or curve-linearity for hair-dressers. If such courses are necessary, and they may well be, they should be built on fundamentals that are quite understandable at some level for every individual.

I hope that we can re-examine some of what I believe to be unfounded educational myths: that girls are more likely than boys to find mathematics and science difficult; that industrial arts as an entry into the understanding of the major technologies that influence our lives is the prerogative of boys. Surely these result from curricular, social, or cultural bias.

6. *Is the secondary school educating for the present or the future* (a) *in its occupational emphases?* Not much has been said to indicate to what extent we have looked ahead in our secondary school planning. It is because I have a wholesome regard for that section of Canadian youth I know, that I would not want to see them sold short. When providing educational offerings for occupational preparation—and in many ways this dominates all that we do—do we consider merely the market of today? We should, it seems to me, be anticipating the vocational requirements of tomorrow. Hence we should prepare for adaptability and flexibility. This is particularly true in our so-called vocational or occupa-

tional programs, but is important too in our so-called academic programs which have a strong occupational dimension.

(b) *in its preparation for citizenship?* If we are educating youth for tomorrow we should be preparing them for the totality of living. This means the development in students of a sense of awareness and interest with respect to future participation as citizens. At one time, I was hopeful that the social studies might serve to accomplish this, and I still believe that, under different conditions, it might. I must confess, however, that I have been disappointed with the results to date. It may be that the school cannot do more than it does; that society must add other stimuli and other means to prepare alert, aggressive, and involved citizens.

(c) *in its preparation for total and enriched living?* We must consider also the problem of education for the amount of leisure that I feel certain will be part of the pattern of living for the mass of our population in the decades ahead. Of course most of what the school does should contribute to the development of the well-rounded individual, of broad interests, and of standards of good taste. There should be more and more attention given to the arts, both the fine and the applied. We have undersold music, art, and drama in our school offerings, as we have limited the industrial arts as a part of general education. What concerns me is not that we fail to provide specialized programs for a few talented young people. Nor do I think that the problem will be solved by adding courses in the arts as an accretion to our secondary programs. No more do I believe that such courses alone are the answer to the use of leisure. I am quite sure that physical education will have to be a major contribution too. But it is the totality that seems important. In some way, and it may well be on an extra-curricular or semi-formal basis, fine and applied arts and all sorts of wholesome athletic and social preparation must be an integral part of educational programs. This will enable more and more adults in future to become active and satisfied participants and enthusiasts, but might well create the basis for greater appreciation of and support for the contributions and achievements of talented individuals and groups who have the potential to add richness to our cultural life in a variety of ways and on more than one level.

7. *Does the secondary school accept excellence and quality in education as a primary objective?* The pursuit of excellence or quality in education is an attitude or state of mind. It must motivate every aspect of our work in every phase of any activity for which the school is responsible. I want to find it in courses in mathematics, drama, or business. It should be reflected in product, process, and performance. "Our need is not merely for more education, but for education of higher quality." The full understanding of growth and change of behavior of the individual has a qualitative factor.

The needs of youth for education in a complex society are themselves varied and often clouded. For this reason, there is bound to be criticism of curriculum, programs, procedures, and results, teachers and teaching, administrators and other educational leaders. We shall have to accept such criticism as a fact of life and as a necessary stimulus to our continued efforts. It is quite obvious to me that those associated with secondary education will have to bear "the brunt of the assault," if only because its products enter immediately into situations where performance is judged by what are presumably the more mature members of the academic, commercial, and industrial community. Nor should we be daunted or discouraged by this prospect.

The direction must be forward. We must be innovative with respect to form, to substance, and to method in planning for secondary education. As weavers of the educational fabric we must experiment with threads having differing textures, with patterns having varied characteristics and artistry, and with processes promising an improved product. As we proceed, we must constantly evaluate the results of our weaving, taking the time for the sort of sober reflection that has motivated us during this Second Conference on the Canadian High School. In doing so we might well be guided by the words of Kahil Gibran's *The Prophet* which provided the title for this paper:

> *You cannot separate the just from the unjust and the good from the wicked;*
> *For they stand together before the face of the sun even as the black thread and the white thread are woven together.*
> *And when the black thread breaks, the weaver shall look into the whole cloth, and he shall examine the loom also.*[2]

---

[2] Kahil Gibran, *The Prophet* (London: William Heinemann Ltd., 1918), p. 47.

IV B-13

Tomorrow's Secondary School*

LAWRENCE W. DOWNEY

•

If, as is generally assumed, criticism and unrest are reasonably accurate indicators of impending change, secondary education in America must surely be on the threshold of major innovation. The field is in a state of ferment and there is a corresponding bustle of activity such as we have seldom witnessed. Secondary education has now entered a new era, and the predominant characteristic of that era is *change*.

What are the implications of this observation for high school teachers? For high school teachers-to-be? For principals of secondary schools? For superintendents? Or for any person interested in the shape of things to come in secondary education? What problems will be faced in the changing secondary school of tomorrow?

There will be the problem of testing new theories operationally. In education, as in so many of the affairs of men, theory often runs far away from practice; for it is one thing to speculate as to what might be done to improve something or other, but it is quite another thing to demonstrate that the proposed theory will, in fact, effect the improvement that is claimed for it. Today, new theories in the field of secondary education are being advanced at an unprecedented rate, but these theories are largely in the nature of hypotheses. They must be tested and found useful in the real world of the secondary school before they can be adopted as the bases for change. So it may be concluded that the testing of unproven hypotheses will be one of the major challenges facing tomorrow's high school educator.

Furthermore, once the hypotheses have been tested, and the nature and direction of change have been decided, there will be the problem of implementing the desired innovations. Our high school is, to a considerable extent, the product of its own past. Prevailing practices have become institutionalized. Frequently things are done as they are simply because tradition says they ought to be, and traditions do not yield easily. Organizations, like people, are naturally resistive to change. The secondary

---

* Reprinted with permission from *The Secondary Phase of Education* (Waltham, Massachusetts: Blaisdell Publishing Company, A Division of Ginn and Company, 1965), pp. 187–206.

school is no exception. Hence it must be realized that establishing the conditions for change will be another major problem facing educators in the secondary school of tomorrow.

It should be recognized further that change and improvement, if it is to be cumulative and significant, must be regarded as a continuous process. Any such process receives its impetus and direction from some sort of "feedback," some indication of the value of the change; but evaluation in education is an extremely complex business. So it may be assumed that assessing the effects of change will be another important task confronting secondary educators in the years ahead.

Each of these three processes, testing untested hypotheses (assessing the educational potential of proposed change), implementing desired innovations (overcoming organizational resistance to change), and evaluating the outcomes of change, deserves the careful and continuing attention of all high school educators in this era of rapid educational transformation.

A good deal of the burden in connection with these changes will fall upon high school teachers. Are they equal to the task? What kind of image of the high school teacher must one have as one speculates about the advancement of secondary education through the efforts of the teaching force? . . .

In this chapter we shall set forth a few untested hypotheses, analyse the dynamics of organizational change, and propose a few guides for the perplexing business of assessing the effects of change. . . .

●

TESTING UNPROVEN HYPOTHESES

An hypothesis, in the scientific sense, is a logical but somewhat speculative proposition growing out of a theoretical formulation. Hypotheses are the "thrusts of the imagination" in which scholars engage when they proceed from the known to the unknown. Once tested and found true, hypotheses become principles or laws. If, however, they are found to be false, they are discarded and replaced by other more tenable hypotheses which are tested and dealt with in like manner. This is the nature of scientific discovery. Observation and practice lead to theory; theory generates hypotheses; hypothesis-testing leads to new knowledge and/or reconstituted theory. And so it goes.

But in education, the testing of hypotheses is often a particularly difficult task. Some educational hypotheses are of a scientific nature and can be tested experimentally in some sort of "laboratory" setting. Other educational hypotheses, notably in the realm of practice, are not readily testable through quantitative analysis or probability theory. They must be resolved by the observations of insightful, artistic teachers. Still other educational hypotheses, largely in the domain of values, are not resolvable through the application of scientific methods or of insightful practice;

Figure 13:1

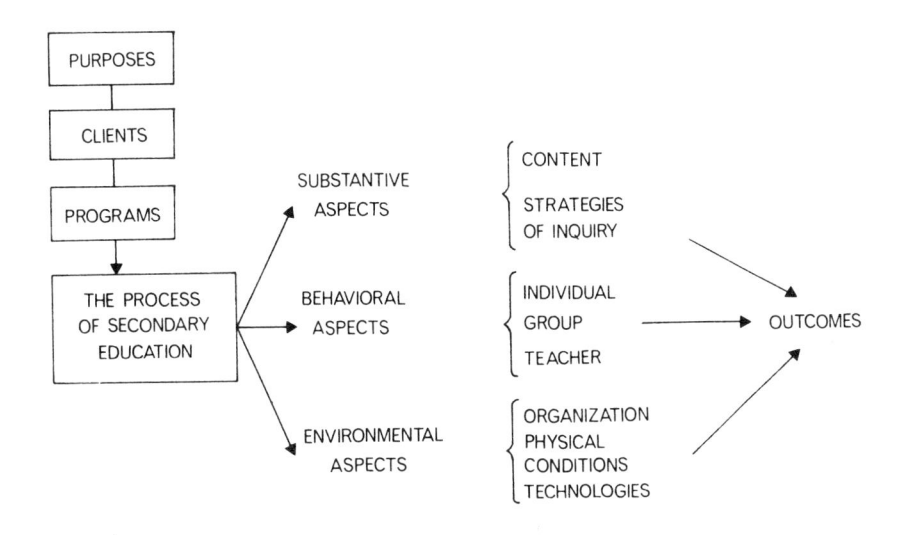

```
PURPOSES
    │
    ▼
CLIENTS
    │
    ▼
PROGRAMS
    │
    ▼
THE PROCESS          SUBSTANTIVE      ┌ CONTENT
OF SECONDARY   ───▶  ASPECTS       ───┤ STRATEGIES
EDUCATION                             └ OF INQUIRY   ───▶
                                                           ┐
                     BEHAVIORAL       ┌ INDIVIDUAL         │
                ───▶ ASPECTS       ───┤ GROUP        ───▶  OUTCOMES
                                      └ TEACHER            │
                                                           ┘
                     ENVIRONMENTAL    ┌ ORGANIZATION
                ───▶ ASPECTS       ───┤ PHYSICAL
                                      │ CONDITIONS
                                      └ TECHNOLOGIES
```

these must be examined in the light of one's philosophical convictions.

The hypotheses to be presented here are of all three types. Some need to be tested experimentally under carefully controlled conditions; others need to be "tried out" operationally by sensitive teachers; still others need to be subjected to debate and dealt with through the insights provided by philosophy and the humanities, illuminated by the reflections of thoughtful educators.

... The process of secondary education ... [has] three major dimensions, the substantive, the procedural or behavioral, and the environmental. But ... the process takes its impetus and direction from its purposes and programs, and from its clients. It leads to certain outcomes (unanticipated though these may sometimes be) which provide it with feedback. So it would appear that there are five major strands to the fabric of secondary education: purposes, clients, programs, processes, and outcomes....

The purposes of secondary education may be specified at either of two levels, though the two are closely related: at the level of ultimate ends, or at the level of immediate tasks. In terms of ultimate ends, the secondary school takes its direction from a philosophy of education—a philosophy that typically incorporated ideals as to the nature and needs of the society which the school serves, the nature of knowledge and how it is acquired, and the nature and rights of the individuals whom the secondary school must educate. In terms of immediate tasks, the secondary school sets as its purpose the transmission of the skills, values, and knowledge which, at any given time, are held to be legitimate outcomes of secondary schooling.

The clients of the secondary school are the young people who elect, are required, or are permitted to avail themselves of its services. Whether they elect or are selected is significant, as is the very wide range of interests, aptitudes, and abilities which the clients inevitably bring to the modern high school.

The programs are the patterns of learning experiences that are planned for various learners or groups of learners.

The processes are the activities that are engaged in as the teaching-learning act takes place. There are a number of aspects to these processes: the substantive, comprising the actual content to be learned and the strategies of inquiry which are called upon in the various fields of study; the behavioral aspects, which encompass the social-psychological dynamics of the individual student, functioning in a group, under the guidance of a teacher; and the environmental aspects, made up of the organizational structure, the prevailing physical environment, and the technological media employed.

The outcomes of secondary education may be defined in terms of the characteristics of the product of the high school and how these contribute to the society in which he lives.

Purposes: From their beginnings, our secondary schools have been characterized by a good deal of confusion as to purpose, both in terms of the ultimate goals of secondary education and in terms of the immediate tasks to be performed.

A number of rather distinctive subcultures exist throughout this continent, with a variety of philosophical positions and systems of values. As one would expect, each subcultural group urges that the secondary school subscribe to one or another basic philosophical position and perpetuate one or another value system. The broad goals of secondary education have developed upon the rather tenuous foundation of competing systems of values. There can be little wonder that high school educators have become society oriented, have tended to take their cues from the demands of contemporary life, and in their assumptions regarding education's goals, have tended to lean in the direction of the prevailing wind.

The tasks which our schools have traditionally assumed developed logically upon this social orientation. Our schools have attempted in varying degrees to train students in the skills demanded by the emerging social and industrial order; they have attempted to imbue students with the values that are most widely accepted in our culture; and they have attempted to transmit the "facts" which have come to be regarded as the possessions of the educated man. To some extent, also, they have attempted to equip students either with the scholastic tools needed for higher education or with the practical skills needed for employment.

One of the most difficult tasks confronting secondary school educators in the years ahead will be the clarification of the purposes and tasks of secondary education. In the future, as in the past, the high school will be expected to preserve and transmit the values inherent in our culture. But which culture? Which values? They will be expected to serve the social and economic needs of society. But which needs? And at what cost to individuality? They will be expected to develop to the fullest the potentialities of every student. But which potentialities?

Our first hypothesis is that if the secondary school does, indeed, have some responsibility for the preservation and transmission and the betterment of our culture—including its inherent values (and this proposition is rather widely accepted), then it follows that all aspects of the responsibility can best be discharged by causing students to learn the crucial aspects of *all* cultural systems, not just their own. If existing value conflicts may be interpreted as large-scale uncertainty as to what values ought to prevail, then surely one of the best ways to remove that uncertainty is to open value questions for the careful study, the reflection, and the debate of the coming generation. Finally, if "discovery" is the process which makes one's learning one's own, then surely students should not be indoctrinated in any particular set of values, but rather should be encouraged to inquire into values and discover for themselves the nature of the good, and the true, and the real.

Although the secondary school does indeed have a responsibility for helping to meet the needs of the industrial and social community which it serves, and although that society may at any given time have specific needs (today, for example, there is a crucial need for technologically trained manpower), if we subscribe to the democratic principle that the individual is more important than the state, then it follows that the high school's paramount function must remain the encouragement of each individual's potential to develop into manhood, not just his potential to become a useful cog in society's industrial machine. In the testing of this hypothesis, educators may have to ask themselves such related questions as: Should other agencies share in the development of social and civic man? Should industry assume the major responsibility for preparing productive men? What are the ethical implications of recent efforts to train students for specific jobs in the adult society? To what extent should individuals be permitted to plot their own destinies?

When these hypotheses have been put to the test of logical reflection and debate, I believe we will move toward a system of secondary education in which the purpose will be simply to engage students in a continuous process of discovery—unrestricted by the prejudices of the adult world, disciplined only by the scholarly modes of inquiry which ascribe to the various domains of knowledge, and limited only by the student's capacity to proceed to ever-higher levels of inquiry. Formal education may then become (as I believe it ought) a prelude to a lifelong pursuit of wisdom and knowledge.

Clients and Programs: One of the most significant changes in our high schools in recent years has been in the clients served and the variety of programs offered. Whereas the secondary school was not long ago an institution that catered to an intellectual and cultural elite, it has recently been called upon to serve an ever-increasing number of students with an ever-widening range of aptitudes, aspirations, and abilities. Many secondary schools have responded to this challenge with the propostion (albeit unspoken) that secondary education as formerly conceived may not be suited to such a vast number and variety of students. And they have proposed that as the clients change, the essence of secondary education should change accordingly!

So we have witnessed in the past few years the development of a whole host of differentiated programs that purport to accommodate the wide range of student interests and abilities (a development which, according to some analysts, is in contradiction to the principle of general education at the secondary level). These programs are designed and organized for "streams" or "tracks" of students. The principle behind this trend may be summarized as follows: educational experiences which differ both in rigor and in basic substance need to be provided to accommodate the range of students' interests, aptitudes, capacities, and career goals (though the latter are often decided by the school rather than by the student).

It is hypothesized that if secondary education is, in fact, general education, and if general education is the process through which the potentialities of the more able students are best developed, then general education may well be the process through which the potentialities of even the less able are best developed.

This hypothesis may become more tenable in light of certain further considerations and related questions. Is there any evidence to indicate that programs which are differentiated in basic content are really answering the conflicting demands for universality and excellence in high school education? Or are they in many cases simply depriving the less able student of an opportunity to become generally educated (at least to a level of minimal competence) and substituting opportunities to learn things they would learn whether they attended school or not, or things which they might more appropriately and more effectively learn in the world of work?

Whether differences among programs offered in our high schools should be differences in kind, differences in depth, differences in pace, or differences in educative procedures is certainly a moot question. But it must be answered, for, in light of the recent demands for quality education at all levels, the problem of numbers takes on serious proportions.

Perhaps in the years ahead, as we lay firm hold on the purposes of education—particularly secondary education—we will conclude that it is not necessary to instruct students in the details of daily life, for such things are learned outside the school anyhow, that it is not economical to train students in the skills of specific jobs, for job opportunities and requisite skills change constantly; and finally, that it is downright folly to condemn any student to an inferior education opportunity on the basis of our assessment of his potential, for none of us really knows what another is capable of becoming.

Processes: It was once thought that formal learning was little more than the simple and direct consequence of teaching. The teacher was viewed as the imparter of knowledge and the student as the receiver. The act of teaching was likened to the process of filling a container. And the act of learning was considered to be a totally passive one. This view of the process implied that being a good teacher involved little more than mastery of subject matter and being a good student involved little more than being able to store away for future recall the knowledge that the teacher attempted to impart.

This view has fallen into disrepute. It has been found that knowledge acquired in this passive fashion is quickly forgotten and not easily generalized or applied. It has been discovered (much to the amazement of some teachers) that what is presumably being taught is frequently not what is being learned. Accordingly, it must be acknowledged that the view of education as an institution where knowledge is dispensed is a naive notion indeed. To improve upon this view, one must arrive at a more tenable concept of the process of learning itself.

It is hypothesized that, if formal education is conceived as a process which facilitates a process of inquiry, leading to discovery on the part of the learner himself, the process will be more effective. It is hypothesized further that the way knowledge was discovered in the first place holds cues as to how it can best be acquired again. To test these hypotheses, educators will have to ask themselves a series of questions: What strategies of inquiry characterize the various domains of knowledge? How do these discipline the process of secondary education? How are student differences accommodated in the process? What role does the teacher play when he wants individuals to discover knowledge within the complex social system of the school? How does one organize for individual inquiry? What is the appropriate environment? What aids may be employed?

Outcomes: The prevailing concept of the ideal school product is of one who is in possession (temporarily at least) of the fund of "facts" which traditionally have been required of high school graduates; one who has learned to adjust graciously to his social environment; one who has accepted the prevailing cultural mores and values; and one who has mastered either the academic tools needed for high education or the practical skills needed for performance in the world of work.

Such a concept has a good deal to commend it. But it includes a number of features which bear careful scrutiny. Are facts in themselves worthwhile outcomes of education? How long does the average individual retain isolated facts? And to what purpose? Is it not logical that in this world of rapidly expanding and changing knowledge, it is much more important for the educated man to have learned *how* to acquire knowledge, *how* to generalize from knowledge, and *how* to apply knowledge than to have mastered fragments of knowledge for their own sake?

At a time when society in general is exerting pressure upon the individual to conform to institutional expectations and adjust to group norms, is it appropriate that the school deliberately attempt to produce conforming, adjusting, citizens? Or is this the very time when the school should be giving more attention to the cultivation of creative and self-directed individuals? By what criterion, or on what authority, does the school decide that prevailing values are the best values? Is it not possible that values, like knowledge, are more meaningful, more lasting, and more precious if they are sought after and discovered through the legitimate process of learning rather than accepted through a process of indoctrination? Finally, one might ask: is a technician, skilled only in the performance of a specific trade, a legitimate product of the public school?

●

ESTABLISHING THE CONDITIONS FOR CHANGE[1]

Historians are fond of pointing out that the most striking characteristic of the North American high school has been its persistent tendency to resist change. The inference in this observation is perfectly clear—and disconcerting to the prophet of educational progress. But I am nonetheless confident that in the years ahead, rapid change will take place in all our institutions of learning, including the secondary school.

Granted, predictions such as this have been made before. The promised panacea for professional practice or the anticipated "breakthrough" in educational knowledge has seldom, if ever, materialized. But there are now two specific signs which appear to me to be compelling indicators of future change in education: First, as one observes the tremendous cultural and scientific advances that have taken place on this continent since the last war, it seems inevitable that these advances will ultimately have their effect upon our educational institutions. Second, as one realizes that the great controversy over secondary education appears at last to have taken a positive turn, and as one notes that the forces of constructive change are now mustering, one must be encouraged to believe that we may be at the threshold of something new—perhaps better—for our high schools.

Anyone who has passed the age of thirty-five must be little short of awed by the phenomenal change that has characterized his time. The fund of human knowledge has virtually exploded; technologies have multiplied the productivity of man a hundred-fold; and advances in the media of communication and transportation have caused the world to shrivel before our eyes. These advances, however, are only dimly reflected in our institutions of learning. New knowledge in the realm of human behavior has not influenced appreciably our concept of the learning process or its facilitation. The clearly demonstrated capacity of technology to increase productivity of workers in other fields has not yet noticeably increased the efficiency of the educator. Similarly, modern communication media, so widely exploited in other phases of our culture, are only beginning to have a real impact upon teaching and learning. If one compares recent advances in education—or rather, the lack thereof—with advances in almost any other field of human endeavor, he will discover that the school seems amazingly primitive by comparison. This paradox cannot prevail; educational institutions will soon be caught in the progress that is sweeping our civilization.

The positive note which seems now to be faintly audible in the controversy over education constitutes my second predictor of educational change. The indiscriminate critic appears to be yielding to the agent of constructive innovation. Universities are realizing, as they did on occasion in the past, that they must assume a major share of the responsibility for the full range of education; the university, in fact, seems prepared to abandon its role as indignant critic of the lower schools and assume positive leadership in the reshaping of education at all levels, particularly the high school. The great foundations, too, are becoming increasingly concerned over education; more than ever before, they see that the stimulation of educational change is a public service in which they should engage. Professional educators themselves appear to be adopting an encouraging attitude; no longer is it heresy for a school man to admit that education is not all that it could or should be.

If one adds to this merger of talents and purposes the impetus currently provided by public sentiment, one is encouraged to predict that genuine educational change must be on the way.

But my purpose is not to argue the likelihood of educational change; the inevitability of change is assumed. Rather, my thesis is that if change is inevitable, we ought to prepare for it and make the best of it. For I do not think that change is all synonymous with improvement. Nor do I believe that the mere initiation of desirable change inevitably leads to improvement on a firm and continuous basis. The history of education is replete with instances of the rise and fall of innovations—changes that educators initiated from time to time for the improvement of their schools. Some of these innovations amounted to little more than fads, and were found out and abandoned before they gained momentum; others appeared to rest upon substantial ideas, but they were aborted by uncontrolled forces in the institution; and still others are, even now, of unknown merit, for their real impact has never been properly appraised.

As one anticipates educational change, and seeks to maintain a sense of direction amid change, one should attempt to establish at least three kinds of basic guidelines. The first has to do with the facilitation and

---

[1] Much of the material in this section first appeared in a slightly different form in Lawrence W. Downey, "Direction Amid Change," *The Phi Delta Kappan*, XLII, 5 (February, 1961).

direction of the educative process itself; it requires a comprehensive image of the dynamics of teaching and learning. The second has to do with the smooth redirection of an organization's course; it involves a sensitivity for the dynamics of institutional change. The third has to do with the cumulative nature of improvement, and it requires a precise design for the continuing evaluation of the outcomes of change....

Once a decision has been made as to the specific nature of the change desired, the next problem is one of initiation and implementation. The implementation of change in any organization requires knowledge of the intricate dynamics of institutional change and skill in dealing with the forces that are inevitably encountered.

In organizational therapy, perhaps the most perplexing phenomenon to be encountered by the therapist is the inherent indifference of organizations to anything new or unusual. In this respect, organizations are rather like individuals. The older they grow, the more fixed they become in their ways and the less inclined they are to view change with enthusiasm. The high school is no exception. The educational institution assumes that one of its functions is the preservation of our cultural heritage and the transmission of that heritage from generation to generation. Insofar as this role is apt to be a guardianship of the cultural status quo, the school is unlikely to become a leading proponent of change.

The innovator can accordingly assume at the outset that inducing or directing change in any organization is not a simple matter; he can assume further that changing the educational enterprise may be something of a special case. Students of organization, however, have proposed a few theories and some procedures which appear to be promising.

One notable characteristic of the typical organization is its tendency to seek a state of equilibrium. That is to say, the organization strives to establish a kind of progressive balance. It attempts to formalize regular patterns of progress: it routinizes the behavior of its members, and it conditions itself to preserve established institutions. Having achieved this state, the organization is said to be in a condition of "no change."[2]

How is this state of equilibrium achieved? How does the organization preserve it? What are its implications for educational change? The condition appears to be achieved and preserved through the interaction of numerous counterbalancing forces. The fact that the forces are counterbalancing explains the condition of equilibrium. The fact that resultant behavior becomes habit-forming accounts for the conditioned state. In most established organizations there is an acquired tradition prescribing that things be done as they have been done in the past; and doing things according to that prescription constitutes a comfortable operation for organization members. But in most modern cultures there are decided preferences for the new and corresponding prejudices against the old. Such cultural values are very much in conflict with the above-noted organizational tradition. These forces may be viewed as counterbalancing. One operates within the organization, the other without. One pushes in one direction, the other pulls back. In time the two forces adjust to each other and the net effect upon the organization becomes the geometric resultant of the two force vectors. The organization accommodates both forces and at the same time moves, under the influence of both, toward the realization of its mission.

This is the essence of organizational equilibrium. The condition is inevitably present, to some degree, in every formal enterprise. It follows rather logically that if one hopes to effect change in an organization, the first objective must be the elimination of these conditions for "no change." This objective is best achieved by upsetting the equilibrium, or creating imbalances in the organization. Imbalances cause reactive discharges of energy; they cause adjustive behavior in the system; and in so doing they provide the most fruitful setting for the initiation of specific changes in procedure.

Now, how can these imbalances be created? Many specific techniques have been suggested. Most of them, however, appear to be subsumed in what has been referred to as the "change agent" technique. The change agent is nothing more than an agitator, a disturber of balance, a stimulation of discomfort or dissatisfaction. Such an agent, acting as a catalyst in the system, causes reactions and provides the setting and the stimulus for innovation.

It should be emphasized that when major imbalances are induced in an organization, the need for direction immediately becomes acute, so it is advisable to use the disequilibrium technique with considerable caution and premeditation. When imbalance is introduced, the consequences are felt throughout the entire organization. Some consequences may be frustrating or even threatening to individuals or groups. It is for this reason that organizations become skillful at reestablishing equilibrium.

It is therefore suggested that, before introducing change, the effects upon all aspects of the organization should be anticipated. If an innovation is introduced in the absence of appropriate conditions for change, the proposal may be overcome by apathy; on the other hand, if excessive imbalances are induced, the proposed change may become subordinate to the resolution of anxieties in organizational members. Keen sensitivity as to the type and amount of disequilibrium appropriate to specific changes is the key to effective direction of change in an institution.

The innovator is advised to consider carefully these minimal precautions:

---

[2] This condition has been described by Kurt Lewin as "stable quasi-stationary equilibrium." The term is an excellent one. The organization is described as if stationary; in reality, however, it continues to function and progress. See K. Lewin, "Problems in Group Dynamics and the Integration of the Social Sciences: I Social Equilibria," *Journal of Human Relations*, I, 1 (1947).

1. Evaluate the worth of the basic idea itself, in terms of the school's purposes and in light of possible procedures for attaining it.

2. Evaluate the proposed innovation with the professional staff, not as an accomplished fact, but rather in light of the need to be met and in terms of a possible procedure for meeting it.

3. Analyze the consequences for the formal organization. Define new roles and provide opportunities for training and experience in new relationships and new skills.

4. Anticipate the impact upon existing informal groups; assess the regroupings likely to be caused by the proposed change; and attempt to plan for the accommodation of emerging interactions.

5. Review individual needs and attempt to anticipate frustrations or threats created by the innovation; institute planned procedures for relieving anxieties.

6. Introduce the change on a trial basis. Failure in an experiment is not nearly as serious as failure in an adopted plan. A test run will provide opportunities for adjusting unanticipated consequences, for acquiring new skills, and for accommodating to new situations.

7. Finally, it is suggested that adequate leadership constitutes the most important prerequisite to successful change. The skillful leader estimates accurately his "degree of freedom" for change. He anticipates in detail the consequences for the organization and for individuals. He stands ready to fill any void which may be created by the change. He times his moves carefully. And when he moves, he inspires in his followers the confidence necessary for success. . . .

•

ASSESSING THE EFFECTS OF CHANGE

Education is undoubtedly something of an art, something of a science and something of a technology. In appraisal of this process, the educator may assume the perspective of the artist, of the scientist and of the technologist. But each of these is, first and above all else, a keen observer. They differ only in the way they use their observations: the artist has a trained sensitivity through which he translates observations into new insights. The scientist's observations become testable theories or hypotheses which he is able to prove or disprove through experimentation and precise measurement. The technologist seeks to adapt scientific knowledge to his practice; he "tries out" new scientific principles and attempts to determine their relevance for his professional activity.

This need for keen observation should be adopted as the first aspect of our perspective on educational evaluation. Further, it might be noted that a well cultivated sensitivity to the total educative process

Figure 13:2

EVALUATION POINTS IN EDUCATIONAL INNOVATION

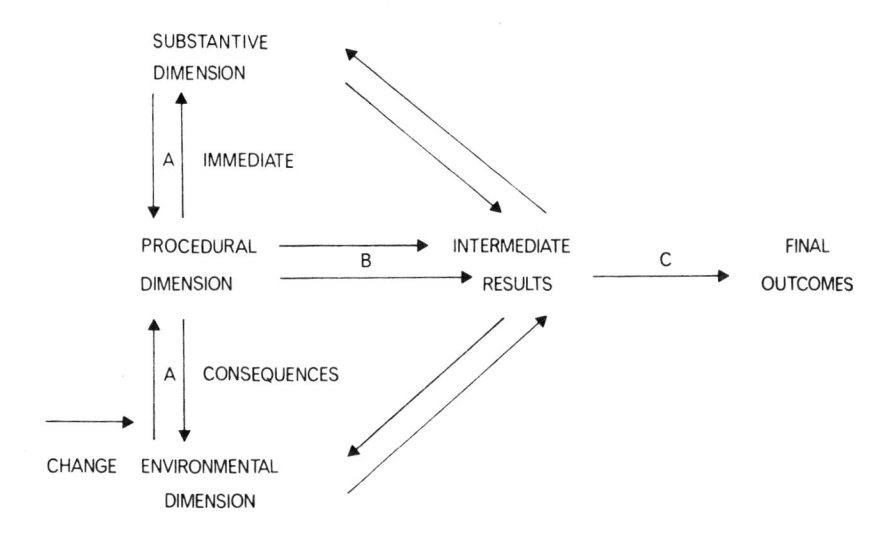

enables one to translate observations into useful insights about the likely consequences of change; that skill with precise measuring devices makes possible the discovery of new knowledge about specific aspects of change; and that simply trying out new ideas leads to improvement in the techniques of educating.

It will be recalled that the educative process was conceived to involve interactions among three basic dimensions: the substantive, the behavioral and the environmental. This view of the process may suggest a useful design for systematic appraisal of change to any aspect of the process.

Suppose, for example, that one introduces a specific change to the environment. Presumably, this interference will first cause a series of immediate consequences by inducing change in all other dimensions; these immediate consequences will react upon the total process and produce intermediate results; and ultimately, through further development of the process, final outcomes will be realized. Figure 13:2 illustrates this cumulative and developmental nature of change. When the change is introduced at the environmental level there are immediate consequences for the other dimensions. These may be observed at point *A*. The intermediate results to follow are observable or measurable at point *B*. Ultimately, final outcomes may be assessed at *C*.

For a specific example, consider the case of introducing an overhead projector into a classroom. This action is a change in the environmental dimension. As depicted in Figure 2, one immediate consequence of this action will be a change in the teacher's role and, perhaps, a change in the mode of inquiry pursued by learners. These in turn may produce, as intermediate effects, improvements in individual student motivations and/or significant alterations in the social climate of the classroom. Eventually, student achievement may be influenced one way or another. These results will be progressively realized, and should somehow be appraised as they occur.

Adequate appraisal procedures involve much more than the measurement of student achievement. Through sensitive observation, one can discover ways of increasing the learning opportunities in specific situations. Skillful appraisal of the intermediate effects of change may suggest further modifications of the educative process, and precise measurement of final outcomes provides a useful basis for retrospection. All these techniques qualify as respectable evaluation devices; each is essential in programs of educational change.

IV C-14 UNIVERSITY EDUCATION

The Modern University*

NEVILLE V. SCARFE

•

In a changing world it is not unnatural that the function, organization, and purpose of a university will change. In the days gone by when only an affluent few had access to higher education, it was possible to design a university which would cater to the leisured classes and provide a delightful retreat from the harsh realities of the world in what has so long been called "the ivory tower." In modern times when higher education has become almost a necessity for many industries and businesses, when a larger proportion of the populace is seeking higher education and when almost everyone has to earn a living through high level skills and knowledge, a university can no longer be a retreat from the world which it serves. It has, on the other hand, to be very much more closely associated with the world of work as well as the professions.

•

THE UNIVERSITY AND THE FUTURE CITIZEN

Very few students now go to a university simply for the joy of studying a subject for its own sake. In fact, a very high proportion of students would disdain this particular attitude. The purpose for which many students go to university relates almost certainly to a particular occupational goal. The modern university has become what the mediaeval university was—a training ground for particular professions. A university is no longer just a place where one can become well informed, where one can acquire knowledge. Of course, it will always be a means of acquiring information and knowledge but now it should be far more than that. It should be a place where one acquires wisdom and important personal qualities which some people describe as mature judgment, intelligent discrimination, creative imagination and ethical character. Put in other words, students no longer simply accumulate information and knowledge; they are expected also to learn how to apply it creatively in some socially useful occupation after leaving the university.

---

* Reprinted with permission from *Canadian Education and Research Digest*, IV, 2 (June, 1964), pp. 102–106.

A modern university should stress more than ever before the importance of logical and scientific thinking, not only in scientific matters but in everyday problems which beset the world. Students at the university need to study the modern world and should be keenly aware of modern ideas in philosophy, sociology, psychology, and politics. All these subjects, however, ought to be pointed towards and focussed on modern problems and be usefully applicable to improving the competence of the future citizen in his chosen profession. Arid erudition and pretentious pedantry have little place in a modern university. Students are needed who are alertly aware and wisely conscious of the connection between theory and practice, between research and its application in the modern world.

In the days gone by, when only the elite attended the university, lecturing skills were unimportant. In fact, most brilliant students gained their wisdom through reading, discussion and disputation as well as through keen observation of the world around. In modern times, when large numbers gain access to the university, lecturing becomes very much more important and teaching skills far more significant in the progress of a university. A university which is not primarily a teaching university, with both graduates and undergraduates, is failing in its real function for society. This is not to say that excellent teaching is not supported and improved by research. In fact, the only way in which teaching can be kept vital, alive and up-to-date is by constant contact with *ingenious developments in modern life.*

A university, however, is still not primarily a research institution. Its money is provided in order to train first class thinkers and exceptionally competent performers in the more skillful and professional occupations of the world. The applied faculties or the professional faculties are, therefore, very important in a good university. In many ways, too, the Faculties of Arts and Science are also professional faculties since they are more often than not training persons for future occupations, but the Faculties of Arts and Science are also service faculties for the rest of the university. It is usually the professional faculties that have closer contact with the world of work and with the realities of life.

In the past, Faculties of Arts and Science tended to become the remote ivory towers and to be solely concerned with the accumulation and communication of knowledge with little or no concern as to its value and use or to the development of wisdom or artistry in the student. Students tended to become well informed rather than competent, erudite rather than wise, good rather than excellent, conformist rather than creative. Real scholarship, real creative imagination, real ingenuity and originality were as likely to be found in professional faculties as in Arts and Science. Unfortunately a very few conservative elements in Arts and Science still seem to equate excellence with the rarefied atmosphere of abstract speculation concerning a massive accumulation of obsolete information.

This is not to decry reflective thought, speculation or contemplation. In fact, this is not to decry thinking at all. It is an attempt to elevate thinking, original ingenuity, and creative imagination to higher levels by making sure that knowledge becomes wisdom and culture.

•

TWO PHILOSOPHIES

Basically there are two philosophies of education which underlie divergencies of view about the organization of and attitudes towards a university. To some extent these depend on the relative emphasis given by university professors to inheritance and to environmental factors in promoting learning and the achievement of wisdom and skill. On this, too, depends the relative amount of sympathy existing between university professor and student.

One attitude says that either a student has inherited competence or he hasn't and there's little that can be done about it. It will not matter much what kind of teaching or home background a student has had or what kind of treatment he gets in university because if he has native ability he will do well. Added to that is usually a belief in an inherent attitude to work. Those who conform to the patterns and ideals of teachers and professors and who assiduously pursue these by developing colossal powers of memory and conscientious devotion to duty will succeed in a university without much effort on the part of the professor. In fact, a "good" student at a university is one who gets first class marks without demanding much lecturing skill from the professor. The inherently clever student who rebels against the drudgery of the system or the conservative outlook or the uselessness of some of the information or the inadequacy of the teaching methods is a nuisance in the university and is classed as lazy. To some professors the university and its methods are never wrong—it is always the student who is wrong—stupid or lazy or an odd ball. He is judged on what is supposed to be an impartial and infallible examination, but one which is often far from a valid or reliable test of a student's full quality or ability. Too often it is a test of memory and conformity. If a professor is a poor teacher he will seek to justify research as the major function of a university. He would also wish to restrict entry to the university to a narrowly academic elite who learn in spite of inadequate teaching.

The second attitude is a belief in the powers of the good teacher to modify, stimulate and promote the potentialities of students. It is a trusting attitude with faith in young people. It believes that a great deal can be done for young people, not in the sense of coddling or nursing them but in the sense of encouragement, stimulation, and discussion. If a student does not seem to be succeeding, the professor will question his own methods and adequacy first before doubting the student's capacity or motivation or powers of concentration. Perhaps by modifying content or method what seems to be a failing student may be helped to succeed. That is to say, the professor does not immediately label a student as innately dull or temperamentally lazy because he believes that environmental influences are as important in the formation of character and the development of potential as inheritance. There is thus greater sympathy between student and professor. Further, a professor with this attitude is usually a good teacher and gives priority to his teaching function, particularly with undergraduates, without any neglect of his own scholarship or interest in research. He is more liberal in his attitude towards admission to a university.

There is no doubt that a more liberal attitude towards university growth and development is needed. Conservatism may have its proper place in the home, in the street and in society but it has little place in a university where radical ideas, adventurous experimentation and advanced thinking should be uppermost. A university is a place where traditional ideas should be challenged, reactionary attitudes opposed and rigid restrictionism liberalized. A university is a place where liberty and equality should reach their ultimate zenith, and where fraternity should mean a community of mutually co-operating scholars.

•

DEVELOPMENT OF THE INDIVIDUAL

Two other important points seem worth stressing. A university can be judged good to the degree to which it is concerned with the individual. Whenever students become anonymous masses and are treated as uniform groups a university has become a factory. The essence of a university is individualism, independence and originality. Every student in a university must be known intimately by one or more professors who make it their business to have personal concern for the continued welfare of a few individuals. This applies as much to first year students as to doctoral candidates, to the near failing student as much as to the gold medallist. If a university accepts a student it accepts a responsibility to see that the neophyte makes the best of his potentialities and grows increasingly to self-controlled independence relying on his own initiative and creative imagination as motivating forces. Caring for individuals does not mean coddling or spoonfeeding. It means stimulus, encouragement, advice and personal concern. This is one of the necessary ways of securing excellence in the university.

Following from this is the essential need to nourish imagination and develop emotional sensitivity. Appreciation of the value of good human relationships and artistic endeavours are just as important as scientific logic or professional perfection. Since, as Sir Herbert Read says, "large areas of human experience are only communicable by non-discussive modes of expression," it follows that a proper balance of personal growth within a university requires opportunities to participate in activities which expand emotional sensitivity as well as those which enlarge the powers of thinking. Creativity in artistic expression should go on side by side with creativity in scientific investigation. While creative imagination should animate university teaching, it should also inspire students to ponder the great riddles of the Universe and lively values which move the human spirit.

IV C-15

The University and Modern Man*

MURRAY G. ROSS

●

A new university can find a precedent for almost anything it may wish to do. Contrary to popular belief, the early universities were highly utilitarian and pragmatic. Masters who depended upon fees for their livelihood found it expedient to be "realistic," to give their students "what they wanted." Says a twelfth-century advertisement by a master in Italy: The course is "... short and practical, with no time wasted on outgrown classical authors, but everything fresh and snappy and up-to-date, ready to be applied the same day if need be." Such appeals are not now respectable. The modern university has little need to recruit students, but if there were such a need, the university today has far more subtle means of presenting the case.

The present conception of the university has emerged but slowly over the centuries. The transition is dramatized, in part, by two books having almost identical titles but published almost one hundred years apart. The first is the famous statement by Cardinal Newman on *The Idea of a University*, and the second is the recent book by the brilliant Karl Jaspers.[1] On many points the authors agree—particularly, it should be noted, on the importance of general and liberal education. On some vital points, however, they differ. For Newman, the university is a relatively select community in which the great truths of the past are learned, where discussion between students and their masters sharpens the intellect, where students acquire wisdom and conviction. Great teaching that elicits intellectual and creative responses in young minds constitutes, for him, the essential university activity. Knowledge he saw as something relatively well-established and familiar; and while he paid lip-service to research and the search for new truth, he had, in fact, little enthusiasm for it. Professor Jaspers, representing rather the nineteenth-century German university point of view, maintains that knowledge is a world constantly being discovered, and that scholarly research and study are the university's principal functions. "The university," he says, "is

---

* Reprinted with permission from *The Journal of Education*, the Faculty and College of Education, University of British Columbia, No. 8 (Vancouver and Victoria: March, 1963), pp. 15–21. This article is an abridged version of the Installation Address given by Dr. Ross on the occasion of his installation as the first President of York University, January 24, 1961.

the corporate realization of man's basic determination to know. Its most immediate aim is to discover what there is to be known and what becomes of us through knowledge." The university must thus do more than train students. It must, as a community of learning, devote itself to the discovery of new knowledge, to the achievement of fresh insights, to the acquisition of new understanding.

Such profound differences as to what the university is to do have run all through university history. How can one, then, say that a new university has any clear inheritance? I think one can. Despite historic differences, there seems today to be reasonably clear and wide agreement about the purpose of a good university and the conditions essential thereto. I find such seeming agreement in three leading ideas.

First, there is a belief in a persistent and relentless search for new knowledge, new truth, and new meaning in discovered truth. The unqualified will to know, the insatiable thirst for knowledge, the unrelenting desire to understand—these are characteristics of the true academic man and the institution in which he functions. The university community has functioned at its best where, and only where, it has been constituted of men with a deep love of learning and a passion for truth. A university must manifest a spirit of investigation, a search for new truth, and a continuing program of research.

The second idea on which I find agreement is that the modern university should devote itself to producing students who have what Coleridge called "the interest of permanence," and who have, as well, what Professor Woodhouse calls "the interest of progression." A concern for students, a desire to expose them to the great civilizations, ideas, and ideals of the past, to train their intellectual capacities, and to help them differentiate between sense and nonsense—these necessities remain. But since the world of knowledge expands now at a tremendously accelerated rate (doubling, it is said, about every ten years), and as university graduation is recognized as a first step in a life-long process of education, to help students develop a capacity for self-education must become a major goal of higher education.

A third agreed necessity is that the university's tasks must be carried out in a context of freedom. Men who do research must be free to pursue disciplined study, however much their study may threaten the established order; and a student must have freedom, that he may learn freedom. It has often been said, in general, that you have to risk your young men if you want to get a generation of men. The university, no less, must take the chance that some of its students will "go to the dogs," rather than restrict the freedom in which the other young men will learn to make their own decisions, develop self-discipline and the capacity to act as persons of independent spirit. We must take risks, but no more effective

---

[1] Karl Jaspers, *The Idea of the University*, trans. by H. A. T. Reiche and H. F. Vanderschmidt (Boston: Beacon Press, 1959).

way of developing character or of discovering the truth has yet been discovered.

This, then, I take it, is our great inheritance: a conception of the university as a community of learning in which research, in its broadest and most developed sense, and teaching, in its highest form, are carried on within a context of freedom.

A new university has a special chance to be sensitive to the social environment in which it is born.

In our day, the social environment is most frequently described in terms of great advances in science and technology. But while these advances bring vast new opportunities to all of us, they also bring problems —and, indeed, threats—to the very civilization they were designed to advance. The "advances" have brought not merely motor-clogged streets, man's submission to the machine, his surrender to mass organization, and his steady, almost rhythmic march towards world disaster—they have also brought the threat of automation of man himself, the loss of faith in himself and of ability to invent and create social forms and institutions to protect and nourish the things he values most.

Our major concerns should not, surely, be how to improve technology (that will continue to improve by sheer momentum), but how to cure man's spiritual impotence; not how to create new forms of transportation, but how to apply creativeness to our social structure; not how to link continents physically, but how to achieve decency in human relations the world over. Hence we must give special emphasis to the humanizing of man, freeing him from those pressures which mechanize the mind, which make for routine thinking, which divorce thinking and feeling, which permit custom to dominate intelligence, which freeze awareness of the human spirit and its potentialities. How free is the human mind and the human spirit in this free society of ours? To free man to use all his creative powers is the fundamental purpose of liberal education. This is also the great need of our day.

Let me speak briefly about some of the human qualities that should particularly concern the modern university.

First, we in the university must nourish imagination. In the lives of many great men, often playing a decisive role in that which distinguished them, one finds the intuitive and imaginative process stimulating and giving impetus to their creative work. It is this process which, on the one hand, produces the "hunch," the shrewd guess, the fertile hypothesis, the ability to take the courageous leap to entirely new concepts; and it is this process which, on the other hand, permits one to combine and relate ideas and images in new ways so that new solutions, or new methods of solution to old problems, are possible. Intuition and imagination seem to be essential equipment of great poets, scientists, historians, administrators, and statesmen. These talents are implicit in all great "breakthroughs": without them, man would never have flown the airplane, submerged in the submarine, written great poetry or novels, or pressed for change in his social institutions.

Some people, strange to say, feel that the university cannot tamper with these human, subtle, and complex characteristics. But surely these are the very qualities in which we should be most interested. As Archibald MacLeish said recently, "... there exists in our society the strange and ignorant belief that the life of the imagination lies at an opposite pole from the life of the enquiring mind ... that men can live and know and master their experience of this darkling earth by accumulating information and no more. Men who believe that have, in effect, surrendered their responsibilities as men."

I agree that it is hard to say exactly what should be done. How intuition and imagination enter into the creative process is none too well understood. But what hampers such insight is understood rather better. Let me illustrate what does *not* help.

Some years ago, a teacher of a Grade 4 class told me she wrote on the blackboard the following problem in addition: $1 + 2 + 3 + 4 + 5 + 6 + 7 + 8 + 9$. She expected that the children, following routine, would require up to ten minutes to find the answer. And she was unprepared when, in one minute, one pupil had not only completed the task, but found a new method. "How," asked the teacher, "did you do it?" "Well," said the pupil, "$5 + 4 = 9$, $6 + 3 = 9$, $7 + 2 = 9$, $8 + 1 = 9$, and $5 \times 9 = 45$." What is shocking is that most of us might have been surprised by the work of this student. We are surprised because most of us have been taught to handle problems like this in a dull, plodding, and unimaginative way: $1 + 2 = 3$, $3 + 3 = 6$, and so on. When I told one of my colleagues this story, he suggested that an imaginative method would have *told* the children to solve the problem by any method *other than* direct addition. An average class, he says, might often find as many as *five* different ways to get a short-cut answer to the problem.

Quite different, in some ways, is the kind of imaginative process involved in the long chain that led from the young Einstein's early dreaming and musing to the overwhelmingly powerful general theory of relativity. Some knowledge of physics, of course, he had to have. But the story does not, as is popularly supposed, begin with a mature Einstein trying to grapple with the scandalous difficulty in physics introduced by the Michelson-Morley experiments with light. (Actually, Einstein only heard of these and saw the relevance of his theory to them much later.) The story begins with a boy, who knows something of light phenomena, asking himself the question, "What would the world look like if I were riding on a beam of light?"—a boy's question not very different from "What would the earth look like if I were on the moon?" Led by this phantasy, dreaming, imagining, working out its consequences in a disciplined way as sought knowledge came to hand, all the elements that were later to yield the mature theory were latent in the bold phantasy, and could probably have come either in no other way or only after generations of more prosaic labors.

Our failure to nourish intuitive and imaginative powers is one reason why so much of the material fed by the high school and the university to young people has little, if any, meaning to them. Unless the student learns to relate facts, to enjoy speculating about them, to receive them into his imagination, the facts remain sterile and largely meaningless. And if we here accept the premise that the university is the beginning rather than the end of education, we surely must be especially concerned with freeing and stimulating those powers in the student which he must bring to bear on new material, if he is to work creatively on his own in the modern world.

The freeing and nourishing of intuition and imagination does not, of course, make hard and disciplined study less important. Intuition and imagination *favor* the prepared mind. Disciplined study and the qualities of which I speak are not antagonistic; they complement each other—indeed, they need each other desperately. At this time in history, particularly, we must make the classroom, the seminar, the whole university, a more lively place—a place in which conjecture and speculation are encouraged, in which even "intelligent absurdities" are considered before being discarded.

We must also learn how to help our students become more emotionally sensitive. By emotional sensitivity, I mean the capacity to be deeply moved and profoundly influenced by the thoughts, feelings, and activities of other people. Imagination is, of course, required, but also something more: the human ability to understand a person or a problem not only with the intellect but also with the emotions. A man who says "I have the feel of the situation" usually means he knows with both his mind and his heart. It is that quality which Shakespeare expresses in "King Lear" when the aged king says "... You see how this world goes" and the blind Gloucester replies "I see it feelingly."

Lack of this capacity to see the world "feelingly" is perhaps the greatest threat to our civilization. For unless we understand the feelings of other people, unless we are able, as George Herbert Mead puts it, "to take the role of the other," unless we are emotionally sensitive, we do not understand the problems of the world in which we live. We stand today on the threshold of a great transition in world power. It is not unlikely that fifty years hence this world will be dominated by non-white people. Only those among us who have some capacity for "the feel of things" as well as "the look of things" will understand what is happening. Recognition of facts and numbers alone—that white people are now outnumbered two to one—does not provide for full understanding. Nor does factual knowledge of the aspirations of the U.S.S.R., or of the People's Republic of China, or of the people of Africa and Asia, give more than a partial picture. We must be able to *feel* what, for example, centuries of white superiority in attitude and practice now mean to the colored peoples. What does it mean to have been treated for so long (even if kindly) as if one were inferior? Unless we have some capacity to know with both our minds and our hearts, we will be unable to cope with this world of change. Thus, without the ability to see the world "feelingly," we cannot hope to develop a world family that can live in peace. Indeed, the questions William Blake raises in his *Songs of Innocence*, "On Another's Sorrow," may be highly relevant for us today:

> *Can I see another's grief,*
> *And not seek for kind relief?*
> *Can I see a falling tear,*
> *And not feel my sorrow's share?*

I will not here attempt to say how emotional sensitivity is to be developed. But I do know that if the university is to develop it, it must be a free academic community in which great literature and history and philosophy and science are taught by people whose emotions are not immobilized by the fear of being human while in academic garb.

Another peculiarly modern problem seems to be that of establishing identity. *Who am I?* is surely the question that most troubles modern man. In one sense, the problem is as old as history, but its nature has changed, and radically so, in the last century. For while in the recent past one conformed to a given pattern of belief and behaviour, one conformed in the sense of "electing" a set of principles in which one had confidence and pride. Today, the tendency is to conform, not to a given set of principles, but to custom, to the prevailing and fashionable belief or practice of the day. And since these beliefs and practices change frequently, there is uncertainty and insecurity. The question *Who am I?* is an acute one for men who are never quite certain in what they believe, or what principles guide their lives, or how they should behave. Like the newest soldier on the drill field, modern man anxiously watches those around him to make sure he stays in step. In our society, as Allan Wheelis suggests, "his character acquires a fine readiness for some unknown undertaking to which it is never committed. He is burdened by a sense of futility and longs for something or someone to give meaning to his life, to tell him who he is, to give him something to live for." The result is that the light touch has supplanted the firm grip, the launcher of trial balloons has replaced the committed man. We appear to avoid final decisions, to maintain all things subject to revision, and stand ready to change course when the winds change. The key words of our time appear to be "flexibility," "adjustment," and "warmth"; the key words of our grandfathers were "work," "thrift," and "will." And the change has not brought comfort, or serenity, or security to modern man. Rather is our day characterized by personal anxiety and personal anguish.

The problem is more evident than the solution. But surely the process by which men discover values and beliefs—indeed, discover themselves

—necessitates searching and striving for personal answers to the fundamental questions of life. There are few places where these fundamental questions can be pursued as effectively as in a university, *if* the university provides opportunities for, and assistance in, the search. It is not the task of the university, of course, to provide definite answers for, or ends to, the search. The function of the university is to help to clarify the questions, to show how great minds of the past have dealt with these questions, to introduce relevant data from contemporary life, to encourage individual students to work through these materials and to find their own answers and their own identity.

The characteristics I have spoken of cannot be directly taught, are not to be placed in neat categories, cannot be worked at for "credits." They must inhere in the *ethos* of the university. If they are not found there, the very spirit of the university will wither.

PART FIVE

Society and the Teacher

V

Introduction

•

In societies throughout the world, teachers have often been looked upon with apathy and even contempt. The situation in Canada has not been an exception. In 1853, the Superintendent of Education in New Brunswick reported, "if a man could get no other work or was incompetent, he tramped the country in search of a school." Up to 1860, it was common practice to pay the teacher in part by requiring him to board in the homes of his pupils. This often led to humiliation and disgust. John Thomas, a teacher in Lunenburg, reported that he was often given straw beds where "mice, fleas, and bugs could be felt at all hours of the night." J. L. Gourlay, in his *History of the Ottawa Valley* (1896), writes that the common schools for the working classes were inundated with "worthless scum under the character of schoolmasters."

The teachers in Canada have gradually raised their social status by keeping abreast of educational ideas in other countries, improving teacher training, developing a sense of profession, and participating in research to improve instructional practices. In the nineteenth century, Canadians followed with great interest the advocacy of science by Thomas Huxley and Herbert Spencer, and the defence of humanities by Cardinal Newman and Matthew Arnold. The exponent of the scientific movement in education in Canada was John Arbuckle of Prince Edward Island who carried on experimental research in education as far back as 1849. Froebel's advocate in Canada was James L. Hughes, who published *Froebel: Educational Laws* in 1897.

A better understanding of the learning process came with the development of child study. The enthusiasm of J. L. Hughes in Toronto and J. H. Putnam in Ottawa influenced the adoption of the "new psychology." There has been a shift from the authoritarian lecture method to a more co-operative method of learning through group participation. The "enterprise" method of teaching with shared activity was popularized in Alberta and Saskatchewan through the writings of Donalda Dickie. Other changes include growth of a distinct science of education, improved human relations between pupils and teachers, and greater concern with the development of each individual child. The need to modify school curricula and teaching methods in the light of research in social sciences and changes in the structure and aspirations of society underlies current teacher training programmes.

Educational research is encouraged in all Canadian provinces. Research is also being done by national organizations such as the Canadian

Council for Research in Education, the Canadian Education Association, and the Canadian Teachers' Federation. The Ontario Institute for Studies in Education, established in 1965, attempts to improve the quality of both teacher education and public school teaching, combining research with its implementation in schools. Its aims include "effective communication of the findings of ... research to those in the educational structure who are aware of difficulties facing them and who desire assistance in solving these difficulties."[1] The need for teachers to utilize research to improve classroom practices has been stressed in recent literature. As Fred T. Tyler said:

> ...we need to prepare teachers who are more aware of the role that research may play in improving instructional practices. We need teachers who have an inventive mind and can translate research into practice: a research report itself cannot tell us how we should teach. There is no doubt that we do not know as much as we should like; but it may also be that we are not making use of the best that is known, possibly because we are not developing inventive minds that will transform research into practice.[2]

Underlying the current emphasis on relating research to teacher training is the assumption that "a school system cannot be better than its teachers."[3]

In addition to research in teacher training, the increase in teachers' salaries in recent years has also contributed toward raising the social status of the profession. The median of school teachers' salaries in Canada was $1,098 in 1944, $1,689 in 1948, $2,308 in 1952, $2,979 in 1956, $4,055 in 1960, and $4,772 in 1964. However, there are still significant regional discrepancies. For example, though the national figure in 1964 was $4,772, the median salary for the Atlantic region was $3,089; for Ontario, $4,992; for the Prairie region, $4,608; and for British Columbia, $5,640.

In this section there are two readings. In the first, Frank MacKinnon shows how the lack of freedom enjoyed by teachers contributes to sterile teaching. In the second reading, Neville V. Scarfe outlines some principles on which improved quality of teacher education may be based.

---

[1] "The Ontario Institute for Studies in Education" (Toronto: The Ontario Institute, 1966), p. 1. The editor is indebted to Dr. Willard Brehaut of the O.I.S.E. for providing information concerning the Institute.
[2] Fred T. Tyler, "Research on Teaching and Learning," *Foundations for the Future* (Ottawa: Canadian Teachers' Federation, 1967), p. 30.
[3] C. Wayne Hall, "A Teacher Educator's Point of View," *Four Viewpoints on Teacher Education* (Ottawa: Canadian Teachers' Federation, 1966), p. 60.

V-16

Teachers as Civil Servants*

FRANK MACKINNON

•

By the time power in education is divided among numerous politicians, trustees, and officials, little is left for teachers. We have come to accept that fact on the assumption that public interest requires public responsibility and that teachers must therefore be responsible to the state. We might well ask, however, whether their responsibility, which in theory seems obviously in the interest of all concerned with education, has not gone too far; and whether in practice it has not become a position of subservience, which may defeat the purposes of education by killing the teaching profession. The present place of teachers and teaching in the school system does indeed provide justification for concern. An excess of administration at the top means for the teachers the humble status of low-rank civil servants. Emphasis on official opinion and practice exposes teaching to the frustrations of bureaucratic routine. One wonders if the result is not inevitable; certainly it is appalling: the teaching profession boasts more ex-members than any other occupation in modern society. Dominated, it is easily taken for granted, and there may here be a threat to the safety of the democratic state in whose interests the system was begun. "The teaching profession," says Leonard Brockington, "is the first the tyrant seeks to destroy and almost the last the free man seeks to honour."[1]

There is nothing wrong with the act of teaching itself. One of the most important, interesting, and rewarding occupations, it can compare favourably with any other profession. When we ask the reason for the acute shortage and high turnover of teachers we must look, not at the work, but at the conditions of work. Over these conditions teachers themselves have little control; the employer, which is the state, has complete responsibility. It is appropriate, therefore, to examine the effect of the state's responsibility on teaching and on the teachers.

Mark Hopkin's famous description of education should now include an official at the middle of the log, for ... the state everywhere comes between teachers and pupils and makes communication between them indirect. Unlike doctors, lawyers, and clergymen—or indeed plumbers,

---

* Reprinted with permission from *The Politics of Education* (Toronto: University of Toronto Press, 1962), pp. 79–88.

carpenters, and electricians—the teacher is not directly employed by those wishing his services. The real relationship is not between him and his pupils, but between the state and the pupils. The service he performs for them is not something determined by him or his profession but follows a set of requirements laid down by the state. Consequently, Mr. Smith of West Street High is a public employee who teaches any thirty pupils assigned to him by the state in much the same way a government clerk inspects the income tax forms placed on his desk; it will be only their good luck if he should be an able scholar at whose feet young people seek to sit.

This relationship is emphasized on the pupils' side by the compulsion of a state service. Unlike the clients, patients, and customers in other occupations, children are a non-paying captive audience required by law to attend school. Neither they nor their parents are able in the state system to seek out the teachers' services; they are ordered to come and get from them certain services which they may or may not wish, and to take them in the form of a curriculum which the teachers who do the providing are nevertheless not able to prescribe. In business, the value attached to goods or services depends greatly on whether the recipient is offering to purchase or the provider is offering to sell. One of the weaknesses of compulsory state education in a democratic system is that the initiative appears to lie with the provider of the service; the teacher is then something of a local agent only and consequently, pupils and parents do not tend to consider him with sufficient seriousness.

It might be fruitful to examine further how the pursuit of knowledge has been affected by this attitude to knowledge as a commodity to be dispensed rather than something for which the pupils must work.

... Unlike other workers, ... the teacher can never assume that his clients really want his services or that they are willing to make the required effort to take full advantage of them. Unfortunately also he cannot assure them of tangible services which will be of immediate benefit. When a contractor builds a house the results are visible and the direct consequence of action by the performer of the service which the owner requests and pays for. Nothing quite so obvious follows from teaching a course in history or algebra: the effects on the mind are not immediately apparent and, indeed, there may be no effects at all if there is insufficient effort on the part of the pupil. In education the customer is never sure of what he wants or what he is going to get, although it is the customer who must exert the main effort. This situation makes education impossible to guarantee, difficult to predict, and hard to understand and appreciate.

It is this particular aspect of education which helps to make it so incompatible with direct governmental administration. When people

---

[1] L. W. Brockington in Robertson Memorial Lecture, Prince of Wales College, 1958.

look to government for action and benefits they tend to expect service that is immediate, tangible, and practical: they count on the government to do what is necessary and produce obvious results. Politicians and civil servants, in turn, because of their need for popular support and of the very nature of their occupations wish to offer the same sort of services, and they too want to see direct action and visible results. Education they are apt to interpret as a political service rather than as an essentially human process. The teacher caught between public and administration, has the greatest difficulty in emphasizing that learning is not a commodity to be thus demanded and dispensed and that the final results depend largely on the pupils.

The dominance of the official attitude thus tends to place education among the social services which are expected to be handed out automatically. Like pensions which come with old age or sickness, like family allowances which are paid out from birth, school certificates are regarded by many as the right of pupils who reach a certain age. Actually, the opportunity for education is the social service; education itself cannot be an automatic right because no one is able to give it. This distinction is vital: if it is not made it becomes impossible to maintain the standards and carry out the responsibilities involved. It is difficult, however, for the state to make this distinction. Its control is so embracing and detailed that it is easy for it to assume, and the public encourages it to assume, that it is giving the education, not just the opportunity. It is then only a short step to an emphasis on the state's *giving* rather than the pupil's *getting,* and the consequent dilution of standards and responsibilities in the interest of "education for all."

The social service outlook inevitably affects the teachers and their work by making it difficult for the public to appreciate the teaching profession and understand its problems. The state, the public, and the pupils are not encouraged to regard teachers as leaders and guides in their fields directing and assisting pupils in their quest for knowledge. Indeed, it is hard for teachers to think of themselves in this role. Since they are expected rather to be dispensers and coaches, their qualifications and achievements tend to become secondary in official and public eyes. So long as there are enough of them to "fill the schools" and expose every boy and girl to some kind of instruction, the state is too easily satisfied and little is done to improve the status of the profession. Under these circumstances the problems of salary, working conditions, training, and supply inevitably appear, and as inevitably remain.

So much has been said about the low level of teachers' salaries that in most places it is taken almost for granted by the public, and considered by officials as being like the weather in that nothing much can be done about it. There is simply not enough recognition of the fact that any good teacher can be lured out of his job by business firms, unless his devotion to teaching is greater than his desire to improve his standard of living, and that the effectiveness of public education declines with every resignation. Admittedly there has always been a tendency for people to underrate the value of culture and to underpay preachers, teachers, and artists, and, as far as teachers are concerned, this tendency is strengthened by the public's attitude that somehow the government should pay less than other employers. There is little to counteract the tendency: if a good teacher resigns and there is no equivalent replacement, a permit or temporary licence can easily be issued to a less competent person so that the job will be filled. The prospect of reform with respect to salary is remote so long as such a practice is possible.

The conditions under which teachers work are, however, a far more serious problem than salaries. The profession is, as has been noted, run like a civil service despite the fact already emphasized that teaching bears no similarity whatever to the functions for which civil service administration is designed.

The classification system illustrates the problem. It is the governmental practice of standardizing and classifying positions and qualifications which has been applied to the teaching profession, so that each teacher is put in a category and appropriately labelled. There are many grades from "superior" to "permit," each divided into classes alphabetically or numerically. Appraisal of this system would involve "merit rating," and this teachers' organizations seem to fear. Now classification may work in the routine of the civil service where it is by and large functions rather than individuals which are classified, but can this arrangement be efficient in teaching where the individual himself is, or should be, paramount? Surely it is no more sensible than it would be to divide doctors, lawyers, clergymen, politicians, and others into first, second, and third class, as well as "temporary" and "permit." The knowledge, methods, and character of teachers simply do not allow them to be standardized and classified without weakening teaching as a whole by subsidizing the incompetent and holding back and discouraging the able. One graduate with a B.A. or one "second class" teacher is not the same as another bearing the same label. A course taught by one teacher is not in effect the same as that taught by another, and no official text, course of study, or regulation will make it so. Mathematics teachers, who are scarce, cannot be classified in the same manner as English teachers who are comparatively plentiful; but the law of supply and demand has not been allowed to operate in education. Indeed, the classification system is one of the chief reasons why good teachers leave, why poor teachers remain, and why the profession is so powerless. "All for one and one for all" is an excellent tactic in its place, but is education necessarily the place for the traditional procedure of convoys that it is the slowest which set the pace?

The practical difficulties which lead to reliance on this classification system are the size of the whole organization and the remoteness of the employer. Teachers do not form a small, closely knit profession with a special and distinct place in the community, but are rather an enormous group with limited association among its members. There are more school teachers in Canada than doctors, lawyers, nurses, engineers, and clergymen combined, and, because the administration of their activities is so centralized, it is difficult, under political control, to accord them the privileges of professional recognition rather than just those of the holding of a job. It is also difficult to recognize ability. Because the minister of education and his departmental officials and the members and staffs of school boards have no real contact with *a* school, they have no sure way of making an official distinction between the teaching ability and professional reputation of Mr. Black and Mr. Brown. They may pay and promote on seniority only. They may favour the academic politician who is popular and knows the right people. They may judge a teacher by the number of committees he sits on or extracurricular activities in which he joins. They may classify on diplomas secured and summer courses attended. They may favour "professional" study in methodology, organization, or administration. What they are almost completely incapable of recognizing and rewarding officially is initial knowledge of the subjects to be taught, renewed or maintained competence in these subjects, natural ability to teach, and productive relations with pupils. The tradition of the classification thus continues strong and, consequently, there is not sufficient reward for the outstanding, incentive to the mediocre, or check on the incompetent.

It would seem that the attainments of pupils would be a particularly revealing means of assessing teachers. But officials have virtually no regular contact with all varieties of school children, and tend to regard them in anything but realistic ways. They often look upon all children as benefiting greatly, perhaps even equally, from their mere presence in school, regardless of the type of teaching they receive or the amount of work they do. They usually regard the completion of a grade or course as bringing a given number of pupils to the same level of attainment. Consequently, mere exposure to teaching and the "passing" of examinations, even at only the 50 per cent level, are magnified out of all proportion to their true significance. Attendance and movement from one grade to another, may tell little about either the pupil or the quality of the instruction he has received, but under the circumstances of the centralized system they count for much and the calibre of the teachers is too easily overlooked.

The classification system combines with the social service outlook to subordinate the qualities of the individual teacher to the arrangement and appearance of the organization. An able science instructor may leave a school and be succeeded by a mediocre one, or a history teacher may lose touch with his subject; no change is apparent as far as the course, the curriculum, or the certificate are concerned, but the essential difference lies where it is most important, but least obvious, in the teaching. With the individual thus subordinated to the job, it is to be expected that the ablest teachers would become discouraged: they may not be paid more than others in the same classification and they may not teach beyond the limits of the official requirements.

Teaching is weakened further by the official necessity of making the system "look good" to the voters. The authorities, who must at all cost retain popular support, are sensitive to failure rates in general and to the adverse fortunes of their constituents' children in particular. They will seek remedies, not in emphasizing that pupils must work—such frankness would be dangerous to the popularity of elected officials—but rather in tinkering with the schools and the curricula. Official interference with teaching standards and practices is common, not so much on behalf of the pupils as because of the need for the vast educational system to show favourable results. This emphasis on the machine rather than on the school adds greatly to the teachers' work. It is virtually impossible, for instance, for them to get the lazy to work if the pupils know that automatic grading is the official policy; and it is hard to convince some parents that what their children will get from school will actually depend far less on the grade reached or the courses "passed" than on the ambition they have, the attention they pay, and the work they do. Officials will not, indeed under the circumstances they cannot, enlighten the pupils or parents by admitting weaknesses. An examination of the annual reports of departments of education reveals the dullest of government documents; they omit everything that might indicate weaknesses and emphasize everything that shows the magnitude of the system and the numbers participating in it.

Of all the results of centralized state control for the practice of teaching, the most powerful, and at the same time, depressing, is the conformity it requires. Teachers must always follow someone else's rules, carry out other people's projects, and depend on persons outside the profession for initiative, judgment, and leadership. A good teacher who loves his subject, his pupils, and his profession would like to do justice to all three, but he must follow the course of study and the assigned textbook, teach no more than what is required, and prepare for examinations set by remote personnel. His work and his method are all laid down in detailed regulations and there is little scope for individual initiative or professional leadership. Power and imagination in teaching are always in danger of being interfered with by those who control the school system. The prevailing official attitude seems to be that somehow the teacher and his profession must be regulated and watched lest either might say something wrong or do something unofficial, and that somehow each school and its work must conform to every other school and its work. The result is inefficiency in a profession where individual ability and character are most important. "A pall is cast over the classrooms," said Justices Black and Douglas in the United States Supreme Court when discussing what happens when teachers are watched too closely.

> There can be no real academic freedom in that environment.... There can be no exercise of the free intellect. Supineness and dogmatism take the place of enquiry. A "party line" lays hold. It is the "party line" of the orthodox view, of the conventional thought, of the accepted approach.... The teacher is no longer a stimulant to adventurous thinking; she becomes instead a pipeline for safe and sound information. A deadening dogma takes the place of free enquiry. Instruction tends to become sterile; pursuit of knowledge is discouraged.... A school system producing students trained as robots threatens to rob a generation of the versatility that has been perhaps our greatest distinction.[2]

The pressure for conformity has yet another unfortunate effect in that it encourages the kind of person who enjoys conforming and who learns how to do it well in a system in which response to political influence is acceptable. The result is an illustration of what Sir Edward Beatty called the chief weakness of public enterprise: the tendency of many public employees to play politics rather than to do their work with full efficiency. Teachers are so dependent on government officials in a system where their worth is indicated by their place in the classification and by "credits" rather than proven by their work, that many of them are often forced to adopt political methods to secure appointment, recognition, and promotion. When actually teaching, they can too easily subordinate their own thinking and efforts to the kind of window dressing which impresses officials and thereby stifle that innate quality of initiative and independence necessary to scholarship. The welfare of schools and the good name of the profession are always damaged by such tactics, and an unfair advantage is taken of teachers who are independent in outlook, who attend to their work, and who have no time or inclination for personal politics.

There is no escaping the fact, however, that in most professions it is often the nonconformist who does the best work. Many of the ablest politicians and businessmen are "characters," and it is often just this fact that makes them successful. Anyone looking back on his school days will remember that some of his best teachers were "different," and, indeed, that they were not always popular. Nevertheless, there is a strong tendency in school administration to distrust difference and ability in favour of sameness and mediocrity. Practically every critic of current educational policy has emphasized the point and given illustrations. From personal experience I can confirm their observations, for, of the official criticisms I have heard of schools and teachers, by far the most numerous have been directed against the better ones and the different ones. Let any two parents test the system by complaining to an official, one to the effect that Miss Smith's standards are too high, and the other to the effect that Miss Jones' standards are too low. The chances are overwhelmingly in favour of Miss Smith getting the official reprimand and Miss Jones going on unhindered.

The mediocrity which the pressure for conformity always encourages is responsible for a remarkable paradox in education, the presence of anti-intellectualism in the very place where it should have no place—the schools. Ill-prepared teachers and indifferent pupils are, of course, prone to excuse their shortcomings by scoffing at those who express ambitions and display exceptional talents. But this attitude is more widely encouraged by the combination of political allegiance and the suppression of individualism which operates for the profession as a whole.

---

[2] *Adler* v. *Board of Education* 342 U.S. (1951) 485.

V-17

Principles of Teacher Education*

NEVILLE V. SCARFE

•

There is no doubt that the demand for excellent teachers will become more urgent and more compelling in the future. The public will demand higher quality performance in schools just as they require higher quality in other services that are provided in an increasingly affluent society. It seems wise, therefore, to debate some of the principles on which improved quality of teacher education may be based, indicating clearly that an improvement in quality always involves an increase in costs.

1. The first principle is that teachers are *made*, not born. This does not mean that, when young people come to a university to seek teacher education, they do not arrive with a considerable number of useful acquired characteristics as well as a few valuable inborn traits. The acquired characteristics, however, are more important than the inborn traits, indicating that young people have a tremendous capacity for learning; indicating, too, that Education of some sort has made a difference to them. The fact that young people can learn, can change as a result of learning, and can be educated, implies that teachers can be educated and trained for their profession. In fact, if we believe in Education at all, we will realize that a great deal can be done to make a teacher out of any intelligent, well-educated individual. In other words, teacher education is both essential and very important.

2. The second principle is that a teacher educates as much by what he *is* as by what he says. It seems that a wise, cultured, mature, well-educated person who has a wide knowledge of society, of human beings, and of new research, will be a promising candidate for the teaching profession. Corollary to this is that a university is a community in which an alert, intelligent person with an open mind may acquire these qualities before or during the training experience. Teaching and learning are far more complicated, far more an expression of what one is than most people suppose. Future teachers should, therefore, come within the influence of the best minds, the best library, the best stimuli to learning, and the best ideals that we can provide.

The community of scholars, which constitutes the university (drawing

---

* Reprinted with permission from *Education 6:16* (Scarborough: W. J. Gage, Ltd., 1967), pp. 107–113.

as it does, students from all over the world and from all walks of life), is a very highly educative community in which students learn a great deal from one another. A university is also a research institution where young people are challenged by original ideas, new knowledge, and experimental outlook. Thus, they can be prepared to serve a future world rather than the present world. Future teachers should all spend least four years on a university campus, engaging to the full in all aspects of university life.

3. The third principle emphasizes that education is a *process*, not a product. Education occurs when young people are stimulated to think, when they are actively inquiring and exploring, when they are experimental and creative. If there are end products, they are the development of attitudes and character, not the acquisition of information; the formulation of ideas, not the storing of facts. This idea of active inquiry, creative endeavor, and thoughtful discussion should animate the educational process in a university as well as in a school. It should be particularly evident in a Faculty of Education. In other words, we should demonstrate to intending teachers examples of the way that we hope they will educate their pupils.

4. The fourth principle is that method is the most important element of a professional teacher-education program. Method is not to be narrowly defined and is not to be equated with techniques alone. In a teacher-education program young people are studying what to teach, why they will teach it, when to teach it, with whom they will teach it, and, subsequently, how they will teach it. *All* this constitutes Methodology. Content cannot be divorced from child psychology, from learning theory, from practice, or from the great themes of educational thought. Method means the careful discussion of all the problems that afflict a teacher in school and in university. It also means the careful translation of theory into practice. Methodology is much bigger and far more important than any outsider or even many teachers suppose.

5. The fifth principle is that the translation of theory into *practice* is very difficult for young people. There is no easy transfer of training from general theory or general method to specific lessons. General method is, therefore, usually quite inappropriate to begin with. The valuable activities for young people are the exact application of theory to specific examples, and enough of these have to be undertaken before any generalizations can be derived by the young teacher himself. It is only through skilfully conducted workshops and discussions, through demonstrations and visits, through meticulous constructive planning, that young people are ever able to make the great transition from theory to practice.

6. The sixth principle is that unenlightened practice on its own is of relatively little use. Experience just by itself does not teach much.

Although it is said that people learn by doing, it is well known that it is learning by "doing-and-thinking," not just by doing. It is what one *thinks* and *feels* as the result of experience or action that makes the difference. Practice that is not carefully planned and discussed ahead of time, and is not carefully analysed and discussed afterwards, is not really very profitable. The time needed for discussion, debate, argument, and investigation is probably longer than the period of simple practice. The stimulation, discussion, and debate of the practical problems of teaching all require the guidance of an extremely skilful, knowledgeable person who is particularly well-versed in the difficulties of young people at their beginning stages. More important still are opportunities for young people to discuss with *each other* the problems they have met, and chances for them to investigate new ideas and fresh approaches *immediately*. This is why long periods of practice without time for contemplation and reflection at a university are of little value.

Simple experience in schools enables a person to learn routines and orthodox teaching techniques under conditions that presently obtain. He does not learn to use new ideas or fresh research, nor does he debate adequately what he sees, without the stimulus of experts from the university. University teacher education must always be in advance of what is going on in the schools, and must constantly be seeking to inject new and important ideas into the school system.

7. The seventh principle states that the success of teacher education is directly proportional to the degree to which it is *particularized* and *individualized*. Another way of viewing this proposition is to emphasize the fundamental importance of the future teacher's understanding himself. Self-analysis, self-appraisal, and self-improvement require the careful guidance of a sympathetic counsellor who can claim the genuine respect of the future teacher. An additional aspect of this hypothesis is the suggestion that a teacher must be primarily a learner, collaborating with other learners as a co-operating team.

Growth is a continuing phenomenon both for the teacher and the pupil. Teachers grow, pupils grow—teaching is, therefore, a continuously changing process. It is not static; there are no cut and dried techniques. Teachers teach differently with the same group of children at the beginning of the year and at the end of the year. The teacher grows and becomes different, and the children grow and become different.

Teachers, therefore, have to learn about human growth, within themselves and within children. They must learn how to change, and how to deal with change. Teachers must learn not to be afraid of children, nor of teaching. They must learn not to be afraid of the child within themselves. If fear is to be cast out, self-knowledge, self-confidence, and self-acceptance must be assured. Knowledge, understanding, and sympathy are necessary both for children and for the subject being taught.

Many of the roadblocks to self-confidence are personal character traits. These become evident during practice-teaching and observation periods. They become ingrained handicaps if allowed to persist, but positive advantages if properly discussed and reviewed in collaboration with an expert and sympathetic counsellor. There is no good substitute for the private discussion and the subsequent reflection which leads to careful study and further enquiry.

Teacher education is, therefore, a very expensive system because it requires a highly trained and very high quality individual to act as tutor. Teachers learn by being put into particular situations that naturally cause them to think. Actual case studies, simulated situations, and vicarious experience through film and video tape are essential to good discussion and individualized help, and may be made more effective by using the recorded micro-teaching involvement technique developed at Berkeley with the use of television.

No two teachers are likely to react in identical fashion to the same set of circumstances. No two teachers should react identically. No two sets of circumstances are exactly the same. Despite the fact that there are certain basic theories or principles or generalizations that are relevant to many circumstances, few teachers apply these in identical fashion. Teaching is personal, unique, and individual. The more the teacher is helped to use his own strengths, and to overcome his own weaknesses— the more confident he becomes, the more he will like his work, the more he will like children, the more respect he will earn, and the more effective will be his teaching. Children learn very little from any teacher for whom they have scant respect.

Not all future teachers need the same kind or amount of training. Some are more suited to one type of circumstance, some to another. Some need much practice on routines, while some need to be freed from an enslavement to them. Some need much encouragement to experiment, others need coaching in the consolidation of learning. For most of their professional life, they will all operate on their own with distinctly different groups of children. Consequently, many aspects of teacher-education programs should be tailored to individual needs, since mass instruction in these aspects is uneconomic and unrewarding.

This does not mean that a person alerted to the problems of teaching and learning cannot gain much from books, from lectures, or from group visits. Thought processes must, however, be highly stimulated, for effective learning does not occur simply by exposure to an experience. It must affect the intellect and the emotions very noticeably. Moreover, solutions to the problems encountered must be available, and plausible, if fear is to be avoided.

8. In the training and education of young teachers a *special kind of skill* is necessary and a *special kind of sympathy* important. It takes several years of study, discussion, research, and observation to train a university professor to become a skilful trainer of teachers. It is true that

every professor who wishes to become a member of the Faculty of Education should first and foremost have been an outstanding teacher, but this does not necessarily qualify him to become an outstanding teacher of teachers. He must have a very wide understanding of the learning process, of adult education, and of adult psychology, and, in particular, a great insight into the problems of the young teachers. Contact with recent research and with recent researchers, and a scholarly awareness of all that has been written in a particular field, are also essential.

Teachers in the classroom, however fine they may be, do not have the special opportunities, nor do they have the need to acquire the same skills that a university professor in Education must acquire. Thus, there is a rather special kind of person needed in the Faculty of Education. Not only must he know a great deal about schools and children and teaching, but he must also have made considerable scholarly study of psychology, sociology, philosophy, and history, in order that research in these various fields can be brought to bear on the problems of the classroom teacher. He is not an armchair philosopher but has regular personal experience in school classrooms.

It is usually quite impossible for a sociologist or a psychologist or a philosopher to come into the field of education from those fields and hope to understand teaching without first having been a schoolteacher. A member of a Faculty of Education must first have been a teacher, have gone into the scholarly disciplines subsequently, and must have made the great attempt to integrate research and theory with practice. Those who are not able or willing to go into school classrooms and help young teachers with their day-to-day teaching problems; those who are unwilling or unable to demonstrate teaching in front of a group of young students; and those who do not enjoy and see the value of methods courses and seminars in training future teachers are not suitable for a Faculty of Education. Equally true is it that persons who are not interested in pursuing experimental work in the classroom or in keeping abreast of the scholarly knowledge available are not suitable persons. Each and every member of the Faculty of Education must integrate within himself, practice and theory, and intense sympathy for teachers, and a great desire to undertake post-graduate experimental work.

9. A ninth principle is that the teacher-education program must be a dynamic, experimental, changing program. Since the university is at the cutting edge of new knowledge and new research, it must constantly re-adapt its plans and its programs to bring within its orbit the new ideas available to the community of teachers, if possible by demonstration. When young teachers from a Faculty of Education go out to a school to practice, they naturally go primed to learn a great deal from the sponsor teacher in the school. The sponsor teacher has also a great deal to learn. The ideal situation is, in fact, where the student teacher and the sponsor

teacher learn mutually one from the other, as a collaborating team exchanging ideas and asking questions.

The ultimate responsibility, however, for the education and training of future teachers must always lie with the university professor. He must keep in constant contact with schools, with children, and with sponsor teachers, and at the same time keep abreast of recent knowledge and research. Only by so doing will he involve young people in situations which cause them to think, debate, discuss, and argue with each other, and with their professors and teachers, about the intricate problems of learning and teaching. Although the sponsor teacher has an all important and essential function in teacher training, he does not have the major function. The university professor must take the major responsibility for the education of teachers *for the future*.

10. A tenth principle would state that teacher education is not a one-shot affair whereby the trainee has learned all there is to know at the end of his university career. Novel research, new ideas, and fresh designs appear so rapidly that every teacher needs a refresher course, at least every ten years, to bring him up to date in his teaching subject and with new pedagogical practices. In the Soviet Union it is compulsory to do this every five years.

And what of the intervening years? Surely the responsibility for keeping practising teachers aware of new thinking, new approaches, new techniques, and new knowledge rests with the training institution. New ideas cannot be left to accumulate on the academic heights, to be released like an avalanche every five or ten years. And how better can theory be translated into practice than to have new ideas tested in the classrooms by practising pragmatists? Teacher education is *continuing* education.

Suggested Readings

Part One: AIMS OF EDUCATION

Althouse, J.G., *Structure and Aims of Canadian Education*, Toronto: W.J. Gage, Ltd., 1949.

Baker, H.S., "Educational Aims: A Further Look," *The Canadian School Principal*, Reeves et al., eds., McClelland and Stewart, Limited, 1962.

Bancroft, George W., "Some Sociological Considerations on Education," *Canadian Education and Research Digest*, March, 1964.

Carter, G. Emmett, *The Catholic Public Schools of Quebec*, Scarborough: W.J. Gage, Ltd., 1957.

Croskery, George G., and Gerald Nason, eds., *Canadian Conference on Education*, Ottawa: Mutual Press, 1958.

Gillett, Margaret, *A History of Education: Thought and Practice*, Toronto: McGraw-Hill Company of Canada, Limited, 1966.

Harris, Robin S., *Quiet Evolution, A Study of the Educational System of Ontario*, Toronto: University of Toronto Press, 1967.

Hodgins, J.G., *Documentary History of Education in Upper Canada, 1792–1876*, 28 vols., Toronto: Warwick Bros. and Rutter, 1894–1904.

Jaspers, K., *The Future of Mankind*, Chicago: University of Chicago Press, 1961.

Kent, T.W., *Social Policy for Canada*, Ottawa: Policy Press, 1962.

Kluckhohn, C., *The Scientific Study of Values*, Toronto: University of Toronto Press (University of Toronto Installation Lectures), 1959.

Koestler, A., *The Yogi and The Commissar and Other Essays*, London: Cape, 1945.

Laskin, Richard, ed., *Social Problems*, Toronto: McGraw-Hill Company of Canada, Limited, 1964.

Lussier, Monseigneur Ivenee, *L'Education Catholique et le Canada Francais*, Scarborough: W.J. Gage, Ltd., 1960.

Macdonald, John, *A Philosophy of Education*, Toronto: W.J. Gage, Ltd., 1965.

Maheux, M. L'Abbe Arthur, "The Foundations of the Canadian Philosophy of Education: The French Canadian Viewpoint," *The Canadian College of Teachers*, Vol. I, 1958.

Maritain, Jacques, *Education at the Crossroads*, New Haven: Yale University Press, 1943.

———, *Man and State*, Chicago: Phoenix Books, 1961.

Oliver, Michael, ed., *Social Purpose for Canada*, Toronto: University of Toronto Press, 1961.

Orwell, G., *Animal Farm*, London: Penguin, 1951.

Phillips, C.E., *The Development of Education in Canada*, Toronto: W.J. Gage, Ltd., 1957.

Porter, John, *The Vertical Mosaic*, Toronto: University of Toronto Press, 1965.

Price, Fred W., ed., *The Second Canadian Conference on Education, A Report*, Toronto: University of Toronto Press, 1962.

Reid, T., ed., *Values in Conflict*, Toronto: University of Toronto Press, 1963.

Russell, Bertrand, *Authority and the Individual*, Boston: Beacon Press, 1963.

Shack, Sybil, "The School in Society," *The Toronto Education Quarterly*, Spring, 1965.

Sissons, C.B., *Church and State in Canadian Education*, Toronto: The Ryerson Press, 1959.

Tillich, Paul, *The Courage To Be*, New Haven: Yale University Press, 1965.

Tönnies, Ferdinand, *Community and Society, Gemeinschaft und Gesellschaft*, New York: Harper and Row, 1965.

Walker, Franklin A., *Catholic Education and Politics in Upper Canada*, Toronto: J.M. Dent and Sons (Canada) Limited, 1955.

Wees, W.R., "Society, Education and the Individual," *The Canadian Secondary School*, L.W. Downey, ed., Toronto: The Macmillan Company of Canada, Limited and W.J. Gage, Ltd., 1963.

Weir, George M., *The Separate School Question in Canada*, Toronto: The Ryerson Press, 1959.

Whitehead, Alfred North, *The Aims of Education*, New York: Mentor, 1949.

●

Part Two: EDUCATION AND DIVERSITY IN CANADIAN SOCIETY

A Preliminary Report of the Royal Commission on Bilingualism and Biculturalism. Ottawa: Queen's Printer, 1965.

Blishen, Bernard R., et al., eds., *Canadian Society: Sociological Perspectives*, Toronto: The Macmillan Company of Canada, Limited, 1961.

Cook, Ramsay, *Canada and the French-Canadian Question*, Toronto: The Macmillan Company of Canada, Limited, 1966.

Courtney, John C., ed., *Voting in Canada*, Scarborough: Prentice-Hall of Canada, Ltd., 1967.

Driver, H.E., *Indians of North America*, Chicago: University of Chicago Press, 1961.

Floud, J.E., ed., *Social Class and Educational Opportunity*, Toronto: William Heinemann, Limited, 1958.

Forsey, Eugene A., "Canada: Two Nations or One," *Canadian Journal of Economics and Political Science*, Vol. XXVIII, 1963.

Honigmann, John J. and Irma, *Eskimo Townsmen*, Canadian Research Centre for Anthropology, University of Ottawa, Ottawa: 1965.

Hostetler, John A., and Calvin Redekop, "Education and Assimilation in Three Ethnic Groups," *The Alberta Journal of Educational Research*, December, 1962.

Jenness, Diamond, *Indians of Canada*, Ottawa: Queen's Printer, 1963.

Jenness, Eileen, *The Indian Tribes of Canada*, Toronto: The Ryerson Press, 1966.

Laskin, Richard, ed., *Social Problems*, Toronto: McGraw-Hill Company of Canada, Limited, 1964.

Leechman, Douglas, *Native Tribes of Canada*, Toronto: W.J. Gage, Ltd., 1965.

Lipset, Seymour Martin, "Canada and the United States: A Comparative View," *The Canadian Review of Sociology and Anthropology*, November, 1964, pp. 173–185.

———, *The First New Nation*, New York: Basic Books, 1963.

Lower, A.R.M., *Canadians in the Making*, Toronto: Longmans Green, 1958.

McFeat, Tom, *Indians of the North Pacific Coast*, Toronto: McClelland and Stewart, Limited, 1966.

Morton, W.L., *The Canadian Identity*, Toronto: University of Toronto Press, 1965.

Naegele, Kasper D., *Canadian Society: Further Reflections*, Bernard R. Blishen *et al.*, eds., Toronto: The Macmillan Company of Canada, Limited, 1964.

Porter, John, *The Vertical Mosaic*, Toronto: University of Toronto Press, 1965.

Reid, T., ed., *Values in Conflict*, 32nd Couchiching Conference, C.I.P.A., Toronto: University of Toronto Press, 1963.

Robertson, R.G., "The Coming Crisis in the North," *Journal of Canadian Studies*, II, 1, February, 1967.

Rolland, Solance Chaput, *My Country, Canada or Quebec?* Toronto: The Macmillan Company of Canada, Limited, 1966.

Russell, Peter, ed., *Nationalism in Canada*, Toronto: McGraw-Hill Company of Canada, Limited, 1966.

Schull, Joseph, *Laurier, The First Canadian*, Toronto: The Macmillan Company of Canada, Limited, 1965.

Scott, Frank, and Michael Oliver, eds., *Quebec States Her Case*, Toronto: The Macmillan Company of Canada, Limited, 1964.

Shimpo, M., and R. Williamson, *Socio-Cultural Disintegration Among the Fringe Saulteaux*, Saskatoon: Centre for Community Studies, 1965, reprinted by Extension Division, University of Saskatchewan.

Sloan, Thomas S., *Quebec, The Not-So-Quiet Revolution*, Toronto: Ryerson Press, 1965.

Valee, F.G., *et al.*, "Ethnic Assimilation and Differentiation in Canada," *Canadian Journal of Economics and Political Science*, XXIII, 4, November, 1957, pp. 540–549.

Valee, F.G., and V.F. Valentine, eds., *The Eskimo*, Toronto: McClelland and Stewart, Limited, 1966.

Part Three: SOCIAL AND ECONOMIC CHANGE

Beattie, Lewis S., *The Development of Student Potential*, Canadian Conference on Education, Ottawa: 1961.

Beck, Robert Holmes, *A Social History of Education*, Foundations of Education Series, Englewood Cliffs, N.J.: Prentice-Hall, Inc., 1965.

Cheal, J.E., *Investment in Canadian Youth*, Toronto: The Macmillan Company of Canada, Limited, 1963.

Clark, S.D., *The Suburban Society*, Toronto: University of Toronto Press, 1966.

———, ed., *Urbanization and the Changing Canadian Society*, Toronto: University of Toronto Press, 1961.

Deutsch, J., et al., ed., *The Canadian Economy*, Toronto: The Macmillan Company of Canada, Limited, 1961.

Dhalla, Nariman K., "Trends in Education," *These Canadians*, Toronto: McGraw-Hill Company of Canada, Limited, 1966, ch. 4, pp. 34–40.

Duffet, W.E., *Education Planning and the Expanding Economy*, Ottawa: Dominion Bureau of Statistics, 1964.

Easterbrook, W.T., and M.H. Watkins, *Approaches to Canadian Economic History*, Toronto: McClelland and Stewart, Limited, 1967.

Economic Council of Canada, *Economic Goals for Canada to 1970, First Annual Review*, Ottawa: Queen's Printer, 1964.

———, *Towards Sustained and Balanced Economic Growth, Second Annual Review*, Ottawa: Queen's Printer, 1965.

Fisher, A.D., "Education and Social Progress," *Alberta Journal of Educational Research*, XII, 4, December, 1966, pp. 257–267.

Financing Higher Education in Canada, Report of a Committee to the Association of Universities and Colleges of Canada, Toronto: University of Toronto Press, 1965.

Goodman, Paul, *Growing Up Absurd*, New York: Vintage Books, 1960.

Harrison, Ernest, *A Church Without God*, Toronto: McClelland and Stewart, Limited, 1966.

Hickerson, Nathaniel, *Education for Alienation*, Englewood Cliffs, N.J.: Prentice-Hall, Inc., 1966.

Hodgkins, R.A., *Education and Change*, London: Oxford University Press, 1957.

Hodgkinson, Harold L., *Education in Social and Cultural Perspectives*, Englewood Cliffs, N.J.: Prentice-Hall, Inc., 1965.

Inman, M.K. and F.R. Anton, *Economics in a Canadian Setting*, Toronto: The Copp Clark Publishing Co., Ltd., 1965.

Jackson, R.W.B., "Education Today for 2000 A.D.," *Education*, Vol. V, W.J. Gage, Ltd., 1965.

Katz, Joseph, ed., *Canadian Education Today*, Toronto: McGraw-Hill Company of Canada, Limited, 1956.

Kelsey, Ian Bruce, "Philosophic Considerations of a Shift in Values,"

The Journal of Education, Vancouver: University of British Columbia, 1965.

Kilbourn, William, ed., *The Restless Church*, Toronto: McClelland and Stewart, Limited, 1966.

Laskin, Richard, ed., *Social Problems*, Toronto: McGraw-Hill Company of Canada, Limited, 1964.

LaZerte, M.E., *The Road Ahead to Better Education*, Canadian School Trustees' Association, Edmonton: The Hamly Press, Ltd., 1955.

McLuhan, Marshall, and Quentin Fiore, *The Medium Is the Massage*, Toronto: Bantam Books, Inc., 1967.

Moore, Wilbert E., *Social Change*, Englewood Cliffs, N.J.: Prentice-Hall, Inc., 1963.

Nordskog, J.E., *Social Change*, Toronto: McGraw-Hill Company of Canada, Limited, 1960.

Ovans, C.D., and L.L. Cunningham, et al., *Educational Change: Problems and Prospects*, Edmonton: Department of Secondary Education, University of Alberta, 1964.

Percival, W.P., "A Sound Philosophy of Education in an Era of Change," *The Educational Review*, January, 1963.

Phillips, C.E., "Changing Attitudes," *The Development of Education in Canada*, Toronto: University of Toronto Press and W.J. Gage, Ltd., 1967.

Pigott, Arthur V., *Education and Employment*, Canadian Conference on Education, Ottawa: 1961.

Porter, John, "The Economic Elite and the Social Structure in Canada," *Canadian Journal of Economics and Political Science*, Vol. XXIII, August, 1957, pp. 377–394.

———, *The Vertical Mosaic*, Toronto: University of Toronto Press, 1965.

Raths, J.D., and J.D. Grambs, *Society and Education*, Englewood Cliffs, N.J.: Prentice-Hall, Inc., 1965.

Reid, T.E.H., ed., *Economic Planning in a Democratic Society*, Toronto: Canadian Institute on Public Affairs, 1963.

Riesman, David, et al., *The Lonely Crowd*, New Haven: Yale University Press, 1964.

Royal Commission on Agriculture and Rural Life, Province of Saskatchewan, *Rural Education*, Regina: Queen's Printer, 1956.

Rudy, Willis, *Schools in an Age of Mass Culture*, Englewood Cliffs, N.J.: Prentice-Hall, Inc., 1965.

Seeley, J.R., et al., *Crestwood Heights*, Toronto: University of Toronto Press, 1956.

Smith, C.E., "Education and Social Change," *Canadian Education Today*, Katz, ed., Toronto: McGraw-Hill Company of Canada, Limited, 1956.

Spinks, J.W.T., "Education for Tomorrow's World," *The Saskatchewan Bulletin*, April, 1963, pp. 24–27.

Vaizey, J., *The Economics of Education*, London: Faber and Faber, Ltd., 1962.
Watkins, M., ed., *Economics: Canada*, McGraw-Hill Company of Canada, Limited, 1963.
Watts, Morrison, "Change Factors in the High School Program," *Education*, Vol. V, Toronto: W.J. Gage, Ltd., 1965.
Whitworth, R.E., "Economics and Education," *Education*, Vol. V, Toronto: W.J. Gage, Ltd., 1965, pp. 23–27.
———, "Education and Manpower," *The Canadian College of Teachers*, Vol. V, 1962, pp. 54–72.
———, "Educational Planning," *Education*, Vol. V, Toronto: W.J. Gage, Ltd., 1960, pp. 71–75.
———, *Skills for Tomorrow*, Canadian Conference on Education, Ottawa: 1962.
Ziel, Henry, "Educating Youth for an Expert Society," a paper read at the Conference on the Canadian High School, *The Canadian Secondary School*, L.W. Downey, ed., Toronto: The Macmillan Company of Canada, Limited and W.J. Gage, Ltd., 1963.

●

Part Four: LEVELS OF EDUCATION

(a) Elementary Education

Elkin, Frederick, *The Family in Canada, 1964*, The Canadian Conference on the Family, Ottawa: 1965.
Heise, B.W., ed., *New Horizons for Canada's Children*, Proceedings of the First Canadian Conference on Children, Toronto: University of Toronto Press, 1961.
Katz, J., ed., *Elementary Education in Canada*, Toronto: McGraw-Hill Company of Canada, Limited, 1961.
Seeley, J.R., et al., *Crestwood Heights*, Toronto: University of Toronto Press, 1956.
The Vanier Institute on the Family, *The Canadian Conference on the Family*, Ottawa: 1965.
Worth, Walter H., *Before Six*, a Report on the Alberta Early Childhood Education Study, The Alberta School Trustees' Association, Edmonton: 1966.

(b) Secondary Education

Belth, Marc, *Education as a Discipline, A Study of the Role of Models in Thinking*, Boston: Allyn and Bacon, 1965.
Campbell, H., *Curriculum Trends in Canadian Education*, The Committee on Education Research, Faculty of Education, University of Alberta, Edmonton: 1959.
Cheal, John E., *Investment in Canadian Youth*, Toronto: The Macmillan Company of Canada, Limited, 1963.

"Composite High Schools in Canada," *Monographs in Education*, The Committee on Education Research, Faculty of Education, University of Alberta, Edmonton: 1959.

Downey, Lawrence W., and L. Ruth Godwin, eds., *The Canadian Secondary School: An Appraisal and a Forecast*, Toronto: The Macmillan Company of Canada, Limited and W.J. Gage, Ltd., 1963.

———, *The Secondary Phase of Education*, New York, Toronto, London: Blaisdell Publishing Company, A Division of Ginn and Company, 1965.

Education of the Gifted, the Fourteenth Yearbook of the Ontario School Inspectors' Association, Toronto: The Copp Clark Publishing Co., Ltd., 1958.

Gathercole, Frederick J., ed., *Secondary Education in Canada, The Canadian Superintendent*, Toronto: The Ryerson Press, 1962.

Konopka, Gisela, *The Adolescent Girl in Conflict*, Englewood Cliffs, N.J.: Prentice-Hall, Inc., 1966.

Ovans, D.D., "The Canadian Secondary School Today," *Education*, Vol. V, Toronto: W.J. Gage, Ltd., 1965.

Phillips, C.E., *Public Secondary Education in Canada*, Toronto: W.J. Gage, Ltd., 1955.

(c) University Education

Beaulieu, Paul J., ed., *Canadian Universities: Research in Science and Engineering*, National Research Council, Ottawa: 1967.

Bissell, C.T., ed., *Canada's Crisis in Higher Education*, Toronto: University of Toronto Press, 1957.

———, "The Importance of Greatness," *CAUT Bulletin*, Vol. XXXV, May, 1965.

Financing Higher Education in Canada, Report of a Committee to the Association of Universities and Colleges of Canada, Toronto: University of Toronto Press, 1965.

Gordon, J.M., "Prairie Universities," *Canadian Geographical Journal*, Vol. LXXI, October, 1965, pp. 112–115.

Griswold, A. Whitney, et al., *The Arts and the University*, Toronto: The Macmillan Company of Canada, Limited, 1965.

Harris, Robin S., ed., *Changing Patterns of Higher Education in Canada*, Toronto: University of Toronto Press, 1966.

———, *Quiet Evolution, A Study of the Educational System of Ontario*, Toronto: University of Toronto Press, 1967.

Hodgetts, J.E., ed., *Higher Education in a Changing Canada*, Royal Society of Canada, Toronto: University of Toronto Press, 1966.

Priestley, F.E.L., *The Humanities in Canada*, a report prepared for the Humanities Research Council of Canada, published for the Council by University of Toronto Press, 1964.

Sheffield, Edward F., "Universities Face the Future," *Education*, Vol. V, W.J. Gage, Ltd., 1965.

Smith, J. Percy, The University and Society, *CAUT Bulletin*, XI, 5, April, 1963.

Spinks, J.W.T., "Education for Tomorow's World," *The Saskatchewan Bulletin*, Saskatoon: April, 1963.

•

Part Five: SOCIETY AND THE TEACHER

Cheal, John E., Harold C. Melsness, and Arthur W. Reeves, *Educational Administration: The Role of the Teacher*, Toronto: The Macmillan Company of Canada, Limited, 1962.

Corsini, R.J., and D.D. Howard, eds., *Critical Incidents in Teaching*, Englewood Cliffs, N.J.: Prentice-Hall, Inc., 1965.

Four Viewpoints on Teacher Education, Canadian Teachers' Federation, Ottawa: 1966.

Gillett, Margaret, *A History of Educational Thought and Practice*, Toronto: McGraw-Hill Company of Canada, Limited, 1966.

Grambs, Jean Dresden, *Schools, Scholars and Society*, Englewood Cliffs, N.J.: Prentice-Hall, Inc., 1965.

Housego, I.E., "Democratic Decision-Making in Education," *The Canadian Administrator*, IV, 8, May, 1965.

Jones, Frank E., "The Social Origins of High School Teachers in a Canadian City," *Canadian Journal of Economics and Political Science*, XXIX, 4, November, 1963.

Kaufman, Bel, *Up the Down Staircase*, Englewood Cliffs, N.J.: Prentice-Hall, Inc., 1965.

Kingett, A.H., "The Role of the Teacher in Society," *Educational Review*, May, 1962.

Lloyd, W.S., *The Role of Government in Canadian Education*, Toronto: W.J. Gage, Ltd., 1959.

Macdonald, John, "A Social Psychologist Looks at Teacher Education," *Education 6:17*, Toronto: W.J. Gage, Ltd., 1967.

MacKinnon, Archie P., "Breaking New Ground in Teacher Education," *The Manitoba Teacher*, May-June, 1966.

MacKinnon, Frank, *The Politics of Education*, Toronto: University of Toronto Press, 1965.

Mahood, D.E., "The School and Controversial Issues," *The Pedagogul*, IX, 4, February 3, 1967.

Neatby, Hilda, *So Little for the Mind, An Indictment of Canadian Education*, Toronto: Clarke, Irwin and Company, Limited, 1953.

Oliver, R.A., *Effective Teaching*, Toronto: J.M. Dent and Sons (Canada), Limited, 1962.

Paton, James M., "Current Thinking on Teacher Education," *Education*, Vol. VA, Toronto: W.J. Gage, Ltd., 1966.

Phillips, Charles E., *The Development of Education in Canada*, Toronto: W.J. Gage, Ltd., 1957.

Ryerson, Egerton, *The Story of My Life*, Toronto: William Briggs, 1883.
Scarfe, N.V., "In Pursuit of Teacher Excellence," *The Toronto Education Quarterly*, IV, 1, Autumn, 1964.
Stinnett, T.M., and Albert J. Huggett, *Professional Problems of Teachers*, Toronto: The Macmillan Company of Canada, Limited, 1963.